SPARKS FROM THE ANVIL

Sparks from the Anvil

The Smith College Poetry Interviews

———◦◦◦———

CHRISTIAN McEWEN

Christian McEwen

BAUHAN PUBLISHING
PETERBOROUGH NEW HAMPSHIRE
2015

Library of Congress Cataloging-in-Publication Data

Sparks from the Anvil : the Smith College poetry interviews / edited by Christian McEwen.
    pages cm
 Includes bibliographical references.
 ISBN 978-0-87233-194-5 (alk. paper)
 1. Poets, American--21st century--Interviews. 2. Poetry--Authorship. I. McEwen,
Christian, 1956- II. Smith College.
 PS326.S63 2015
 811'.609--dc23
 [B]

                              2015005176

Book design by Kirsty Anderson
Typeset in Sabon LT Std
Cover design by Henry James
Printed by Versa Press, East Peoria, Illinois

BAUHAN
PUBLISHING LLC
PO BOX 117 PETERBOROUGH NEW HAMPSHIRE 03458
 603-567-4430
WWW.BAUHANPUBLISHING.COM

In memory of
ALASTAIR REID
(1926–2014)

and

BARBARA MOR
(1936–2015)
beloved friend & mentor

CONTENTS

INTRODUCTION

Listening to Poets/Poets Listening

"What do you do?" someone asked William Carlos Williams.
"I listen to the water falling," he answered. "That is my only occupation."
—Ann Armbrecht

When W. S. Merwin was a little boy, he was perfectly happy playing by himself. His mother remembered him sitting on the kitchen floor with two copper bowls and a box of dried peas, pouring the peas from one bowl to another, "listening to the sound of rain." Eighty-some years later, when he came to Smith, he spoke to me about the art of listening: *open, undirected, utterly attentive.*

For the past five years I've been listening to poets, in a series of extended conversations modeled on *The Paris Review Interviews*. When I first proposed this project, in the winter of 2009, I had no idea what to call it. But my mother's mother was from Donegal, and back in the old country, in Ireland, Brigid was the patron saint of poetry, and of smithcraft too; also, it must be said, of midwifery. And there we were at Smith College. So I came up with a name that paid quiet tribute to St. Brigid, and at the same time brought together all those different kinds of making. I called the project "Sparks from the Anvil," with the "sparks" as the brilliant insights, the casually dazzling remarks that are thrown off in the course of hammering away in the "smithy" that is poetry. Hence, of course, the title of this book.

Between the spring of 2009 and the fall of 2013, I interviewed a total of thirty-three poets, all of whom had come to read at Smith, and sixteen of whom are featured here. We would sit together in a little insulated booth in the Center for Media Production, crammed side by side in two awkwardly angled chairs, and my friend Daisy Mathias would "mind the computer" while I conducted the interview. Many of the *Sparks* writers were new to me, and I was almost always obsessively well prepared. I'd have a sheaf of single-spaced pages jam-packed with quotes and questions, which would inevitably proliferate in the course of the conversation. "When did you first encounter poetry as a child? Whose work inspired you? Who encouraged you once you began to write?"

The answers that emerged were poised and lucid, quietly authoritative; they were tentative and shy; they were giddy, exhilarated, sprawling, fresh, and new. I rejoiced in all of them. But most of the interviews lasted for well over an hour, and the transcripts were correspondingly unwieldy. In preparing this manuscript, I edited each one in the service of length and clarity, and made minor changes in tense and usage too. The poets contributed revisions and additions of their own, which at times were edited yet again by me, until we were all agreed upon the final text. The versions that follow are in most cases about half their original length. A short biography has been added for each poet, and lists of their publications appear in a bibliography at the end.

Looking back over the completed text, I recognize a familiar set of themes, having to do with early childhood memories: family, landscape, books; gradually opening into more professional adult issues: challenges and obstructions, daily writing practice, sources of delight and inspiration. Each poet has a private tale to tell. And yet it is also possible to braid those tales together, and to read them as a kind of composite biography centered on poetry itself: where it comes from, what forms it can take, what circumstances encourage it to flourish. If the poet is indeed a blacksmith, what does her smithy look like? How does she swing her hammer? How smoldering-bright her coals? If poetry is a tree, how does the forester prepare the soil? What gives him faith that little sapling will take root?

***

The African American poet Nikky Finney grew up on a farm in South Carolina. "I listened for a very long time as a girl," she says. "I was incredibly quiet." Even as a small child, when her grandmother would wheel her out into the garden—"hot sun, mosquitoes, flies"—she would just sit quietly and listen.

"Sound traced the day," Finney remembers. "The rooster crowing, the milk truck stopping half a mile up the road (I can still hear the brakes!), the pickup, my grandmother, the postman—everything was situated by sound and sight." She sees it now as a kind of poetic apprenticeship. "That was my sensory perception growing bigger and getting fed."

Many of the writers I spoke to had similar stories. They were child naturalists, child mystics, child adventurers, quietly attuned to both inner and outer landscapes. Most of them first came to poetry through the voices of women: mothers and grandmothers, nannies, sisters, aunts. When W. S. Merwin was a little boy, his mother read him Tennyson's "The Brook" and "Where Go the Boats?" by Robert Louis Stevenson. "Do you remember that lovely poem?" he asked me. "'Dark brown is the river. / Golden is the sand. / It flows along for ever . . .' They're river poems. They're water poems. Water and boats. And that's a kind of freedom. It's a water freedom, you know."

As a child, Merwin read those poems over and over again. From early on, he knew that he too wanted to be a poet. "It had to do with the great moments of language that I'd heard. I wanted to find the way to them myself. And I always was going to do that, always, from four on."

Again and again, the writers I spoke to would name that moment of astonished gratitude, when poetry ceased to be "a school thing, a skirt thing" (as Saul Bellow put it) and became a passion and obsession of their own. When Chase Twichell read Keats for the first time, she understood "language as a door to go somewhere else." Michael Dickman was transported by Neruda. By the time Edward Hirsch encountered Gerard Manley Hopkins, he was already a college freshman. "I remember reading 'I Wake and Feel the Fell of Dark Not Day,' and it just took the top of my head off. It took me a while to realize that it was even a sonnet. I just was so moved by the desolation."

* * *

Reading and rereading, learning poetry by heart, can take place in the most casual of circumstances. But for almost everyone I spoke with, there was a more formal initiation too: a poetry workshop or creative writing program. Here at last, the apprentice writer encounters like-minded friends and mentors, and, if he or she is lucky, the encouragement of a professional working poet.

For Gwyneth Lewis, that poet was the Russian writer Joseph Brodsky. "His intelligence was extraordinary," she says now. "And his sense of poetic tradition. He taught us to put ourselves in relation to Auden, to Frost—and behind Brodsky himself was Akhmatova—so I've had a sense of poetry as a communal activity ever since."

At times there can be worldly consequences to such camaraderie: a teaching opportunity, a grant, a publication. But in most cases, friendship really is its own reward, translating back, very directly, into the work itself. When Jean Valentine won the Yale Series of Younger Poets Award, she was approached, privately, by Adrienne Rich and Jane Cooper, who became her friends (and steady, supportive readers) for the rest of their long lives. Deep into old age, Maxine Kumin and Donald Hall still traded worksheets, using a specially dedicated fax. The tribe of poet-friends remains minute and potent to this day. Gerald Stern put it best, perhaps, exulting in his own moment of emergence. "I wrote a book, it won a bunch of prizes, and suddenly I knew all the poets in America."

* * *

For the young poet, just moving out into the world, such connections can be marvelously sustaining. But external encouragement goes only so far. There are also the long years of apprenticeship (and all too often, penury and anonymity) in which the writer learns to listen inward, to sit with silence and bewilderment: begins, in other words, to find a voice. When W. S. Merwin was eighteen years old, he went to visit the aged poet Ezra Pound. "One of the things he said was, 'If you're going to be a poet, you have to take it, and yourself, seriously. You have to work at it every day.' And he said, 'You don't have enough to write about every day. You think you do, but you don't; your life at eighteen is really not that interesting.' So, he said, 'Learn languages and translate. That's the best way of learning your own language there is.' And that's absolutely true."

Over the years, translation provided Merwin with a daily task, teaching him a great deal about language, and something too of the art of listening. "Listening is where it all begins," he says. "The origin of poetry comes from hearing something, not from understanding it."

Annie Boutelle agrees. "I think it's true—that silent listening is probably, quite frequently, where a poem begins. Something comes to us, however it comes to us. It's all a little bit mysterious. It might be just a word that suddenly looks as if it wants to be in a poem, or it could be a whole little phrase."

Boutelle experienced this viscerally when she wrote the poems in *Becoming Bone*. She'd been planning to write a novel about Celia Thaxter, and had accumulated a great deal of information. But when she sat down to work, the book "just refused to be written." And then suddenly, out of the blue, a little poem appeared, which, it was clear, was the first poem of a series, and from then on, she knew what she was doing. "I was writing poems, and they were satisfyingly little, too, so that you got one little glimpse, and then the next one and the next."

* * *

The poems in *Becoming Bone* are written in the voice of Celia Thaxter, as the poems in Boutelle's *This Caravaggio* are, many of them, written in the voice of Caravaggio. Whether it is Edward Hirsch speaking in the voice of Gertrude Stein, Rita Dove embodying the prodigy George Bridgetower, or Patrick Donnelly writing in the voice of his dead mother's ashes, the persona poem is especially popular with contemporary poets. Some of the most astonishing examples can be found in Patricia Smith's *Blood Dazzler*, where Smith gives voice not just to the victims of Hurricane Katrina, but also to the hurricane itself.

> I become
> a mouth, thrashing hair, an overdone eye

she writes.

[E]very woman begins as weather,
sips slow thunder, knows her hips. Every woman
harbors a chaos . . .

One of the great joys of conducting the *Sparks* interviews was the chance to encounter such work, much of it "hot off the anvil," before it had even made it into print. Another was the sheer range of practices on display, from Matthew Dickman's "bright colorful building blocks" to Jean Valentine's enigmatic dream fragments and Jane Hirshfield's koan-like "sentencings," described by her as "shooting stars of thought." Each of the poets I spoke with had different aims and literary ambitions, along with a correspondingly varied sense of where support and inspiration might be found. Maxine Kumin, with her childhood grounding in prosody, laid great store by the mastery of traditional form. The first time she taught graduate students, she was appalled. "They couldn't tell a trochee from a tree limb!" In her own case, established forms provided the necessary "asbestos gloves" with which to tackle the most challenging of subjects— her late poems about Guantanamo, for example, or Abu Ghraib. She had to pound it into form, she told me, or she couldn't write it.

Yusef Komunyakaa was also drawn to tightly orchestrated forms. In high school, he wrote a hundred-line poem, all in rhymed quatrains. But then he discovered Langston Hughes, and his style began to change. "I grew up with the blues without even knowing it was the blues; everything around me was the blues. And I realized that embracing free verse, blank verse, I could sing in a different way, and maybe one that was truer to my experience."

For him, there is a kind of "singing underneath things," both in jazz and in what he calls "the deep silence of nature" —beauty and terror lying side by side. "And one doesn't know if one is being beckoned or—if it's the opposite of that." In either case, he says, "it's very tangible." He listens hard, and tries to give it voice.

* * *

It is not easy to be open to such mysteries, especially now, in a world crammed with ersatz connectivity. During the years I conducted the *Sparks* interviews, I was working on a book called *World Enough & Time: On Creativity and Slowing Down*. It was clear to me, as it was to many of the poets, that a certain kind of deep, wide-ranging receptivity was under siege. How best to find that spacious time again, that private smithy, in which to focus undistracted on the work of poetry?

Each of the *Sparks* writers has a different set of answers to that question. Some turn their backs on the new media and retreat to plain lined paper, pencil, pen. "I love the ritual of writing," says Chase Twichell. "If I had my way, I'd be writing with a stylus on wet clay." Others find sustenance in prayer and meditation, or, like Edward Hirsch, in rich and concentrated reading. Yet others rely on the fresh perspective offered by a daily walk.

For Merwin, here, as always, what matters most is the simple act of listening.

If you ask people to listen, they immediately want to know, "Listen to what?" But as Merwin told me, "That's what you have to find out. Only you can tell you what to listen for. But listen. If you hear the silence in the room, that's something. If you hear your own breath, that's something. If you hear the empty stream bed. If you hear the birds waking up in the morning. If you hear the car shrieking to a stop at the red light. *Whatever it may be. You're listening to it. Listening, listening, listening.*"

If you are lucky and attentive, such listening can intensify into a profound receptivity, heightening the senses and making space for what's to come. It is in that crucial moment of surrender, of self-loss, bafflement, and welcome, that the old assumptions vanish and new clarities can be hammered into shape. Or, as Merwin put it, with the calm authority of his eighty-five years, "*Poetry does not come from what you know. All that you know is very important, and not to be put down and ignored. But finally, it is from the unknown that poetry comes to you.*"

Christian McEwen
Northampton, 2015

ANNIE BOUTELLE

Interviewed April 25, 2012

It gives me great pleasure that this collection of interviews should open with the name of Annie Boutelle, both as a fellow Scot and as the founder of the Smith College Poetry Center. When *Sparks from the Anvil* first flickered into life, it was Boutelle who gave me her approval and encouragement, Boutelle whose enthusiastic "Yes!" first fanned the flames.

Thank you, thank you.

Annie Boutelle was born and grew up in Scotland, and now lives with her husband in western Massachusetts. She wrote her first poem as a child in 1953, in honor of Queen Elizabeth's coronation. In high school, her English teacher was Iain Crichton Smith, then writing poems both in Gaelic and in English. Boutelle read his work attentively, was much inspired, and published several poems in the school magazine. As a student at St. Andrew's University, she wrote her thesis on the poetry of Hugh MacDiarmid, and continued to work on poems of her own.

At the age of twenty, Boutelle moved to the United States to teach French in a private girls' school. Soon after, she got married and had three children. Though she taught in the English Department at Smith College, she wrote no poems for almost thirty years. She was struggling with a novel about the nineteenth-century writer Celia Thaxter, when, as she explains here, poetry came back to her, "and suddenly I was able to do this wonderful thing again." *Becoming Bone* was published in 2005. Since then, she has published three more books of poems. As she says, laughing, "There was no stopping me, after I got moving."

As I walked down the track to the river the morning of our interview, a lanky, long-bodied young fox paused on the slope ahead of me. Its color was astonishing, that sharp chestnut, the vivid flag of its tail. I stood there, watching it, for several minutes. "Hello," I wanted to say to it. "Hello, hello . . ." Sparks from some heavenly anvil: both encouragement and blessing.

Words

When did I forget how to plowter, how
to be scunnert, how to look for foozle

under the bed? When, afraid of sounding
twee, did I stop saying wee? Who snatched

away douce and douchty? I lost my spurtle,
grew too proud to be wabbit, avoided any

kind of big stramash. Even when my Libra
soul pendulumed alarmingly, I didn't swither.

I quarreled with the Bens, sent the burns
into exile. Did they creep slowly off, little

gray mice looking for another home (no
sleekit rodents this side of the pond)?

How proper it all became, no screech
of pipes, no eightsome reels, no raucous

ceilidhs, no cailleachs with their thin white
hairs and whisperings, no burach spreading

out across the floor. Nuala sees her
language as a boat, a coracle to launch

in the bulrushes and send off to "some
Pharaoh's daughter." I saw mine as

something like a wart, a fart, a sneeze.
And, oh, my lost darlings, I run after you

now, wrap treacherous arms round
you, dust you off, feed you kippers

from Loch Fyne and whiskey from Islay,
then pin you on the page, as witness.

Christian McEwen: You published your first two books back in 2005. They both came out in that same year, pitch-perfect, perfectly honed. And I wondered if there was a long private incubation before that, or whether you just returned to poetry after a number of years.

Annie Boutelle: Yes, I did return to poetry after a number of years. I had been surrounded by poetry in my childhood and I wrote a lot of poems, especially when I was at St. Andrews University. When I first came to the United States—I was twenty—I was teaching at a private school in New Jersey. And I think that it was impossible for me at that time to figure out who exactly I was, and if I wanted to be writing poems, *what would these poems be like?* I mean, could I write American poems? I was a little dubious because here I was, a stranger in a strange land. Would I continue to write Scottish poems?

So, for whatever reason, I just stopped. I absolutely stopped writing poems. And when the first poem arrived in connection to the Isles of Shoals book, it was just as if a treasure had suddenly dropped into my arms! [Laughs.] I was deep into writing poetry before I knew it, and I felt as if I had come home at last. The years in between of course were busy with many things, including the births of three children and my teaching at Smith. But I certainly have been delighted to be immersed back into the poetry world.

CM: Did you think during those years that you had renounced poetry?

AB: I'm not sure I'd say "renounced," but I had certainly put it aside. Let's just say that.

CM: How long was it between that first Isle of Shoals poem till the date of publication?

AB: I'd guess something like two years. I know I wrote it pretty quickly. Once I started, it was clear where it was going. The script, in a way, was already written by what had happened to Celia Thaxter—the woman I was writing about. I remember it as being quite a quick process.

CM: How wonderful. That something can be lost, and then so completely found.

AB: Yes. And it was all thanks to my dear friend Annie Raskin. I was staying at her place down at Cape Cod when the ice melted or—I don't know what metaphor to use—when suddenly I was back, and I was able to do this wonderful thing again.

CM: Such a joy.
    I loved those poems from *Nest of Thistles*, "Girl" and "Rockfield Primary School," which are about yourself as a child. And I wondered if you'd say something about yourself as a little girl, and how you first came to poetry.

AB: "Girl" is actually set in Aberfeldy in Perthshire. Most of my growing up happened in Oban on the west coast, but I was born in Aberfeldy and that's where I spent the first few years of my life.

CM: How old would you have been at that time?

AB: Oh . . . I was four or five, I'd guess.

CM: You've said that your father loved Coleridge, and your mother loved recitation. And that your own first poem was written for the Queen's Coronation in 1952.

AB: Right, yes.

CM: So I wondered what you learned about poetry as a child. Whether your parents read to you, and what you were taught at school, between, say, the ages of four and twelve.

AB: Oh, yes! Once we moved to Oban, and I was sent to the Rockfield

Primary School, there certainly was a lot of poetry. It was part of the regular program. I particularly remember one teacher. "O the Young Lochinvar has come out of the west, / Through all the wide Borders his steed was the best." She'd get so excited, and she'd wave her arms up and down as she read to us.

And we were expected as children to memorize poems and then to be able to recite them back, and I've always felt very grateful for having that as a beginning, and for the real focus that was put on poetry in those days.

CM: And then in high school, Iain Crichton Smith was your English teacher.

AB: Iain Crichton Smith was my English teacher. And he was a wonderfully funny man. I have been very grateful to him over the years. I loved knowing him as a friend when I got older and he was no longer teaching. I would always stop and visit him whenever I was back in the area.

CM: Were you reading his poems as a young girl in the high school?

AB: I was, yes. He of course wouldn't read his poems to us at the time, but I would buy whatever books he was bringing out, and I really love his work. I think it's fantastic. Especially his use of slant rhymes. And the knowledge that he was writing poems in Gaelic as well as in English is quite amazing. And writing plays in Gaelic as well as in English. He was very talented.

CM: Were you writing your own poems at that time?

AB: In high school, yes. I was writing poems in the high school. One or two were published in a little magazine that they brought out once a year. I don't think I shared them very much with people.

The high school was a fantastic school. John Maclean was the rector, and he'd grown up on Raasay, and was a wonderful classics scholar. He always walked around with a copy of the *Odyssey* in his pocket. And if a teacher were ill, he would stand in for that teacher. He'd pull out the *Odyssey* and he'd translate it in his head into Gaelic, and then into English, and he'd read us the English version, the final version. And that would keep us going until the bell rang, and we moved on to the next class.

There was also an amazing history teacher called Mr. Murray. He had a very distinctive way of teaching that involved students pretending that they were, let's say, in a little tiny village on the west coast of Scotland, with the Vikings pillaging and slaughtering people.

There was this effort of trying to imagine yourself into history.

CM: That's so interesting, because you yourself have done both those things. You've translated from the French and the German. And two of your books, the Celia Thaxter and the Caravaggio, both center around persona poems—becoming other.

AB: Yes.

CM: So, one could trace that way, way back perhaps . . .

AB: I think you're right.

And then the other wonderful thing about Mr. Murray was that he started a climbing club, and anyone who had a good pair of boots was welcome to come along. It was a wonderful social occasion for us. A chance not only to get to know Mr. Murray differently, but also to get to know our fellow students more completely than we would have otherwise. We had a class reunion last year, and Mr. Murray's name came up over and over again. It was clear that one of the most important things that had happened to us was knowing Mr. Murray.

CM: That's wonderful.

I'm looking at your first book, *Nest of Thistles*. I was very moved by the poems about your lost brother, and the later ones about your mother suffering with Alzheimer's. I wondered if you'd talk about the satisfactions, and also the anxiety, of giving form to such intimate stories?

AB: I wrote the poems about my mother only after she was dead. I don't think I could've written them while she was alive. And the ones about my brother, who [had] Down syndrome and was sent off to a [special needs] home—I think I really needed to write those poems. I think, maybe, it's a Scottish thing that a lot of that stuff is kept pretty private.

And yet it had been something truly momentous in my life when my brother was sent to the home, because I had been very fond of him. And the reason he was sent to the home was that I had begun imitating how he talked, and this disturbed my parents so much they decided he would have to go away. That must have been a huge loss that I had no way of even talking about or exploring.

So I think that it was a book that was good for me to write, and allowed me to face up to some stuff that otherwise I wouldn't have the courage.

I was quite scared of what my sister would think of all of this, because I hadn't asked her permission. I had just written the poems and I had dedicated the book to my sister, and then I sent it off to her in the mail. And after it was off in the mail I thought, "Oh, my God! Maybe she is going to hate this book."

So, after I thought that it would've arrived, I called her up and said, "Are you all right with this?" and she said, "I've just been crying for the last two hours," and she said, "Tears and soup don't really go very well together!" But she said, "I really, really love this book." And I had such a huge feeling of release because I had just really blindly pushed forward, and assumed that this would be all right with her. And, my sister and I are very close now. We were not close as children. We were always squabbling over one thing or another. But one of the absolute delights of my adulthood has been rediscovering that sister, and she's been rediscovering me over the years as well.

CM: Wonderful! What a story! What a story, and a tribute to your courage too.

AB: Thank you.

CM: There's a thread of melancholy in your work that maybe has to do partly with being a foreigner. I wondered if you'd say something about what that long exile has meant. I'm thinking of poems like "Bens" and, of course, "Nest of Thistles" and "Words," which is my own favorite.

AB: Oh, I love "Words" too. It's hard for me to reconstruct now what it was like to write this book. But I felt instinctively that it was a book that had to be written. I had great pleasure writing it as well. There's obviously quite a bit of sadness in it, too. But I felt I was reconnecting in a major way with where I came from and, as you know, it is such a beautiful country. Every time I'm there I just spend my time looking at the hills and looking some more at the hills. It's gorgeous in its severity. [Laughs.] I try to get back at least once every year and if I don't get back any given year, I feel something is wrong in my life. I need to touch base with Scotland whenever I possibly can.

CM: And do you keep in touch with Scottish poetry?

AB: I went to StAnza one year and that was very interesting. I don't read as much in the way of Scottish poems as I should, although, like you, I visit the Scottish Poetry Library every time I'm in Edinburgh and steep myself in the poems that are there. And I also listen always to Iain Crichton Smith. They've got some wonderful recordings of him going to Aberdeen as a young man and seeing a train for the first time ever. He'd never been off the island before that!

CM: What other poets and writers have inspired you?

AB: I have to say that Eavan Boland has had a big effect on me. She was the very first reader that we had at the Poetry Center at Smith, and I absolutely adore this woman's work, and have done since I read "Pomegranate" in *The New Yorker* a long, long time ago. I would follow that woman anywhere. She's been crucially important.

And I loved the Dickman brothers, Matthew and Michael. I was entranced by what they were up to, the two of them. You know how very different their two kinds of poems were. But I thought that they were really great. Jack Gilbert was a big favorite of mine, and I miss his presence in the Valley, which was delightful in many ways. I'm *hugely* indebted to Elizabeth Alexander with the work she did getting the Poetry Center off to this amazing start. We really owe her a huge amount.

CM: One of the things I love about your poems is their clarity, their precision. I'm thinking of phrases like "braided gold" for the barley in your "Ghost" poem. You have such a delicate, delicious gift for metaphor. And I wondered if you'd talk about what was involved for you in preserving that clear eye, that grace and accuracy.

AB: I don't know! I mean it's just the way I am. It's built into me; I don't have a choice! [Laughs.]

CM: It's a delicacy and a sensibility that gives me tremendous joy, I have to say.

This connects to something Edward Hirsch said when I interviewed him. He talked about the din of the culture, the noise of America today, and the ways in which that can distract young people in particular, pull them off course. I suppose I see your gift for clarity as an achievement of contemplation, of stillness. And I wondered if you had any particular antidotes to the rush, the overwhelm.

AB: I'm thinking of W. S. Merwin now, and something he said. Something like, "The important thing is listening." This morning I was in the Poetry Center and there's a quotation there. And again, the main message is, "Listening is where it really all begins." I think that's true—that silent listening is, quite frequently, where a poem begins. Where we, the writers, don't really know, but something comes to us, however it comes to us. It's all a little bit mysterious. . . . It might be just a word that suddenly looks as if it wants to be in a poem, or it could be a whole little phrase.

And I know that if I find myself with a little phrase that has just popped into my head, I always take that really seriously. I always, if I can possibly do it, write it down. Because if it's not written down, it will vanish. And it's usually the sign of something that's wanting to break through and become a poem.

CM: How do you teach that gift of receptivity, that listening skill to students?

AB: Well, I'm ready to talk about it, and I have talked about it with students over the years. But I've found my students to be wildly inventive and bold about what they're ready to write about. It's amazing to see what can happen within a semester. Someone who has begun in a very tentative way gradually begins to discover what she's capable of. It's like little planes at an airport: suddenly they're up in the air, and are doing amazing things that they hadn't expected.

CM: I wondered if you'd say more about your persona poems, and how it is to write as someone else.

AB: Oh! I think it's a great privilege to be able to be somebody else, and to think your way into somebody else's head. Of course, you may be completely wrong about what you've discovered. But there is a freedom not to be writing about the self. I know that if I find too many "I's" cropping up, I get quite distressed.

CM: Could you explain about what drew you to Celia Thaxter?

AB: When our children were young, we used to go out to Star Island, on the Isle of Shoals, for a week every summer. My husband would be the doctor on the island, and we were given a lovely little cottage to live in. And there's no way you can be on the islands without learning about Celia Thaxter. I bought some books about her, and enjoyed reading them. My mother-in-law, who had come with us, instantly thought that I ought to write a children's book called "Celia's Lighthouse." She thought it would be a very good children's book. [Laughs.] My mother-in-law was always suggesting things to people and sometimes they would go along with it and sometimes they would say, "Sorry, no, this is not for me."

So I had the, "Sorry, this is not for me" response, but at the same time, with every given year, I was learning a little more about Celia Thaxter. I thought I was going to write a novel about her, and I did a lot of work preparing for this. And after I had accumulated all of this information, I sat down to write it, and, damn it all, it just refused to be written! Just, no way! I thought, "Well, this is awful. You know, *what do I do now?*" And suddenly, this little poem appeared, which, it was clear, was the first poem of a series, and that was what broke the silence. For thirty years, I had not written. But that poem, it was as if it fell down from heaven and into my lap!

From that point on it was easy. I now knew what I was doing. I was writing poems, and they were satisfyingly little, too, so that you got one little glimpse and then the next one and then the next.

CM: Perhaps you could read one. Maybe "Sea Baby," which I adore.

AB: OK.

[Annie Boutelle reads "Sea Baby."]

AB: It's been years since I've read that poem, so it almost felt like the poem of a stranger. [Laughs.] *"What is she meaning by that?"*

CM: I think her meaning is pretty clear!

So finally this brand new venture, *This Caravaggio*. Would you talk a little about how you came to write that book? What was so impressive to me was your own faith in the impetus that carried you forward. It seemed as if you were touched by fire, by Caravaggio, and you said, "Yes!"

AB: I think that's pretty accurate, actually. My husband and I were in Venice, and I said to him, "If we're going to be in Venice, shouldn't we also go to Rome? It's not that far away and I would really, really like to see Rome." And he's very indulgent, so he said, "Sure, that's OK with me." And off to Rome we went. In the first few days, I managed to get the two of us to the Borghese Gallery, where there are these incredibly beautiful Caravaggio paintings. I soaked them all in as best I could. Then, after that, we went around the churches in Rome, which are beautiful, and in many of them there are wonderful Caravaggio paintings just where he painted them. I was thrilled by what I was seeing. There was something about the directness of it that bowled me over.

And I knew that when I went back to the United States, I would really, really want to find out more about the man who'd made this beautiful work. The Smith library was enormously useful to me. I filled up my entire office with Caravaggio books, and read and read and read and read as much as I possibly could. I had really no idea that I was going to write about him. It was just plain old curiosity. I wanted to discover as much as I possibly could. And when I finished the reading, I remember feeling a great sense of sadness because he had become a part of my life.

But the thought eventually moved through my head that, "Maybe you could write a poem about Caravaggio." In a way it was easy, because I approached it chronologically. I began with him as a child, and then gradually allowed him to get older. I loved doing the extra research that

I did then, and the pure pleasure of looking at these paintings, over and over and over again, and reading some of the stuff that art historians had said—sometimes disagreeing violently with what they were saying. And other times feeling as if I was really learning a lot from them, as well as from the paintings directly. It was really such pure pleasure.

CM: What was it like to allow someone else's images to give rise to your words, as opposed to, say, knowing the story of Celia Thaxter and coming up with the images yourself? So many of your Caravaggio poems involve very precise mirroring of what is there in the painting. In a sense you become subservient to what is there already.

AB: Yes! And I felt very happy about being subservient to it. They're so amazing, those paintings, and, I guess, partly it was a mission to get more and more people knowing about them. Not that there aren't people in the world who know about them already! [Laughs.] So it's maybe a little cheeky for me to think that I was opening doors. But I know that it was an important book for me, not only to write, but to get out there in the world. Really, I had such faith in the paintings that I thought they would carry me through. That, and the character of the man are at the core of the book.

CM: Yes, the character of the man, Caravaggio. As you've said, there's a certain hubris or courage that's required in taking on a masculine voice. Could you speak about that?

AB: I was always scared to do it. That's the main thing. I'm relieved to think that nobody thought it was too terrible, that I was up there as a woman pretending to know a lot about Caravaggio. I think if you have enough confidence in the work, you can somehow make it work, in a way that it wouldn't otherwise. I just had to be bold, and you know, that's one of the delights at Smith. Our students are ready to be bold, and in many ways they are models for us to follow. I am constantly inspired by the boldness of my students.

CM: That's lovely to hear.

What do you feel most delighted to have accomplished in the Caravaggio book? What surprised you most, astonished you most? You've spoken, for example, of the variety of different forms and the stretching that was involved with that.

AB: Yes. I wanted that deliberately. I wanted people not to know what kind of shape they'd see when they'd turn the page. I very deliberately played with form in a way that's unusual for me, and allowed poems to get very, very skinny or short and fat or whatever. Someone was asking me recently about the "Tour de Nona" poem, which is in this block shape, and that was when Caravaggio was imprisoned in Rome. I specifically wanted it to have this feeling of entrapment.

CM: It's literally a concrete poem or a stone poem.

AB: Yes, a stone poem.

[**AB** reads "Tour de Nona".]

CM: Wonderful.

So how do you think your work is going to change now that you have more time to give to it?

AB: I have absolutely no idea! You know, in my experience something grabs me. This has happened often enough for me to feel totally confident that it will happen. I don't need to go out looking for it. It will find me. But, I have not a clue as to what I will do next. I will just wait and see, and keep myself busy in other ways than in writing poetry.

CM: You have already a new book in the works.

AB: It's called *How They Fell,* which is a reference to what happened in New York with the towers. But it's a weird book. It's about desire, and it's also about various boyfriends of mine from my years in Scotland and Vienna. It was really interesting thinking back to these various guys, some of whom were quite wonderful and others less so. It's a really quite wild mixture of things. "How They Fell" applies to Adam and Eve as well as to the towers. I haven't actually looked at it for a while. And it will be interesting to see what kind of revisions I may want to do when I go back to it. The next challenge, obviously, is to make it the best book I can.

CM: So you've got the mythological or the theological. You've got the political, and you've got Scotland and America and Europe.

AB: Yes. And I've got some really rather nasty characters who do rather nasty things, too. But I won't tell you more than that. [Laughs.]

CM: I have just a couple more questions.

I wondered if you had a few words for the young writers who may be reading this—anything you wished you'd understood at their age, and that maybe you'd hoped to share with them as a teacher, and as the founder of the Poetry Center.

AB: I think that it is extraordinarily useful for young writers to get a community of other writers around them. We can learn so much from other people. We all have huge blinkers on in relationship to our own poems, and it is phenomenally useful to have somebody else to take a look, and to let us know where the black holes are in our own work.

I always encourage my students to attend as many poetry events as they possibly can. The more you can steep yourself in poetry, whether it's attending poetry readings or just reading poetry books that you've discovered and love, and reading them over and over again, the more you learn about how the writer is doing something.

It's an exciting time for poetry in the United States. There are a lot more people open to it than was the case before. We've certainly been amazed at the audience at the Poetry Center right from the get-go. We had no idea there would be over four hundred people showing up for Eavan Boland's reading, that very first time.

And I will always remember this: There was a German student who was studying at Smith, and she came to me early on, saying that she was impressed and somewhat horrified by the amount of stress on the campus. In the German university she was from, the stress was nothing like what it is at Smith. She said that some students solve it by being active physically, and that's what they're often encouraged to do—to go to the gym or to be on the rugby team or whatever.

But, she said, there are a lot of people who don't like those physical activities, and for them, the Poetry Center was playing a role in reducing stress. She said, "There's something about going to a reading. You don't have to put up your hand and ask questions. You don't have to do anything, other than be there and listen."

And she thought that was one of the best methods for reducing stress.

I had never thought of it in that way, but I think she was right. I think that's why we see so many students attending the readings. There's a way the Poetry Center feels like a kind of home that is different from the rest of Smith, and they appreciate what comes to that home and treat it delicately.

MATTHEW DICKMAN

Interviewed November 3, 2009

When I asked Annie Boutelle whose work she particularly admired, she praised the Irish poet, Eavan Boland, and, immediately afterwards, the twin brothers Matthew and Michael Dickman, who had read at Smith not long before. "I was entranced by what they were up to, the two of them." She recognized how very differently they wrote, Matthew in long, exuberant, ecstatic catalogues, Michael more fragmentary and austere. But, she emphasized, "I thought that they were really great."

Matthew Dickman grew up in Portland, Oregon, with his brother, Michael and their little sister, Elizabeth. Their mother, Wendy, was a single mom, and those early years weren't easy. There were drugs and gangs and skinheads, casual violence. "In retrospect," says Matthew, "I feel like a bullet had gone by my head." He first came to poetry through rap music. "Someone had a boom box and played Ice T's first album, and I thought, "What is this? This is great." He and Michael began to read voraciously in high school, and to write poems too. By the mid '90s, they were both writing seriously, along with their friends Michael McGriff and Carl Adamshick.

When Matthew's first book was published in 2008, it won the American Poetry Review/Honickman First Book Prize, selected by the poet, Tony Hoagland. Since then, he has published two more books (one co-written with his brother) and his work has appeared in *Ploughshares, The London Review of Books, Narrative Magazine,* and *The New Yorker,* among others. He is the poetry editor of *Tin House Magazine,* and still lives in Portland, Oregon.

Country Music

When the dogs in my neighborhood go wild
over the patrol car's red and blue scream, the lights hitting
someone's window like electric tickertape
and I know some of those dogs are biters
because I was someone they bit,
I begin to think about the lives of men
and how we carry the heavy load of muscle, the rumble and ruckus,
without a single complaint
while vulnerability barely lifts its face from the newspaper.
But I've been drinking. I'm a little messed up
and there's something about cigars and bourbon I no longer want
to be part of. I remember how Kate would slip out
of her jeans, her bra. How she appled my body;
all that sweet skin and core, the full mouth and pulp.
She was like a country song
playing underneath an Egyptian cotton sheet, the easy kindness
of her body finding its way into mine.
But I have a father somewhere. I have a way
I'm supposed to walk down the street like a violent decision
that hasn't been made yet.
I don't care how many hours you put in
weeding the garden
or how much you love modern dance. You'll still slip back
into your knuckles.
You can carry your groceries home in your public radio tote bag.
You can organize a book club.
You can date an Indonesian hippie with dread-locks
but you are never far from breaking someone's jaw.
When I was twenty-three I went to a party,
drank two Coronas, and slapped my girlfriend across the face.
I wanted someone to beat me.
I wanted to get thrown into the traffic
I had made of my life,

to go flying over the couch
where two skater kids were smoking pot out of a Pepsi can
and talking about a friend
who ollied over a parked car the same day he got stabbed
at the mall.

Christian McEwen: I wanted to ask, first of all, if you'd talk a little about your growing up.

Matthew Dickman: I grew up in a neighborhood called the Lents District in Portland, Oregon. I grew up with my twin brother, Michael, my little sister, Elizabeth, and our single mom, Wendy Dickman. I grew up in a really wonderful, supportive household in a fairly rough, very lower blue-collar neighborhood.

CM: Could you tell me about the ways in which being a twin has influenced your work? What strikes me is that your brother and you write such different poems. Did you consciously decide to divide the language of poetry between you?

MD: Consciously being a twin did not dictate how I would or wouldn't write a poem. Michael and I started writing poems pretty furiously in the mid '90s with two other poets, Michael McGriff and our friend Carl Adamshick. At the time we all wrote poems that were very similar and often sounded like the work of poets we really loved and were reading at the time.

Now all four of us write very differently. I think that that change happened out of our own characters and who we are as people, but perhaps it was in some way subconsciously setting apart a little piece of land for each of us.

CM: That makes a lot of sense. There's a reference in the *New Yorker* article about Michael and you "waking from the same dream, the same nightmare." Do you still find that your psychic lives are entwined in that way?

MD: Maybe not as intimately as when we were children. I think we share a lot of the same anxieties. We have the same sense of humor. When we're together we can finish each other's sentences. And I acutely know how my brother is feeling, and sometimes I wonder if he doesn't know how I'm feeling even before I do.

CM: You spoke of him, your brother Michael, as "that great and mythic friend of mine, that lucky charm." And I wondered whether knowing him so deeply, and with such affection, made it hard to connect with other friends, even perhaps girlfriends and lovers.

MD: That's a great question. I think that's a question not just for twins, but for siblings who may have been born near the same time as each other. When you are that close with somebody—even if it's a friend, but certainly a twin—they fulfill a lot of things for you as a human being that maybe a lover or another friend might fulfill—support systems and things like that. So I'm sure that's there somewhere, but luckily we seem to be fairly well adjusted, and we both have important and deep relationships outside of our friendship and our fellowship and our relationship as twins.

CM: Going back to your childhood in Lents, what was your relationship to poetry in those days? How old were you when you first found books and began to write?

MD: I found books and began to write in high school. My experience with poetry in my neighborhood was . . . none. My first memory of poetry actually has to do with music, listening to rap music in the neighborhood. I was in seventh grade. I remember it distinctly. Someone had a boom box and they played Ice T's first album, and I thought, "What is this? This is great." So my earliest experience with any sort of poetry was rap music. Then later, in high school, I fell in love with a young girl much older than me—she was a junior. She read Anne Sexton, and then I started falling in love with Anne Sexton.

CM: What is your own writing process? Do you find yourself guided toward a poem primarily by its music and its rhythm, or by its subject matter?

MD: I think the answer has to be music and rhythm. Years ago I'd think of a poem for a long time and I'd have a story that I'd make up, and I would write it in my head and rework it in my head, and then write it down on the page.

But then I stopped writing poems for a little under a year, and when I started again all these rules I had made for myself seemed to have disappeared with the therapy I was getting that year, and I could just sit down and write whatever I wanted to write. And so I started looking at it like bright colorful building blocks, where a blue block would appear, and then I would put a red one there, and then a green one. It sounds silly and sort of naïve, but I like the expansiveness of beginning a poem in that place rather than having a distinct idea of what I'm going to write.

CM: I think of the line of yours, where you describe your heart as "president of the Association for Random Desire." That links beautifully with what you just said about the colored blocks. There's a courage there, and a readiness to be distracted, and to follow the distraction to its glorious destination, which I really admire, in the sense of trusting your feelings, your intuition, your luck, almost.

MD: Luck, and also I'm a big fan of failure. I think failure is a great thing we get to have in our lives, and poor failure is so talked down to and marred that I like the idea that I'm able to fail. I'm OK with my heart being whatever my heart is going to be, and letting my writing come out of that in whatever way it's going to come, whether it's silly or a little clichéd or deep and heavy or funny. Whatever it is, I'm OK with it.

CM: You spoke earlier of the more formal self, if you will, and now this trust in the randomness, the trust in the colored blocks. When you reached that place of trust after that year of therapy, was that what you would call the moment when you "began to find your voice"? Or do you not think in terms of voice, because in a sense each poem is its own new voice?

MD: That's a great question. I'm not sure exactly where I stand on voice. Writing the poems that ended up in *All-American Poem* and starting to do readings here and there, I started getting this fear that people would one day realize that it was just me talking. Once I felt that fear, maybe that was a sign that I had found my own voice in my poems.

CM: I'm particularly in love with your zany metaphors. I love the line "snow falls like really expensive French sea salt." "My watch with the time inside it bravely marching forward." "The moon with his black dinner jacket." "The sweet mollusk of the tongue." Wonderful, wonderful language. Who do you think helped model those metaphors for you? They come from you, obviously, but somebody out in the poetry world also showed you that such things could be done. So who were your teachers?

MD: Immediately, I think of Anne Sexton. I think her metaphors are often wild. Dorianne Laux has a huge talent and big heart for metaphor, as do Sharon Olds and many other poets. The weird thing about metaphor is that it's a mystery. Nobody knows where it came from. We can't study it in our language; we can't go back far enough. It's that great human impulse to describe something, to get at the truth of it. "He ran like . . . he was running" doesn't tell you what he ran like. "He ran like a train, out of control, through a bottle of whiskey"—although that may not make total sense, emotionally it does. And that's the strange, wonderful thing about metaphors.

CM: You mentioned Sharon Olds, and of course her father was your step-grandfather, which must have had its complications. So I was wondering when you first read her poems, and indeed when you first crossed paths with her as another poet.

MD: There weren't actually that many complications for Michael and me, or our little sister, with our grandfather. By the time we got to know him he was sober, and also very, very ill. He was a much different man than he was with Sharon growing up, certainly, and even with my mother, Wendy, or my aunt, Lori. So that part wasn't that complicated or difficult. And even Sharon—we knew Sharon as a half sort of aunt. We didn't grow up listening to her poems or reading her poems—well, reading any poems at all, really.

It was only much, much later, when Michael and I started writing poems on our own, that suddenly there was this link. But our friendship with Sharon is mainly out of deep love and mutual admiration of really great donuts and, um, trying to be sane and human in this world that we all share.

CM: Could you talk about family life and the encroachments of that difficult outside world? I'm thinking now of poems like "Lents District." The *New Yorker* piece said that you guys were drinking at the age of twelve, and there were a lot of drugs and shoot-ups in your neighborhood, so I wondered how it was to have that private safety and sensibility, and then those challenges just beyond the gate.

MD: In retrospect, I feel like a bullet had gone by my head. You know, having the stability of a mother like Wendy, and our house. It says something that a lot of our friends were always coming over to the house. Not because you could drink there or party there, but because there was always food there, no one was getting beaten there, no one was getting harassed. I didn't know at the time—although I could probably sense it some ways— that it was a haven for Michael and me, our little sister, and many friends.

I would go over to pals of mine—their homes—and their parents would be ill with drug-abuse and alcoholism. There were some places we'd stay, and you'd just know that you would get hit along with the kids, the other kids. So it was an incredible thing that our mom was able to have there in that neighborhood. Later she started reading our poems, and thought, "God, I didn't know it was that bad." Because she worked all day into the night and came home and was trying to put food on the table and have her own life, and it was Michael and I and Elizabeth who were going out into the neighborhood and kinda knew more about it.

CM: Are you still in touch with your friends from those days?

MD: Not really. I've bumped into a couple of them. Some of them are dead. I don't really go back to my old neighborhood, partly because it's changed so much, and a lot of the things that I used to do there I don't do anymore. [Laughs.]

You know, I don't do drugs anymore. But I have one or two friends I'm still in touch with and who survived the neighborhood and survived their childhood.

CM: I wanted to ask if you'd talk about men and manhood as they show up in your life and in writing. I'm thinking of a poem called "Country Music," where you refer to "the lives of men, and how we carry the heavy load of muscle," and then that amazing line, "I'm supposed to walk down the street like a violent decision that hasn't been made yet."

I wondered whether having a brother, whom you so clearly loved and could be truthful with, as well as a single mom, whom you clearly admire and respect, meant that you were able to avoid that false armor that so many adult men are burdened by.

MD: I think that's exactly right. I think that having Michael, and Michael having me, really saved us from a lot of that. A lot of it, when we were growing up, was unavoidable. You know, Michael and I grew up and we were in fights. I've lived in some neighborhoods where if you are walking down the street, two men passing each other, you just say, "Hey. Good evening, how's it going?" And someone asks for a light. But in my neighborhood growing up, if two men were passing each other, they would check in with each other, not, like, saying "Good evening," but, *Are you dangerous? What's gonna happen? Is there something that's gonna happen?"*

For me, something that was incredible was early on in high school, when I started reading about the Beatniks and the Beat poets, and especially the community of men around Allen Ginsberg and Jack Kerouac and Burroughs. Because this was a group of men who were coming together and not causing violence. And I mean, *violence.* There was heartbreak and people were cruel to lovers and that kinda thing. But in the neighborhood I'm thinking about, and many neighborhoods like it, if a group of men are together on the corner it's not gonna be to write poems. And I thought that was revolutionary, really revolutionary.

It's one of the reasons Michael and I were attracted to our friend Carl and our friend Mike. We were once all four on a panel and someone said, "It's strange that there's not a woman on the panel with you." And although we have dear, intimate female friends who are poets and writers, I think we have this bond because all four of us came from similar neighborhoods, and we were all men who were choosing not to hit our wives, not to flunk out on our kids. We were these four weirdos who were choosing to write poems together.

CM: It interests me very much, the notion of a male role model who's doing something that the world perceives as "sissy." For example, when

I worked as a writer-in-the-schools in New York City, for a poet to come in who was a man was very different for the children than for a poet to come in who was a female, because a woman would be expected to have a soft, open heart and a gentle way with her, whereas a man who was both strong and gentle was modeling something tremendously important for those children.

MD: I think it's a really moving thing, and not just because of the neighborhood that Michael and I grew up with, but because I am a man I think about masculinity a lot. In that poem you talked about, "Country Music"—I don't think that men are ever very far from violence. Now I think that men are hopefully more and more, from generation to generation, making the choice against it. And that's the courageous thing.

CM: I'm going to ask you to read "Country Music," because I think we need it right now, at this moment.

[**MD** reads "Country Music." See page 34.]

CM: Thank you so much. Tell me what that word "ollied" means.

MD: [Laughs.] It's a skateboarding term. When you ollie over something, you snap the back of the board down at the same time as you drag the side of your foot up the grip tape at the front, and you pop up into the air.

CM: Brilliant!

How do you know when something's done, especially perhaps those long, ecstatic catalogues like the ones in *All-American Poem*?

MD: That's a hard question to answer. I mean, poetry is so funny because it's always complete. But it's always unfinished as well. In a very real way, in a way that interacts with a reader, or someone listening to it, it's complete. And I think always sort of unfinished for the writer.

Lists are hard because lists can go on forever and ever and ever and ever and ever. So for me the way a poem finishes—and this may be a little woo-woo—but it just feels done to me. It's like when you meet someone you fall in love with the first time you meet them. You understand them, you see them, and the feeling is of *Oh! Oh, there you are! Right. OK. Fine.*

You know. And that's the feeling for me at the end of a list. And also, you know, if I read a list in a poem, or if I have a poem that jumps around for too long while I'm reading it to myself, if I feel like I've just encountered someone at a party who will not stop talking to me, I know it's time to use the bathroom, you know what I mean? I know it's time to, like, cut it [laughs] and look at it again.

CM: Apart from your brother, where have you found your best readers and encouragement? I know your high school teacher was very helpful, but more recently than that?

MD: More recently than that, I would say other poets I've been lucky enough to meet. My poet friend Matthew Lippman, who's a great poet, he is always encouraging, and a great reader for me. Dorianne Laux, Joseph Millar, these other poets. And I should say that the greatest thing I feel I've gotten out of poetry—besides, I think, it really saving my life as a young person—is the friendships with other artists, other poets, with painters, with fiction writers. And that is wholly enriching and absolutely important beyond anything else, beyond publications or awards, or, you know, some attention. Because the good news is that there is actually no fame or money in poetry. There's none. People sometimes feel like there is. But the elephant in the room is that it's actually just poems.

But I also find encouragement outside of that immediate world of poetry. I share my poems with people who don't often read or write poems. They're really encouraging, but they're encouraging in a great way, because they don't understand totally why I'm doing it, but they don't care because they love me. They think it's really weird, like, "Oh man, keep making those spacesuits made out of jello. It's awesome. It makes you happy." You know, that's kinda like the energy. And it helps, too, because if I share a poem of mine with, like, a friend of mine who works at Starbucks, who plays in a heavy metal band and only reads, like, dark vampire novels, if he reads my poem about love and he understands it and feels it, then I feel, "Good, I'm not getting too far away, not just from him but from myself."

CM: That makes a lot of sense. I know the two of you have worked in the food service industries, and I wondered whether you're still doing that now that your poetry is so much better known.

MD: I work right now at a Whole Foods in Portland, Oregon. I started there a year ago washing dishes, and now I work in the wine and cheese department. It's very fancy. [Laughs.] But they're great. They give me time off to come to readings, like at Smith College, or wherever. So, no, I still do that. I still work in places like that. I was a baker for years. I'm guest teaching right now at Portland State University, an intro to poetry class, which is really fun. But I imagine that my life may always be partly these kinds of jobs, which, um, I don't dislike. At all.

CM: When I look at your acknowledgments, I see Naomi Shihab Nye. I see Joe Millar, Marie Howe, Kenneth Koch, Frank O'Hara, Pablo Neruda. Who are you reading and rereading at this point?

MD: One of the things I'm reading is this incredible book of poems by James Allen Hall. He has his first book out, called *Now You're the Enemy*. This is a brave, brave, poet, who writes beautiful, heartbreaking poems. I'm also reading some poems by a friend of mine, Jillian Weise, who wrote this great book, *The Amputee's Guide to Sex*. Another really brave, wonderful book. I have those two by my bed, and then I read a lot of things that aren't poems. So I'm reading a memoir right now by Ann Hood called *Comfort,* and I am reading—actually, for the first time in my life, and I can't believe it—I'm always coming late to a party, and it's sort of embarrassing at first, but then I'm just like, you know, fuck it, I'm here, and it'll be great. I'm reading *On the Road* for the first time. I'm blushing as I say it. It's in my hotel room right now. And I think it's grand.

CM: I remember, as a student in London, reading it all night long until four in the morning.

MD: I bet. It's so great.

CM: I wondered if you had any special advice for young writers starting out, and also those who are older and maybe more discouraged?

MD: My advice would be the advice that I try to take for myself, which is not always successful. One, I think whoever suggested that people writing should avoid the influence of other writers should be sent to the corner, and have to sit on their hands quietly and think about the bad, bad thing that they've just said, and no dessert for them! I think we should be open to influence. I think that's the great thing about human beings, that we are open to influence, and that we can synchronize with people, and then break away, and then synchronize with other people. It's a magical thing, and I don't think you should worry if you're reading a lot of poems by Sylvia Plath and you're "sounding like Plath."

One of the reasons I think you should be influenced by people, and actually try to be, is it helps you as a reader to understand their work, and you get closer to that writer, which is an especially meaningful experience when the writer is no longer alive. And the other thing is you learn about writing in a way that you might not if you just hole up in your house, not read anybody else's poems, and try to figure out what your voice is or what you're doing.

So my advice is to be open to influences, other poets' music, to try to relieve yourself of an anxiety of intellect. I know it's hard when that anxiety runs rampant in schools, to try to let that go, to say, "I'm a human being, and one day I get to die, and in between now and then I get to run and fall and get up and I can do anything." Larry Levis, the great Larry Levis, said, "Out here I can say anything."

And that's something else that's great about writing. We live in a world where you can't always do anything you want: you are constantly having to follow rules. And when you sit down with a pencil or a pen and a piece of paper, this is a world that has no rules for you. You can say anything, you can be anybody you want, and that is going to—along with maybe gardening—help you live much longer. So I think that's some advice.

And then the other thing is for poets who are starting to send work out to be published—like, I sent poems out for six years or something, and got rejection after rejection after rejection. It's that the more you can separate your writing life from this other life of publishing or awards, the better. It's like church and state. Writing is the mystical, religious life. And then publishing and that sort of thing is the secular life. Both are exciting for their own reasons, but I think it's healthy for us if we can separate the artist that we are from the secretary that we can be.

CM: There's a question that the poet Nikky Finney asked Lucille Clifton—Nikky Finney was the poet-in-residence here at Smith for a couple of years—and she said, "Think of a moment in your life so precious that if you could wear it you would. A moment so divine." And I realize this is a little bit of a woo-woo question, but I wondered, what would you say?

MD: Oh, I love woo-woo questions. Hmm . . . I think . . . well, I have many. I could put together a whole suit, with a hat, out of them. One, of course, is the first time that I kissed somebody. *Ohhh, man!* If I could wear that around I would be floating. I was probably like thirteen years old. Twelve or thirteen years old. Now, in my neighborhood, you know, I got rapidly mature in the next year. But that first kiss was so . . . sweet. I mean, if you painted it, it would look so overly romanticized. It was under a weeping willow. In a park. I actually wrote about it a little bit in a poem called "Public Parks." But, weeping willow, slight drizzle, some ducks, I mean, like, get out! And if that could be a coat I could wear around, I think I would no longer be afraid of dentists or flying, or ever getting my heart broken. I don't know—have you ever had to take Oxycontin? [Laughs.] You'd feel like that.

CM: You answered that so beautifully, thank you. So is there anything else that you would like to add?

MD: I don't think so. Except for this: that I'd like to ask anyone who ever reads this interview, this conversation that you and I have had—to go out and get a book of poems or print up a couple of poems that you really like, and send them to someone who doesn't read poems. Because they need them, more than you know, and more than they know. I think poems, more than any other art, help us to be OK with being here on earth. And I think we should try to share that as much as we can.

MICHAEL DICKMAN

Interviewed November 3, 2009

Both Dickman brothers are over six feet tall, with pale skin, sandy hair, and blue-green eyes. As I sat with Michael in the recording booth, it was hard not to feel that I was simply picking up my conversation with Matthew where it had last left off. But despite the physical similarity, Michael has a very different presence: warier, more cerebral, more abstract. He is, in fact, the older of the Dickman twins, born August 20, 1975, just two minutes earlier than his brother, Matthew. Both boys grew up in Lents, a working-class neighborhood in Portland, Oregon, with their mother, Wendy, and younger sister, Elizabeth. Michael started reading poetry in high school, inspired by Neruda's book *The Captain's Verses*. "I read it from cover to cover, and by the end I was in tears. I couldn't believe that you could do what Neruda was doing with language."

In the years that followed, he too began to write seriously, publishing his first book in 2009. His second book, *Flies,* won the Academy of American Poets' James Laughlin Award. In 2009, he was appointed the Hodder Fellow at Princeton University. He has also received residencies and fellowships from the Lannan Foundation, the Vermont Studio Center, and the Provincetown Fine Arts Work Center. Like his brother, Matthew, he still lives in Portland, Oregon.

Some of the Men (excerpt)

I had to walk around for a long time before I could see anything

The leaves
circling down the street
imitating the insides of seashells
imitating
my fingerprints

I could sense my father
sitting alone in his little white Le Car
staring off at the empty parking lot

No radio
No wind
No birds

Just some guy in his car looking out at the blacktop and the shadows
of telephone wires

It isn't a sad scene, not really

Some of us are getting
exactly what we asked for

Some of us
don't even have
to wait

*

Think of my grandfather, still drunk or asleep, passed out on top of my
grandmother
so she has to wait for him
to come to

along with the late
Redwood City morning
the light skipping in
across

the swimming pool

The smell of failed sex
bourbon and
chlorine

Dead cigars

He taught me how to swim

with one of his hands beneath my legs and another beneath my stomach
how to cup my hands, how
to turn my head

Inhale and exhale
and move gracefully
through liquid

*

Look at
Josh's father—

Stumbling into the bedroom at three in the morning the two of us asleep
        and all that moonlight
        and beat his son's
        head against

the headboard

You fucker you fucker you asked for it

The moon

His jaw splashed across the pillowcase

*

The Parietal   Temporal   Occipital

The Atlas and Axis
Spheroid and

Spheroid

The real smile
real grin

Your movable and immovable joints

Your eyes

your orbits

Sutures

If given the chance
I would

break them all

*

For a long time my grandfather
tried to kill anyone
who came near him

Wives
Daughters
Stepdaughters

What is it called when insects are stuck forever in a kind of amber?

Then he got sick
and he was going to die anyway
and he stopped
trying to kill people

Then we could fall in love

Christian McEwen: Would you talk a bit about your growing up?

Michael Dickman: Sure. I was raised by a single mother in Portland, Oregon, in a working class neighborhood of Portland called Lents. Raised with my twin brother, Matthew, also a writer, and then also with my little sister, Elizabeth. My mother, Wendy, raised all three of us single-handedly. She worked lots of different jobs, mostly in the insurance business.

CM: In what way has being a twin influenced your work? It's very clear how differently your brother and you each write poems. I wondered whether your imaginative take on things was always so distinct.

MD: One of the great things—because Matthew and I always got on so well—was that no matter what we were doing, whether it was theater and drama or writing, we always had someone there as a support, critic, or cheerleader. And it's really, really, really, really important, for anyone trying to make something, to keep hearing a voice that says, "It's worth doing, what you're doing is worth doing," which is something I heard from Matthew over and over again.

But even in acting we had very different approaches. I would come from underneath or beneath a character, whereas Matthew came from on top, producing performances that were very, very, very different. So much so that I think it was distracting for directors and casting directors. So we'd have conversations like, "How much do you want this part? Who is it better for? I'll go. And now it's your turn to go audition."

And then in the poetry—Matthew's poetry is very often much more giving than mine, sort of fiercely celebratory, and mine is, I would say, not exactly that. And physically on the page they look wildly different. That just happened. There was never a conscious moment where I thought, "Well, if we're both going to be doing this, then it better be very, very different." It just sort of happened through our separate reading, and the things that we were falling in love with on our own. There were writers I was drawn to and writers Matthew was drawn to.

CM: What was your relationship to poetry as a child? How old were you when you first began to write?

MD: I'm almost sure that there were books read to us as children, but I don't have a memory of this. I have a memory of movies and television. You talk to some people and they say, "Oh, well, my father or mother read The *Odyssey* to me when I was one year old and I've always remembered that." But there was nothing like that. I started reading for the first time as a sophomore in high school. The book that got me excited was *Lord of the Flies*.

But poetry was a different matter. It happened around the same time. A friend of mine told me I should buy this book, and it was a book of poetry by Pablo Neruda called *The Captain's Verses*. I didn't read it for a couple weeks and I thought, "I should read this because then I can talk to my friend about it, and impress this person." And so I read it cover to cover, and at the end I was in tears. It was very strange. I had never had an experience like that before, reading. I could not believe that you could do what Neruda was doing with language. And more than that, I didn't know that you could be a man and say certain things in a certain way, and so that got me wanting to read everything of his.

And then, both Matthew and I had a drama instructor named Ernie Casciato who became a mentor and a kind of surrogate father. And Ernie's message was that it's OK to be an artist; in fact, it's important, we need artists, and you could be one if you wanted to. And so the combination of those things, an adult saying, "It's fine, and important, and you should, and you could," and then coming across a genius like Neruda was really what got things started.

CM: Are there any artists in your immediate family?

MD: No, not really. Both Matthew and I know so little of our father. He's around, but just not a part of our lives. I've heard that as a child he was interested in painting. But unlike the two of us, he did not have anyone supporting him, and in fact, he experienced a violent retribution from his parents. I guess he was to become a businessman, which he did. [Laughs.]

CM: What does it mean for you to work at a poem? From outside it seems like a more delicate, more cerebral process than Matthew's, the slivering together of those explosive little shards of memory. And from outside, as a reader, there's perhaps less of the comfort of music and momentum. So I'm wondering how it is for you to make a poem, and how you even know when you're done.

MD: This will sound very surreal, but for me, often it will start with—I'm sort of more and more from the poetic school of guided-by-voices; so I will hear something on a walk, on a run, waking up, going to sleep, sometimes a phrase, part of a phrase. Like on a run in Provincetown. I was running and I heard this voice in my head, not a crazy voice, but a voice that said, "What are you going to do? Describe the light falling through the pitch pines again?" I hadn't been writing in a while, and I was wondering what to do, but it sounded to me like a way into a poem, and it became a way into a poem called "Late Meditation." So sometimes there'll be something like that and I'll write it down.

I carry around these little, tiny spiral Mead notebooks that can fit in the palm of your hand. Joan Didion has this great thing about, "The difference between being a writer and not being a writer is the capability to write something down at any moment." Which is really important to me because things are so fleeting in my mind.

So I'll write things down, more and more things, and then they'll start to add up, or stack up, and have a relationship with each other, and when it gets to that point, then I'll start to type out what I think is going to be a poem.

And theater continues to be important to me in the making of poems, because I can see a kind of dramatic arc in the sequences of the poems, and I want them to arrive, or fall, by the end of the poem, in the same way that a very tight play by Caryl Churchill has affected me.

And then the other thing, besides phrases, is that I'm very image-driven, and it's how I can express whatever it is I'm trying to get across in a poem, which often, to me, is very, very mysterious until the very end, or even for months and months afterwards. And then it takes me—the shortest time it's taken me to write a poem I think is two months, and then the longest is ten years.

CM: So an average poem would have how many revisions?

MD: You know, the average poem in *The End of the West* probably was revised fifty times.

CM: Thank you for saying that. It's especially important for beginning writers to know.

MD: Almost the only thing I'm interested in as a writer is revision. And it's mostly what I'm interested in hearing about from other writers. It wasn't always like this, but more and more I've tried to become purposefully more relentless with my revision, with my editing, and I've learned this from older writers whom I admire. I remember an experience with a poet named Marie Howe. I had this really long, like ten-page, poem, and it wasn't working, and I was depressed by it; I didn't know what to do. I showed it to her and she said, "You should very quickly, without thinking too much, just go through and cut the poem by 75 percent." And I said, "Oh yeah, sure, I'll do that." You know, "*Never!*" And then I thought I'd just say thanks and leave. And she said, "No, no, honey, now. *Now, now, now!*"

I was petrified. It was so frightening. But I went through. I cut almost 90 percent of the poem. She said, "Read to me what you have." I read it to her. And it wasn't fixed, it wasn't a perfect poem, but I could suddenly see a way into the poem again that was exciting to me, that could breathe new life into it. "Revision" is "to see again" what's in front of you, and I can only do it by being very relentless.

CM: So is revision mostly about cutting out? Or is it also about sharpening, clarifying, rephrasing, putting in white space?

MD: All those things. You know, for me the first thing is to cut away things that are burying the images, that are slowing the thing down too much, or that are speeding it up in places where I don't want the poem sped up. And also as a way to remind myself that language is cheap. I didn't pay for it; it's not a painting; I don't have to pay hundreds of dollars. Like William Stafford said, "a poem is not a monument," it's something malleable. But then, also, you're right, it's for me very much so about clarifying, about getting a four-word statement to say exactly what it means. And then, and this is really, in a way, sacrilegious, but visually, how the poem looks on the page is very important to me, how it draws your eye, how it makes you read it. I want to fasten the poem to the page so that if I read it out loud, and you haven't heard it, but you read it out loud at home, we sound almost alike.

So, yeah, all of those things.

CM: Thank you. You described that beautifully. Could you talk a little bit about the white space and the line breaks? When I look at your poems I see, as it were, the branch of a tree, and also the white sky behind the tree. And if the poem really takes off that sky changes color, you might say. [Laughs.] You're working so much more with white space than most poets do.

MD: Looking back on things, of course, sometimes it sounds more purposeful than it really is. But if I think about it, there was the desire to take more time, to be able to slow down, and with white space I felt like, not as a science, or as a scientist, that I could manipulate how quickly we understood, I understood, what was happening in the poem.

And then also, maybe somewhere I wanted to be a painter. [Laughs.] The visual arts are very important to me, and I love painting especially, and sculpture, and I've read countless interviews with contemporary painters, people like Barnett Newman who work with trying to measure out a sort of music or movement in a painting, and they do it often with white space. I thought that was fascinating. And you can do that to some extent with line breaks, causing pauses like Pinter does in his plays. You can cause this thing to happen where you can be moving down the page in a stanza or a strophe very quickly, and depending on the next break you can have this sort of sigh that happens, which I think is exciting.

CM: Are there poets who work with white space in a way that inspires you?

MD: Yes, there are. Jean Valentine does this incredibly well. And someone like Rae Armantrout, who has a new book out called *Versed*, which is just stunning, it's mind-bogglingly good. In fact it's so good that when I read it I think, "This is what I want to do." But the job of being Rae Armantrout is filled by Rae Armantrout, so you have to do your own thing.

CM: I wondered whether there was a moment when you felt you'd begun to "find your voice," and what made that possible for you.

MD: I think there was, and if not voice, certainly a kind of poem that I wanted—where I finally felt, "This is what I want to try to write." That happened for me in graduate school when I was, oh, twenty-seven or something. I was working on a poem called "Some of the Men," and it wasn't working out, and I had been writing it like I'd been writing a lot of things, sort of columnar poems that move very quickly, they move very fast. They still weren't as exuberant as, say, Matthew's work, or someone like James Schuyler, but they were more like a very quick Levine poem, those beautiful books like *1933*. But I felt like it just dropped off the table for me; I'd write it and it would just fall on the floor and I couldn't find it.

And then I was reading more and more short contemporary plays that often were in three sections or five sections, that did not use a lot of language, and I thought, "I'm moved by this so much more than a lot of contemporary poetry. How can I try to yoke these two things together? *That's what I want to do.*" And so I cut ninety percent of that poem and split it up into sections, and also started pinning it up on a wall and moving the sections around to see what kind of a story came out, on the assumption that the first story I wanted to tell is maybe not the best one, and that the poem itself might have something else to say.

Which is actually something that I started doing because of reading an interview with Walter Murch, the great film editor. Michael Ondaatje interviewed him for days and days, and one of the things he talked about was editing a film sequence. We don't understand the world in a straightforward narrative sense, and if you showed a movie that showed a sequence of shots that were shot one right after the other, we'd have no idea what was happening. Even if it was a movie about someone walking across a room, we'd be confused. Like, sitting here now, I'm talking to you, so I'm noticing what you're wearing, I'm also noticing the things on the table, the paperclips, the person out there who's making a note. All these things make up how I understand the world. So Murch would put up these stills on a light board, and then he'd start to take them out, until some action or movement or story started to unfold, and in some minor way I wanted to try to do that with a poem.

CM: It's very skillful, how you reach a certain arc in the course of each poem. And also the way you work with pace. Some of your poems are fast, some are slow, and yet they're all like sticks on the white page, floating on the white page, the white river of the page.

I wanted to ask you about "Some of the Men," because it's such a strong, powerful poem. Maybe you could talk about men and manhood as they showed up in your life. I think of those lines in "Some of the Men" about standing in the yard with your "hands in your pockets, curled into tiny fists."

Do you think that having a brother like Matthew, and a single mom whom both of you so clearly love and respect, meant that you could avoid some of the false armor that adult men are burdened by?

MD: Absolutely. Talking to male friends of mine, artists, talking about their childhoods, there are many things that we did not, I did not, have to deal with day to day. Certainly there were times I spent with my father, and his advice was always like that, "full of armor," sort of aggressive, not very helpful. And then also, the fathers of friends in the neighborhood I grew up in, hardly was there one you could look up to as a strong, healthy male. You know, they were drinkers. They worked their asses off. They were exhausted. And mean-spirited. And disappointed. And so I think having Matthew helped a lot, and of course our mother.

We grew up in a house full of women—my mother, my little sister—and so there was that, there was a very strong influence. But also we were very lucky, we had, early on, a very healthy strong, male mentor who did not have that sort of armament, who was just interested in lots of different things, but mostly in me, that I was healthy, happy. You know, "What are you doing?" "This." "Great." So that was also really helpful.

CM: Could you name some of those men?

MD: Well, Ernie Casciato was one of them. My friend Jerry Atkin, he and his partner Lee were great friends of mine when I was in my early twenties, and Jerry has been involved in the labor movement for years. He was someone who showed me how you could be angry as a man in America, very angry, and not cause harm. Which is really important because you know, in my neighborhood, in my past, if you were a man and you were angry, violence ensued of some kind, period. So Jerry was like that. And Ernie—in high school, and also now. And then when we were much younger we had John Polak, the father of my oldest friend, Andrew Polak, who's fantastic. When we were really little, like two, three, four, five years old, John was a great example of someone who was very strong, very creative, very helpful. Again, he was someone who, you could see how you could be a man, be a certain way, and not have to fall into these terrible holes that many, many men I knew did.

CM: Could you talk about that difficult outside world? I'm thinking about poems like "My Dead Friends Come Back," and the little details that came out in the *New Yorker* article, about the drugs and the drinking and the trouble when you were in your teens.

MD: Mm-hmm. I was very lucky because of my own cowardliness when it came to certain things. I was willing, at twelve, to drink for hours and hours and hours on end, and do other sorts of drugs, but I literally was afraid of needles. And also, our family was very small and very kind of tight, and I knew that there were things that I could do where my mother, my sister, my brother would be disappointed or upset. I also knew that there were things there'd be no coming back from, and I wasn't willing to sacrifice that. One of them would be heroin. I'd go into stores, I'd steal things, I'd graffiti things, but I never pointed a gun at anyone—although I had the opportunity to. I passed that by, happily.

And also, more and more as I got older those things in my neighborhood became less and less exciting and more tiring. I remember at a certain point being out with friends and thinking, "This night is endless and I don't want to do it anymore." And other things started to take up more of my time, like theater and art.

CM: I was full of admiration for the wit, the playfulness in your work. I'm thinking of lines like "the napkins, folded into paper boats, contain invisible Japanese poems." And also in reading your poems I found this thread of . . . I hardly know what to call it, but spirituality, God stuff. And I wondered what part that played in your life.

MD: Well first, I'm very, very happy if you found anything witty or humorous, because I think there are things that are witty and humorous in these poems, but they're often not visible to people. There's a line where this mother leaves needles in the couch cushion for us to sit on—oh, it's a poem called "Scary Parents." And it's true, and I also thought it was very funny, like some sort of horrible whoopee cushion, but no, it never gets a laugh.

But you know, we were raised in Catholic school. We went to church. I don't go. I don't practice in any real, active sense. I feel like I have a healthy—if not spiritual life—a healthy spiritual wondering, and sometimes intense questioning of the world. But I think that at some point—because of Catholic school, and because of going to church—you're given certain images, almost birth images, these very organic things that you cannot shake, but have to wonder at in art.

Someone this is true for, who writes amazing poems on the subject, is the poet Charles Wright, who is also one of our best image-makers. He talks about how early on there are certain things that are truly burned into us, and you're left to deal with those for your adult life. And certainly for me the idea of salvation, especially from a male figure like Jesus, is something that is a real struggle, and something to think about, for sure.

CM: Because the males in your life were so problematic that the idea of being saved by a male is itself somehow problematic?

MD: For sure, that's part of it. And then just the idea that there's something that wants to do the saving, that we need saving at all, questions like this. And on top of that, all of the imagery is amazing in Catholicism and also something I can't get away from, because it's really, truly burned into my head. Even looking at painters I find that I'm drawn to certain things. Barnett Newman has these amazing paintings—"Onement" is an amazing painting—but then I find that I'm drawn to a painting that's a sequence called "Stations" and then also the subject matter is the Stations of the Cross, and I can't get away from it.

CM: Does "Onement" have to do with atonement in some way?

MD: I think it could. I think for Newman it had to do with atonement for the kind of art that he was making before he really found his voice.

CM: I was reading *The End of the West* and I was thinking about your mother as Annie Oakley. This valiant, bold, heroic girl, and how she modeled courage in comparison to your grandma. And I wondered if you'd speak more about your mother, because clearly in both your poems and your brother's poems there's this heroic, hardworking, single mom.

MD: She certainly was. People say this about their mothers, but she is one of the most amazing people I've ever met. A very, very strong, sometimes single-minded woman. Single-mindedness being, "My family will survive and we will be fine." You know, someone who raised three children on her own, worked full time, beat breast cancer, went back to school as an adult to get an MSW, all the time while making house payments. Sort of amazing. And so that is definitely there.

And also, there's something about her as Annie Oakley in this poem, and in a sense this poem gives real-life characters a way to live out a kind of life that they wanted but weren't allowed to have. What my mother ended up having was a family, but at some point, certainly, what she wanted was another horse, and a life that was more independent: independent of family, definitely, of course, independent of men, and more free.

CM: I don't know how to describe this except in terms of, like, an aura or a halo. You've given us the character of the real people, your mom, your grandma, and so forth, and you've also provided the surrounding dream, or the surrounding fantasy, like the Annie Oakley fantasy. And you manage to tell both the lived story and the dreamed-for story at the same time. It's a piece of very skillful legerdemain. . . . [Laughs.]

MD: I'm glad you think so. The only place I have to start from is my own life, and after that my hope is that things get much stranger and that the imagination takes over, because it's a piece of art, not autobiography. But these are the people, the characters of my life.

CM: Your brother tells me he still works at Whole Foods and I was wondering where you were working now.

MD: Right now I'm very lucky. Since September I've had a Hodder Fellowship at Princeton University, where I don't have to work, don't have to teach; the only requirement is that you live there in that town, and that you write for ten months. Before that, as recently as last July and August, I was working as a prep cook. You know, the same old story, $9.25 an hour, no health insurance, cutting up onions in a basement basically for beer money [laughs] and then, of course, writing on my days off.

When I have a job like that I can't write during the day. Cooking is so physically demanding, which is how I've made a living for the past ten years, that it has to be a day off where I can pull everything together for what it takes to start to make a poem.

CM: How are you enjoying Princeton?

MD: The fellowship is great. The town, we're just getting to know. There are some beautiful things about it. The canal is beautiful. And I've been very lucky: the staff there, the creative writing staff, has been unbelievably pleasant, inviting, encouraging, and so there's a way in which you can be as active in that community, or as un-active, as you'd like. And either way is fine.

CM: I'm wondering whom you're reading right now. When I look at your acknowledgments I see Joe Millar, Marie Howe, Denis Johnson. Who else do you admire?

MD: I read a lot of poetry, especially—or almost all—contemporary poetry. So it changes a lot. But there are certain books that will hit me, and there is a short pile of them that I have at home right now that I read over and over and over again. There's a poet named Jay Hopler who has a book called *Green Squall,* which was a Yale pick a few years ago, which is just stunning. It's the kind of book that I read, and I put down, and I think, "How do I begin again knowing that this is in the world?" More recently, a woman named Arda Collins published a book called *It Is Daylight,* which reminds me of Mark Strand around the time of *The Late Hour,* strange, weird, beautiful persona poems and monologues. And then I have a long list of things that I need to read to fill out my mostly self-education: Stevens, Milton . . . [laughs] are both on the top of that list.

CM: Stevens will give you enormous joy.

MD: I'm looking forward to it. I really am.

CM: Now that you're in Princeton, how do you keep up with your friendships, your poetic network?

MD: It's a combination of things and it's always linked so personally with whomever it is I want to be in touch with. One of my best friends and a great poet, Carl Adamshick, he will not send an email, he won't do it, and so we write letters back and forth through the mail. And then with Matthew, we talk on the phone once a day, and read things to each other over the phone. With other people—my great friend and mentor Franz Wright, it's mostly only through email. And the same with someone like Denis [Johnson]; I'll send drafts of things, either in the mail or through email to these people, who are very kind and somehow always make time to read the thing and send me some notes back.

CM: What advice would you give to young writers starting out?

MD: I can only talk about what's been helpful for me, right? So when I was a younger writer than I am now, reading was what helped, I mean just reading, reading, as much as you can. And also, you're lucky if you have some obsessions. And then the other thing is keeping in mind that it's a gift to get to write the poem. That's the deal. That's actually the whole deal. It's very hard, because we have egos, but after that anything else is just sort of extra: publications, things like that. Which is really almost impossible to remember when you're sending things out.

But I think having tried to be an actor really helped, because as an actor you go to fifty auditions in a week and you hear forty-nine times, "No, you're wrong. You're not for us." And then the fiftieth time you hear, "Well, come back next week," and then you hear, "No." So I was, like, very prepared, and I sent things out for seven years straight before anything was taken. And then it only happened very slowly. And then when I was discouraged, always going back to a poem that I found exciting or a book that was very dear to me reminded me over and over again: *This is why. This is why.* And with poetry, also, it's a little easier because there's no real money at stake. Quiet as it's kept, I was paid, like, less than a thousand dollars for *End of the West.* So keeping that in mind, I think, is good.

PATRICK DONNELLY

Interviewed May 25, 2012

Patrick Donnelly was born in Tucson, Arizona, in 1956, the elder of two children. His mother, Dorothy, read to him from an early age, not just Whitman and Dickinson and Yeats, but Swinburne too. As a child, he became a voracious reader. "My mom is absolutely the reason I'm a poet today," he says now, crediting her too for his love of theater, opera, and classical music.

When *Jesus Christ Superstar* came out, Donnelly was in his teens. He played the record over and over, and, though he had grown up in an atheist household, found himself captivated by the story of Jesus. In the years that followed, he set out to explore most of the major religions, from Judaism to Catholicism to Buddhism, arriving, finally, at some sort of personal synthesis. For a while he thought seriously of becoming a priest; later, he studied as an opera singer. It was not until his early thirties that he began to write, then study poetry.

Donnelly's first book (drawn from his MFA thesis) was published in 2003, and his second book some nine years later. His poems have appeared in a number of journals, including *The American Poetry Review, The Massachusetts Review, Ploughshares,* and *Slate,* and in anthologies including *The Book of Irish American Poetry from the 18th Century to the Present,* and *From the Fishhouse: An Anthology of Poems that Sing, Rhyme, Resound, Syncopate, Alliterate, and Just Plain Sound Great.*

Donnelly currently teaches poetry at Smith College. He is also director of the Poetry Seminar at The Frost Place in Franconia, New Hampshire. He works as an associate editor of *Poetry International,* and translates classical Japanese poetry and drama with his spouse, Stephen D. Miller, associate professor of Japanese language and literature at the University of Massachusetts, Amherst.

Cradle Song

When I signed for her ashes

I received her, as once
    she received me
into her lyric hold
    and let me ride anchor there,
smaller than the letter *alif.*

They gave her into my hands,
    seven pounds, two ounces,
as once they had given
    me into her hands.

I set her on the hearth shrine,
    as she set me once a place at her table,
among her other needy charities.

After nine months I scattered her
    back to that cold, delphine Atlantic of hers,
to tidal squalls that rip
    and sigh their salt across the rocks,

as once she let me fall

unready
    onto this world's
gasping, shouting, love-stained shore.

The Mother's Ashes Reply

when he put—when that man put my
    ashes in the water,
for the space of four
        green waves

I held together as a knot of
        milk

then a fifth thing of—water?—broke
        open my last

seals and—

      delivered

me to be

                no body

      and no body's

              mama

Christian McEwen: You published your first book in 2003, just past your middle forties. And I wondered how far back those early poems go, and if you had in fact been writing privately for many years.

Patrick Donnelly: Some of the poems in *The Charge* go back about twenty years. I did write as a young person, but it was not my main focus. I tried to be a priest, and then an opera singer, then I worked in nonprofit. Writing didn't really come on to the front burner until the '90s, when I started studying in earnest with some good poets. I finished the book as my thesis for an MFA program. And then it was taken and published within about a year, which I'm sure you know is like being struck by lightning. [Laughs.] It just doesn't happen!

CM: Congratulations! That's a great story. I love all the different threads in your life—the opera singer and the priest. One starts to think what each identity implies, and how you're using your poetry to satisfy those same goals.

PD: I have a class in mind about Maria Callas, who to me is the absolute exemplar of the artist. I don't know whether this would be an opera queen class [laughs] in which I'd just listen to my favorite recordings and make other people listen too. But it would have to do with not looking for safety: about learning one's craft to the utmost, so that one can make it a tool for expression without struggling with technique.

CM: When did you start to translate, was that only after you met Stephen Miller?

PD: Stephen and I met in 2002, and were married in 2005. We started to put our toes into the pool of translating about 2004. Before that, I knew absolutely nothing about Japan, except what everyone knows, and Stephen really opened that whole world to me. I'd heard of other poet/linguist/translator teams. I knew that Stanley Kunitz had translated Akhmatova, and did not speak Russian, so I said to Stephen, "Why don't we just try it?" And we did.

CM: What effect would you say it has had on your own work?

PD: Enormous. I already had the very short poem as one way to work. And I love that, and I try to encourage my students to use it. But because the poems we work on are so incredibly compressed, thirty-one syllables in the original, they have pushed me even further in that direction. How much you can say in a very little space, by using implication and hints that throw off an aura that is huger than the real estate that a poem takes up. Translation has been huge in pushing me toward lyric compression.

CM: You write in your poem "Your One Stone," "My father gave me a stone, and I ate it." But you also describe that father running to embrace the prodigal son "like a deer running to the smell of apples." I wondered if you'd say something about yourself as a child.

PD: Both of those poems are from my first book, and I would say that the first book, again by a system of hints and implications, suggests that the speaker has a fraught relationship with his own father.

A lot of threads came together in "Your One Stone." Probably the most obvious is Jesus's parable from the gospels, illustrating the goodness of God the Father. "If a son asks his father for a loaf of bread, will he give him a stone?" It's a rhetorical question, and the answer is, "Of course not." But in the real world, sons ask for loaves of bread and they do get stones, and they have to eat them, they have to make the best of them.

My dad is eighty-three now, and we have a very warm and cordial relationship, but it wasn't always so. You know, for a man of his generation to wrap his mind around having a gay son, and a son who wasn't interested in any of the professions he had in mind for me, has not been easy. We butted heads for many, many years and were estranged for part of that time, and yet somehow, luckily, we've worked our way back toward a relationship.

None of us know when we're going to leave life. It's nice to leave things a little more peaceful than the struggles we had when we were young.

CM: I understand you had a sister too.

PD: I have one sister who is eight years younger than I am, and she's represented by one poem in the new book. None of my family relationships have been particularly easy, and the poem that is in her voice is sort of a critique of the speaker, who is "me."

CM: I thought you did that beautifully. And since we're talking about family dynamics—you have that wonderful line about your father laying "the y of ice" next to your mother's "x of fire." Perhaps you'd talk a little about your mom and her x of fire.

PD: Mm-hmm. Well, my mom is absolutely the reason I'm a poet today.

She loved poetry, she loved all the arts, and she was a very creative person in her own way. She was also very troubled and unhappy, and I think today would have received some diagnosis and probably treatment, and might have been happier. I don't know. But to love her, or even to be in a relationship with her, was always difficult, and when she died I started writing poems about her, and her life and death. I thought, after four or five poems that would probably be it.

But it wasn't. The poems about her eventually made up the entire middle section of the new book, *Nocturnes*. And that felt right. I've always used poems to scratch an itch or to assuage an ache in myself, and though I hope they're not just therapeutic, they do scratch the itch and assuage the ache, and I don't feel the same way after I have gotten them on the page.

So writing this second book with the big section about her helped me to resolve a lot of feelings that were left over about our relationship.

CM: Among my favorites are two poems you wrote to your mother, the pair called "Cradle Song" and "The Mother's Ashes Reply." "Cradle Song" is about a son dealing with his mother's ashes, but the poem in which the ashes reply is an astonishing tour de force. I think many people could have decided to write that first poem, but to give that parent a voice in death is astonishing to me.

PD: Thank you.

CM: I wonder what inspired you to write the poem in just that way.

PD: This idea of poems in dialogue with one another—maybe more literally than we usually mean that—is something I stole from the Japanese imperial anthologies. There you will find what you call *zōtōka*: which is to say, "poem and reply." The Japanese were poetry nuts for about a thousand years. A lot of the time they enclosed poems with messages, or they sent poems as messages to one another, and you were expected to write a poem back, and a lot of these exchanges—*zōtōka*—were preserved in the imperial anthologies. It hit me like a tidal wave, this idea of the communal writer and these different voices speaking and replying. Plus they're very sly about how they do it, which I love; they are not literal in their replies. Often someone will ask a question in the first poem, and the replier does not answer the question, or asks another question.

Nocturnes is actually full of poems that talk to one another. There's a pair of Japanese poems that talk to one another in that way, and then there are these two poems, which I will now read.

[PD reads "Cradle Song" and "The Mother's Ashes Reply." See pages 66 and 67.]

CM: You read that beautifully. The bewilderment of the ashes at finding themselves to be ashes, and the way you pace that, it's very, very powerful.

PD: That second poem, "The Ashes Reply," was a way of really releasing my mother. I love Rip van Winkle stories, and the terrible lonely way they make you feel. And for me, one of those stories is, "What if my mother had not had children, or not become my mother?" In many ways she was not suited to be a parent, and might have been happier without children. But that was not an option that was open to women of her generation. So this poem is my way of acknowledging that there might have been an alternate universe where my mother was not my mother, and that the ashes have now gone on into that universe and the last seals are broken open, and the connection with the unhappiness is gone.

It's a terribly lonely thought, to think that your mother might not have been your mother. But it's also freeing, not just for her or for me.

CM: Your mother's name was Dorothy Best, and you thank her often for your love of poetry. I wondered, as a child, were you much of a reader, and how did she bring poetry to you?

PD: I was, I think people would say, almost too much of a reader. I was a fearful child. I grew up in New Mexico at a time when it was, probably still is, expected that boys would be athletic, and outgoing, and be interested in boy things, and I was not. I very much hid in books, which were not only a safe world for me, but an exciting and romantic one. My parents were both hyper-literate, and they bought me my own books from a very early age.

And as far as my mother's love of poetry, yeah, she read me poems from an early age. She loved some things that everyone loves, but she also had some eccentric tastes, like she loved Swinburne. [Laughs.] Nobody loves Swinburne anymore. And Yeats, Yeats was really important to her, and Whitman and Dickinson.

I knew which poems she loved, and these were the poems Stephen and I read when we put her ashes into the water. So, yeah, there's a long history of love, and not just for poetry, but for theater, opera, music, classical music.

CM: I was moved by how many of your poems have to do with passion and compassion, poems of loss, poems written also in the long shadow of AIDS. You refer at one point to an Indian teacher called Baba, and use the Arabic phrase *bismillah,* which is "In the name of God." Could you talk a little about your spiritual practice, and what has allowed you to hold that amount of loss?

PD: Well, the simple narrative fact is that I've passed through most of the great world religions at this point, and come out the other end. But I was not raised in any religion. My parents were both atheists, my mother in a very aggressive way, and my father in a gently agnostic way. To my mother, religion represented the worst of human nature: dark superstitious ignorance. She had absolutely no respect for it at all, and I sort of parroted those ideas from her as a kid. And then when I was a teenager, a bunch of things happened all at once. My parents got divorced and my stepmother, who was an artist, was a very different kind of person, and she started to gently and not so gently challenge some of the received ideas I was parroting from my mother. She was not selling any particular spiritual tradition, but that sort of opened my mind.

And then *Jesus Christ Superstar* came out, and I listened to it repeatedly in my room. I wore out the record. And I started to get interested in Jesus, just as a person. I was attracted, I'd say now, to the poetry of the story, the human poetry of it. And so I started making an exploration. I grew up in Santa Fe, New Mexico, and I thought in my naive way that I'd just go and ask people about these things, and my first stop was at a synagogue. But I was turned away. I now know that this is a tradition of Judaism, that when a non-Jew comes to inquire about Judaism, they are discouraged at first, to see if their interest is real.

My next stop was the Catholic Church [laughs], which of course is a huge presence in New Mexico, and I was lucky to meet a wonderful priest who gave me instruction to come into the church. My parents were absolutely horrified. It was the worst possible thing they could imagine, which pleased me in and of itself. I went off to the seminary, and I tried to become a priest, unsuccessfully. And I stayed a Catholic for a number of years until the conflict of being gay just became too great and my self-respect carried me out of the church.

I studied Buddhism after that, and after that Sufism, which is a mystical teaching within Islam. And now having come out the other end, I think I have achieved a synthesis of all those things. I've kept pieces of them that work for me, which is what all the religions complain about [laughs], and I'm just lucky we don't live in a time where you can be persecuted for synthetic beliefs.

CM: I hadn't understood there was quite such a pilgrimage involved.

PD: Yeah. And I'm in a strange place now, where I've almost come back full circle. What I'm interested in is the poetry of the stories, of all the various traditions, and what I'd call the essence at the center of those stories is everything to me. That is what I lean on just to walk through life. I'm not interested in participating in the traditions according to their rules anymore, so that creates some friction, but for the most part I'm at peace with it.

CM: So you're getting from spiritual practice the beauty of the language and the narrative, but not what it often wants to offer, which is the courage to keep going. Or perhaps the beauty becomes the courage?

PD: Beauty can only carry you so far. What I reject from the spiritual traditions is their dualisms and some of their legalisms. It's not that I have risen beyond the need for them, but I don't consider them useful in navigating daily life or in understanding the world.

CM: I was moved by "Nocturnes for the Brothel of Ruin" and "Pantoum of the Brothel of Ruin," which are very brave and intimate poems, and I wondered if you'd describe how it is to give voice to such stories.

PD: The title poem of the book, *Nocturnes for the Brothel of Ruin*, I have only read once in public, and that's partly because it's long, in sections, and it runs about five or six pages. But also, I know it's a hard poem for people to hear, it has some ugliness in it, some very raw sensual specifics, about what it was like to go to a gay bathhouse in the late '80s, early '90s in New York City.

At the same time, I love the poem. For a while I was kind of ashamed of it. I read it once at the Massachusetts Poetry Festival, as part of a panel about "shocking poems," for which it was completely apropos. People were shocked, and I got absolutely nothing back after or during the reading, so I haven't tested it out a lot. . . . I think I may have absorbed some of the people's shock about it.

And then I went back to it and read through it as I was considering this year of readings, and I found that I love this poem, and I'm proud of it as a poem. Also it carries the history of a quite specific time and place into the future, and to me that is extremely important.

The pantoum that follows it, "Pantoum of the Brothel of Ruin," is the same narrative setting—and originally it was part of the first poem. But it wasn't working in its then-form, it was kind of prosey, so I cut it loose and thought, "Well, I'll just leave that, I won't try and work that in." And then it occurred to me, "This is a kind of memory that will not go away; well, what forms are appropriate for writing about memories which cannot be suppressed?" And in English there are two: the villanelle, which has returning lines, and the pantoum, which we imported through Malaysia, and which is an even more obsessive form. You have very few lines to move forward because you're constantly bringing up these other lines that have already appeared. And so the poem wrote itself once I decided it was going to be a pantoum, and I'm very happy with that too.

CM: Could you talk a little more about form? A pantoum feels like such a useful shape to contain that ongoing mystery, that unanswered question, and you use a lot of anaphora too, and that's very powerful.

PD: I love formal poems in other people's writing when they are skillful. But I'm not particularly skillful in received forms like the sonnet. I have tried many times, and I always end up with something very stiff. Also I just completely run off the rails; the form runs away with me. A lot of people say that's one of the benefits of form, to subvert agenda and intention, and I can agree with that in theory. You can imagine some Elizabethan paradise, where people were writing in form all the time, and they really got good at it. But you'd have to have fifty or a hundred really bad ones before you could write a good one, and I guess that's been my issue with form, that I haven't written a hundred bad ones yet.

CM: In terms of friends, colleagues, contemporary poets, whose work do you find yourself returning to? Whose work are you inspired by?

PD: I'd say Bach or Shakespeare are my great models as artists, people who didn't pull away from the hard parts of living in the marketplace, and the necessity of producing art in part just to earn some money and in part to achieve something incomparable.

I interact with a lot of poets, either through teaching or publishing or in other ways, so the list is almost too long. But I'll just throw off a few. Laura Kasischke is doing amazing work right now; my mentor, Martha Rhodes, every book of hers is more incredible to me, and more brave. I don't know anyone who panders less to certain ideas about how to get along in the poetry world, and she is a poet working in the marketplace; she is a publisher, she's a teacher; she's helping a lot of people, she's giving other people a lot of opportunities. But her poetry is completely uncompromising, it does not play nice, and I really admire that about her.

Let's see . . . Mark Halliday is a poet whose work I really admire. Of an earlier generation, oh so many! Jack Gilbert, Ellen Bryant Voigt, Steve Orlen, Larry Levis. The richness of late twentieth-century American poetry is just incredible. Stanley Kunitz, Donald Justice. The list goes on and on. Elizabeth Bishop . . .

CM: If you went back into the deep past: Christopher Smart, William Blake . . .

PD: Or even further back, to the Greeks. I'm always really moved by Anne Carson's *Sappho,* for instance, or the Hebrew psalms.

CM: And of course now all the Japanese.

PD: Yeah, there's that whole other world, which is now part of my work.

CM: Now this is a curious question perhaps, but what has it meant to your work to be so enormously tall? You write in one of your poems, "my tallness that sees over things." I wondered what that's given you as a seer, and what too it may have deprived you of.

PD: I'd say, for most of my life I've been uncomfortable in my own body, and unforgiving of the ways in which my body did not line up with ideas of male beauty when I was in the marketplace, you know, to try and find love. That caused me a lot of suffering. My father is also very tall, in fact he's taller than I am, he's six feet eight and I'm six feet six. We both had this sort of adversarial attitude when people wanted to talk to us about that, partly because we're shy, and it's sort of strange to have strangers coming up to you and talking about your body, even though they invariably mean it in a very nice way. But I'll give you an example of something I grew up with: Have you ever heard the expression micro-aggression?

As the term implies, it's not a huge traumatic act, but a system of little "nibbled-to-death by goldfish" attacks on the psyche and self-esteem. So growing up in the '60s and '70s in New Mexico meant playing basketball for tall people, there just was no option, and I was not interested and I was not good at it. I made a trip home recently to New Mexico, and Stephen and I went up to Taos just to look around. We stepped into a curio store on the plaza, and started to have a conversation with the proprietors, an old Hispanic man and woman, and there might have been some Native American mixed in there too. The old guy, like a lot of older people in New Mexico, was very concerned with lineage, so once he learned I was from New Mexico, he wanted to know who I was, who were my people. "I know them, *et cetera, . . .*"

So the next question was "Did you play basketball?" I said no, and I explained that not only had I not been very interested, but that I wasn't good at it, and he said, "If you had been my son, I would have made you play whether you wanted to or not." And he meant this, I think, in a nice way, but that's an example of the kinds of micro-aggression not just I, but all kinds of young people who either are different or feel different, have to endure. Now why would he have made me, you know? And why should any child have to butt heads with a parent about that kind of thing?

So at fifty-six, I do tai chi, I do yoga. I've found a way into my body, to inhabit it. I have taken care of my health with a tremendous amount of work since I've become infected with HIV, so obviously I decided to stay in my body. And I would say that every front has a back. The benefit of my being tall is that I'm different, and that I stand out and I can't be forgotten in the ways other people can be. But I still think about the gay community, and the pressure to be beautiful, and I still don't meet those standards, and I guess the sad thing is that I still care and wonder to what extent that holds me back. It's a delicate dance. I wish I didn't care, which is, I guess, what I'm working toward, but it isn't entirely true.

CM: There's a thread of melancholy in your work, a deep consciousness of your own mortality, and the mortality indeed of an entire generation. Reading your work, I felt almost as if you had been schooled by death, by loss, by illness to a point where death was somehow the truest of all life experiences, some kind of apprenticeship almost. There are lines in one of your books where you're talking to a dead lover, "Thank you for the hollow / you left in this pillow. / I practice / putting my bones here." And there's a teacher or a friend who scolds you, "At fifty-one you are too young to think of death so much."

I'm not sure what the question is, but I wondered if you could comment on my fumblings here, and say where they feel true to you, and what in fact death, mortality, has meant to you.

PD: I don't think you're fumbling at all; I think you've hit it on the head. It has been an apprenticeship, and this is the gift of HIV to me. I said before, "Every front has a back," and the front of HIV is terrible, but there is a gift to every negative thing that happens. And in terms of the literary community, this morning someone wrote that he had longed for fame as long as he had longed to be a poet. Now I can imagine feeling that as a young person, but that's not a way I would like to end my life. Those are not values that I aspire to. The knowledge of my own mortality, and watching so many people die during the late '80s and early '90s, was a splash of cold water in my face, both about how I was acting and how I thought about myself, and what I thought the world was and what it is for. I still don't know the answers to a lot of those questions, but I know that the time is short, and I've lived with that now for almost thirty years. Remember the Flannery O'Connor short story, "A Hard Man Is Good to Find" . . .

CM: "A Good Man Is Hard to Find."

PD: [Laughs.] "A Good Man Is Hard to Find." Hmmm. A Freudian slip. Where one of the characters says about the old woman, "She would have been a good woman if it had been somebody there to shoot her every minute of her life."

The Japanese poems that Stephen and I are working on are Buddhist poems from eight hundred or a thousand years ago, and they are incredibly aware of impermanence and mortality. Everything is passing away from these speakers, it just slips through their hands, and this is the reality of the world we live in. And I am glad to be aware of it, absolutely it has infused my writing; this is what my writing is for. I'm not at all comfortable with this situation. I want to shake the bars about the way human life is designed. We come into the world in a very difficult way, causing pain to others, and we struggle, and then there's only one way to get out of it, and the end of life is ugly whether it comes early or late, it's painful, and there's suffering and indignity . . .

Both Stephen and I have had aging parents; now his whole family is gone. It is awesome, in the literal meaning of that word, to watch. And to me it's really the only subject other than love. There's a letter of Emily Dickinson's, where she's writing to someone about her nephew's death from typhoid at a very young age, and apparently right before he died he asked for the door to be opened: "*Who* were waiting for him, all we possess we would give to know . . . though *is* there more? More than Love and Death? Then tell me it's [sic] name!" So this, to me, is the poet's landscape. There are other subjects that are subordinate to these, and they are a lot of fun and even comedic and farcical and neurotic subjects, but it all boils down to a variation for me on those two.

CM: Saul Bellow has this line about poetry being "a skirt thing, a church thing" in America today. And I wondered if you'd talk about what's been involved in protecting a certain tenderness, a certain luminosity in your spirit in a world where that's not so welcome.

PD: For someone who lives and breathes poetry, it's almost hard to imagine those people outside the charmed circle, for whom poetry means nothing. I'm surrounded with poets, many of my closest friends are working poets, working artists, and this is important to us, and so if someone else doesn't think it's important then that's fine.

About the tenderness, or what you call luminosity, that's how I see things: at the center of everything, no matter how hard or ugly the shell, there is light, there is luminosity, there is tenderness. I could be wrong about that; but I don't care, that is the way I choose to live my life and the way I choose to interpret everything that comes at me.

There's a thing that happens and it's almost impossible to describe. I've experienced it with music, with opera, with poetry certainly, with works of visual art, when an artist is working, usually over a whole life, producing a lot of work, and some of it is at a very high level. But then there's something else that happens, and I'm not sure that it's absolutely under the control of the artist, or is a result of all the choices that go into making a work of art. But on my end as a consumer or receiver of the art, it's as though something cracks open and you have a view suddenly into something sublime, something of supernatural beauty. I can remember a moment at the Brooklyn Academy of Music, listening to a performance of Handel's *Orlando,* beautiful music throughout, but there is a trio in one of the acts, and something happens there. It's beyond even genius. It opens the door into something incomparable. So that is how I see the world, even the ordinary world that we walk around in, that there is something of great tenderness and incomparable beauty inside and sometimes outside.

CM: Thank you. You said that so beautifully.

If you were trying to explain that to a group of younger writers, to help them protect that part of themselves, so that they too could become poets or opera singers or whatever they ought to be, what might you say, by way of advice?

PD: I'm not sure there's anything anyone can say to protect young people from mistakes, and I'm not even sure that's a good idea. My own life has been a stumbling from one mistake to another, and some of those have been the most valuable experiences of my life in terms of teaching me about the world.

In terms of the students that I have charge of, who are working with me, it's all about craft and learning the tools. I often compare it to working with clay. If I poke the clay this way, what will happen? If I poke it with a wet hand, what will happen? If I poke it with a stick, if I fire it at 1500 degrees? You have to learn control of your tools as in any craft. If you're going to be an athlete, if you're going to be a dancer, you have to learn control. So I try to keep the focus there when I'm working with young people, as my best teachers did too, and really away from any idea of material achievement that can come through writing but is sort of beside the point. We all have to live. It's a shame that Mozart died at thirty-five with no money, that's a scandal, but the money is not the point. There are teachers I cross paths with who are encouraging young people to publish or to concern themselves with social media before it's really time to think about those things. So I regret that.

CM: When I talked to Edward Hirsch about the growing din of the culture, he said something like, "Our lives are so speeded up we've almost lost the capacity for stillness." So I'd suggest that in order to work with the clay, one needs to create some protective space around the clay.

PD: There needs to be a cloister, and sometimes that means protected periods of time. But for somebody who's working in the marketplace, it's hard to protect that time. I think it's a spiritual practice. You have to find the inner place where you can work, and of course that's not easy. It's an ongoing struggle, but necessary.

CM: One more question: I know that you left Brooklyn and New York for western Massachusetts, and I wondered if there's anything you enjoy about living here, and anything you particularly miss from city life.

PD: I left New York City in 2004 after twenty-four years, and I didn't think I was ready because I still loved it, and I was still very interested in my life there. But I'm a gardener, and I have a huge garden here, and I really enjoy that. And there are so many writers here, wonderful writers. I can drive ten minutes to one of the great shrines of human achievement at Emily Dickinson's house. And that's part of living in western Massachusetts, the presence of all the people who have worked here and achieved enormous things. I'm extremely happy to be here. I don't know what life holds for Stephen and me, no one ever knows, but I love this place. We have put down deep roots here, and people have been welcoming. I feel very happy and lucky to be here.

RITA DOVE

Interviewed September 28, 2010

Rita Dove has a striking presence: modest, authoritative, graceful. She was born in Akron, Ohio, in 1952. By the age of six, she was well able to read, and by seven or eight she was already writing her own poems. "I grew up in a household that had books," she says. "That, I think, made all the difference."

At eighteen, Dove was named a Presidential Scholar, one of the top one hundred high school graduates in the country. As a brilliant young African-American, the expectation was that she would go on to study law or medicine in order to be a credit to her race. Instead, she attended the University of Miami in Ohio, changing her major a number of times before finally settling on English. "So I got to do what I loved to do, which was to read and write about books."

In the years since, Dove has made a tremendously successful career as a writer, publishing nine books of poetry as well as a novel, a play, and collections of both essays and short stories. In 1987, she received the Pulitzer Prize for her collection *Thomas and Beulah,* based on the story of her maternal grandparents, and in 1993 was named the U.S. Poet Laureate, the youngest poet ever elected to that position. Among Dove's numerous honors are the 1996 National Humanities Medal from President Clinton and the 2011 National Medal of Arts from President Obama, making her the only poet with both presidential medals to her credit. She is currently Commonwealth Professor of English at the University of Virginia in Charlottesville.

Concert at Hanover Square

June 2, 1790. George Bridgetower and
Franz Clement: child prodigies, of an age

Do not think for a moment
that we were boys. Souls
in a like anguish, perhaps;
or when in a fortunate instant
we forgot ourselves—gray mice
biting each others' tails,
rolling in the grass in our woolen knickers.

We did not understand how to covet.
We knew hatred
because we could smell it
all around us, it sang in the cool glasses
tinkling over our heads,
the carefully tended laughter,
the curious glint
of a widow's appraisal.

As for competition—ah, well.
Want was a quality I could taste,
music set my body a-roil,
I was nothing if not everything
when the music was in me.
I could be fierce, I could shred
the heads off flowers for breakfast
with my bare teeth, simply because
I deserved such loveliness.

If this was ambition, or hatred,
or envy—then I was all
those things, and so was he.

Two rag dolls set out for tea
in our smart red waistcoats,
we suffered their delight,
we did not fail our parts—
not as boys nor rivals even
but men: broken, then improperly
mended; abandoned
far beyond the province
of the innocent.

Addendum:

Rita Dove: George Bridgetower was a violinist, a biracial prodigy playing the stages and courts of Europe from the age of nine, wowing high society with his music. He was born in 1780 of a mother who was from what is now Poland, and a father who billed himself as the African prince. In "Concert at Hanover Square," little ten-year-old George is playing a concert with another ten-year-old prodigy, a French boy by the name of Franz Clement. The idea was these two talented boys, one white and one who was dark, would cause quite a sensation—ivory and ebony, playing together. In the poem Bridgetower himself is speaking.

Christian McEwen: In one of your essays you said that you loved to read by the age of six, and by seven or eight you were already writing your own poems. I wondered if you'd talk a little bit about your growing up.

Rita Dove: I grew up in a household that had books. That, I think, made all the difference. My father was a research chemist. My mother was a housewife, but she had read and memorized Shakespeare in that old tradition of memorizing poems. And so every once in a while she would quote something that was appropriate. Like cutting the roast, she would say, "Is this a dagger that I see before me?" So when I read Shakespeare, it didn't frighten me because I'd heard some of those words before.

The key thing was that I felt comfortable about picking up any book and seeing what new worlds were in it. I read all the books on my parents' shelves. My parents didn't restrict me. They figured that if I could understand a book, I was old enough to read it. On the top shelf was the biggest book: *The Complete Shakespeare.* I don't know if my parents had read the entire volume. Most probably they hadn't. But I was determined to read it all. So I just dug in and loved it. I was around ten years old.

By the time I was six or so, I was reading and I loved to read. When I began to write myself, I started imitating the things I read. It seemed like the natural outcome of reading. My brother would always start a newspaper in the summer, and I would become chief reporter. We also wrote comic books. We made up our own little comic book characters. That was all part of our childhood play, except that we were playing with words.

CM: I remember reading about those comic book heroines: the Jet Girl, the Remarkable Girl, the Space Girl, the Lightning Bolt. And I wondered whether those magical girls ever showed up in your later work.

RD: Not by name, though what they did, I think, infused the women characters in my poems. Jet Girl was smart and whippet-thin. Remarkable Girl had imagination, because she was remarkable, of course! They were modeled on Wonder Woman, when I think back on it. Wonder Woman had everything. She was smart. She was sassy. She had that incredible invisible plane.

CM: But you also said of yourself at that time, "Though I loved books, I had no aspiration of being a writer."

RD: I had no aspiration to be a writer because I had never met a writer, and didn't think of writing as an occupation or something that a living person did. To me every writer was firmly frozen between the covers of some book. And most of them were white males. I wrote, though. I wrote. And sometimes I would show my writing to my teachers. But when I got into the adolescent years, I didn't show it to anyone, because you never do when you're an adolescent.

It wasn't until I was in eleventh grade that an inkling of that possibility began to emerge in my thoughts. The very first day of school my English teacher walked into class and dissected the first paragraph of Thomas

Hardy's *The Return of the Native*. She showed us how the music of that paragraph matched the mood of the heath. No one had ever done that before. No one had ever shown us how the power of writing was built by the author. And then she arranged for me, and a few of my classmates, to go to a book signing by John Ciardi. At that point I didn't know who John Ciardi was. He was in town to promote his translations of Dante, and so I met a real live author. I talked to him. I saw his name on a book and I saw the author himself—a normal person. And I got his book signed. It began to dawn on me: "Oh, writers are real people. This is something that is possible to achieve."

So she was really, really instrumental in my evolution as a writer, yet I had never shown her a single one of my poems. Years later I asked her, "How did you know?" She said, "You just had this gleam in your eye when we talked about the whole mechanics, the structure of writing." So that was a first inkling.

Still, I hadn't admitted to myself that I wanted to be a poet because, come on: there was no visible means of income. I didn't know anything about MFA programs. And also I was very good scholastically. At that age, I labored under expectations that I would become a credit to my race as a doctor or lawyer or possibly teacher. And so I went to college with those expectations in mind. I changed my major about six times in the first quarter. Finally I settled on English because I could say it was pre-law, and obfuscate a little bit. So I got to do what I loved to do, which was to read and to talk about books.

Writing with a serious purpose happened almost by accident. I was taking an advanced composition class, and my professor became ill a few weeks into the semester and was replaced by the fiction writing professor. He came into the room—I'll never forget it—in an electric blue Italian suit and said, "We're going to tell stories, and we're going to learn how to construct those stories. And by then, you'll know everything you need to know about composition." So I was kind of hijacked into the creative writing program. After a while, it became clear to me that all I really wanted to do was to write, And that maybe I should be thinking about finding a job that would support this habit.

CM: And at that point, were you sharing your work with the other students?

Or were you still quite private about it?

RD: I was sharing my work in writing workshops. I learned, first of all, the incredible fear of sharing, but soon followed by the incredible elation that comes when something one has written resonates in another person's experience. At the same time, I learned how to differentiate between my personal self and the writing self. In other words, not to take criticism personally, but just to tell myself, "OK. I'm not getting this across. But I'd like to connect with the reader. That's the end game, so let's revise." I grew to love revision. It sounds masochistic, but that's where a lot of discoveries happen.

CM: When did you tell your parents that you wanted to be a writer?

RD: I didn't let on until my junior year. I went home for Christmas, and told my mother that I wanted to be a poet, and she said, "You'd better tell your father yourself." So I did. Sure, I was the odd duck in the family. My brother was in computer science. My younger sisters were also trained in the sciences. To his credit, my father simply said, "Well, I've never understood poetry. Don't be upset if I don't read it." Which was fair enough, as far as I was concerned.

CM: What were you reading in those days, apart from John Ciardi?

RD: I was always reading Shakespeare. Langston Hughes entered the picture before I reached high school. In college I read Sylvia Plath and Anne Sexton, Mark Strand and James Wright, Robert Bly. And I was devouring a lot of British fiction, too. Before I left high school, I had read all of Thomas Hardy's novels because I loved them so much. I remember thinking, "I must finish these before I graduate. Then maybe I will be ready for college."

CM: Did you read Thomas Hardy's poems at that time?

RD: I did not. I wasn't introduced to his poems until college. I still remember my professor quoting a Hardy poem and I'm thinking, "Oh my gosh! The poems are amazing too!" And off I went to find them. One of the things I'd taken from that childhood reading was that if I was interested in someone—if I found just one poem I loved—then I wanted to read them all. So I'd go off on my own and read the rest.

CM: In *The Poet's World* you talk about deliberately trying to remain ignorant of your own poetic process in order to keep the left side of the brain from colonizing the right. And I wondered whether you still feel that way, or whether it has grown easier to talk about the process in these last years.

RD: It has become easier to talk about the process; however, I still keep myself ignorant of that essential last bit of magic. I'm not going to examine it too closely. But the physical, external process, that I can talk about.

I like to write by hand, initially. I need that physical contact with the paper. And I do get kind of particular about what I'm using. It's strange, although I believe that everybody does that to a certain extent. I don't like pencils. Fountain pens are too prissy. Maybe I kind of got frozen in what I used when I first had that spark in college. So I tend to write on college-ruled notebook paper at first. With a *Bic* pen.

CM: And then you go to the computer and print it out?

RD: Yes. At the point where I can no longer see the poem or imagine the visual shape of the poem on the page, I will type it up on the computer and print it out. Then I immediately start revising by hand. Occasionally, I go back and copy the entire poem out by hand again, because when I'm writing it out with a pen, I hear how long the line is. I hear it in my head. I also hear the silences.

I love to revise and so I have lots of revisions, with each revision paper-clipped on top of the next. And then comes the problem of how you file those little devils! I discovered early on that I could not write a poem from beginning to end. That's not the way I live. I tend to do many things at once. If I walk across the room, I'm going to pick up five things along the way to distribute somewhere else. So I decided to try to organize my writing life that way. I work in fragments. Often I will start a poem and can't get any further with it, so it needs to be filed. I can't file it by topic or by theme. That doesn't make much sense to me. The themes change. So I file my poems according to color, which is a way of keeping it intuitive. I do love color. And the colors correspond more or less to my mood. So, for instance, a revision may go into the red folder. And then if I come in to write one day—and I try to write every day when I'm at home—and I don't really have an idea in my head, or I'm trying to remember where a certain poem is, if I feel like I'm red that day, I'll go pick up the red folder. This system works pretty well for me. And in the process, poems might change their colors too.

CM: That's a lovely system. I love how you balance the formal and the intuitive. It's such a sweet marriage of those two things.

RD: Thank you.

CM: In *The Poet's World,* you mentioned the number of American poems that have been set in backyards, inside a house looking through a window at a yard. You said at that point, "American poets rarely step into the outside world." I was wondering whether you yourself had consciously tried to change the rules since then, particularly in your last book, *Sonata Mulattica,* which has many, many journeys in it. Lots of outside stories. Lots of outside poems.

RD: It did go outside, didn't it? Well, I wouldn't say that I consciously tried to do that, but once I was aware that many modern and contemporary American poets rarely stepped outside, I would push myself to step out every once in a while. I even try to make my students step outside. On the first day of class, I ask them what they're passionate about. And typically, they respond, "Reading." I probe further, "Well, what else?" And they say, "Well, poetry." And I won't let go: "Well, what else?" Then I follow up, "You must be passionate about life. Passionate about something in life, at least—something outside of these walls in order to write anything of meaning to you."

Sonata Mulattica does step quite a bit outside of the walls. I wanted to bring the world back to the intimate, as opposed to the intimate staying very carefully within itself, and only daydreaming about the world. [*Sonata Mulattica* re-creates the life of George Bridgetower, best remembered for being the first performer, and the initial dedicatee, of Beethoven's *Kreutzer Sonata.*]

CM: How much research and preparation did you do in writing these poems?

In a sense it must feel like a lifetime's research because of your own journey as a musician.

RD: You know, that's well put: it was a lifetime's journey. When I look back on it, it seems almost inevitable that I would write this book. When I became aware of George Bridgetower, I thought to myself, "This story is so amazing, and it not only deserves—it *needs* to be told." I know German, and I've been playing the cello for many years, so I'm familiar with classical music. I am familiar with the territory in which he moved. When I began writing the poems for the book, the sole research I had in hand were a few snippets I had taken off the Internet. Just the basic outline of his life, plus a couple of articles from old musical quarterlies.

I wrote until I realized, "Well, I can't go any further here because I don't know what London looked like in 1790. I don't know what this ten-year-old boy would have seen walking down the street, how many black people he would have seen, and how they would have reacted." So I had to go back and do research. I would write, research, write, research. One thing I did try to do was to keep the research under the surface of my awareness every time I sat down to write. I did not want to become too enamored of the facts. I think that one of the things that can happen in, let's say, a bad costume drama, is that one becomes enamored of the era and forgets the fact that human beings, basically, have had similar emotions since the beginning of time. All the basic emotions are the same.

CM: You have some extraordinary stories in these poems, about Haydn's death and the Napoleonic soldiers, for instance. But often I was just drawn along by your depiction of Bridgetower as a little boy, or as a young man as he moved through that very different world.

RD: What really interested me from the beginning—fascinated me—was to try to discover how he had felt. That was always what pushed me. *How did he feel? How did it feel to even be in this position?* No doubt this has something to do with the empathy that I, as an African-American and a poet, felt for him, and also as someone who herself had chosen to step a bit off the beaten path. When I was growing up, I often felt a little bit out of sync with the rest of the world, and yet I went on to find recognition and praise in the smaller world that I had chosen, the world of poetry. I wanted my readers to become fellow travelers on this journey through Bridgetower's life, and to realize that this era was not anything to be studied under a glass globe. It was as vibrant, strange, and quirky as contemporary life. I didn't want my readers to be stifled by reverence for the classical era. I wanted them to think, "Gosh, they were just as loopy then as we are now!"

CM: When I hear you read, I'm struck by how much of the joy of that book has to do with the number of voices in it, and how well you inhabit them all. Was that something you consciously set out to do?

RD: At the very beginning of my writing about George Polgreen Bridgetower, I started small. I thought, "I'm going to write a poem or two about this young man who premiered Beethoven's *Kreutzer Sonata*." That's his claim to fame. But then the project began to grow, and with it my curiosity: "Well, how did he *become* the young man who premiered Beethoven's sonata?" Fairly early on I realized that in order to grasp who he was and how he had become what he was, I needed to imagine and recreate for myself the world around him, his personal circles and the wider circles of history that he was embedded in, which meant many voices. Now, I love the theater. I love the way voices sound in the air and what they tell you or can't tell you. So the prospect of bringing in many voices was a delight to me. I can't explain how much fun it was to have all of these characters around me. And I miss them now, you know? I miss Haydn and I miss George Bridgetower and Black Billy Waters and "Prinny," a.k.a. the Prince of Wales.

CM: Is working with other voices something you encourage your students to try?

RD: Yes. I do try to help my students go in that direction, or at least to attempt to go in that direction, because I know that one of the hardest things for young writers is to get over their self-consciousness, that sudden sense of "Oh, this is my voice. I am actually saying this. I'm going to have to read this." Writing in different voices can be a very useful way to channel your emotions. As a writer, you can tell yourself, "This is not me. I'm just imagining what it would be like if I were in this character's position." It's a very helpful method for students to practice.

CM: This question goes back to what you were saying about helping students find their passions other than reading, other than books. And also to something you said in *The Poet's World* about the outside world and "the little window" of the television screen. People talk nowadays about "nature deficit disorder" and young people not having sufficient time outside in the great green world or the great ochre-colored world. I'm wondering if that's come up for you with your students, whether you feel they are almost too wedded to their screens and their machines.

RD: I don't worry because of technology, per se—the fact that they have all of these great tools like Google and the Internet. But I do worry that they communicate too exclusively via technology, that it has become their major mode of communication. I worry when they text each other across the room and when Facebook has become more fascinating to them than hanging out with friends. Even in my own life I notice how technology interferes, which can be at once comforting and disturbing. In the summer, the air conditioning is on, and so I don't hear the birds and I don't hear the frogs at the pond. I don't hear even the mosquitoes. There's a whole layer missing—well, many, many layers and textures are actually disappearing, for better or worse.

To be fair, such considerations do often pop up in the work of my students—the sense that there is a deficit, especially once they have learned to ask themselves the right questions, like, "Well, OK. So he broke your heart. But where did he do it and what could you hear and smell around you?" To be aware that we are still and foremost physical beings. To be aware that anything we experience in life has all these little ambient sensations. And even if we no longer encounter birds and bees all summer long and feel the grass on our bare feet, we should at least savor other small sensations, like the cool touch of the table or the warmth of it, or the way the chair fabric bristles under you—all the details that elevate our experiences beyond the mundane.

CM: Absolutely. The recent edition of the *Oxford Children's Dictionary* actually left out words like "gerbil," "hamster," "goldfish," "primrose," "dandelion," and replaced them with words like "blog" and "voicemail." I wondered what you might say about this.

RD: That's outrageous. It's horrific! My first impulse is to say, "Why do you have to take words out? Why can't you just add words?" Sure, words like "blog" need to be in there, but I don't see why "gerbil" should disappear because of that. You've just struck me dumb! It's distressing, because children get their cues from adults. If you take out the word "gerbil," they will think, "Gerbils aren't important." So that's quite alarming.

CM: What would you tell the students who'll be reading this interview—what would you advise them, to help keep their poetry rich?

RD: I used to advise students to *read, read, read.* The older I get, the more I also want to tell them to *live, live, live*—while they *read, read, read,* of course! If they live intensely, they're also going to read intensely, because they'll want to see what others have done. When I first went into a library as a young kid, I was struck by the notion that here were worlds to explore, worlds I might not be able to get to physically—but I could read about them and experience them through books. And soon enough, I decided that this didn't mean I wasn't going to try to get to those worlds; someday, intense reading and intense living might converge. As they did, eventually.

So the students should live intensely. That's what I'd advise.

NIKKY FINNEY

Interviewed June 2, 2009

Now in her late fifties, Nikky Finney is a striking presence, a passionately articulate poet-shaman. Born in Conway, South Carolina, in 1957, she was especially influenced by her grandmother, Beulah Davenport, and by her father, "the justice man," who taught her that "you can knock down barriers in the sweetest way, many times, with language, words."

Finney was an attentive listener from an early age. "There was music before there was language," she says, "music before there was poetry." She started writing in her teens, but didn't show her work for almost a decade. At twenty-one, she began to study with Toni Cade Bambara. "Then I was a writer drawn to pretty words," she tells me. "Toni Cade Bambara was the first person to say to me, 'OK, Nikky, you can write a pretty poem. So what? What's the plan? What are you going to write next?'"

In the years that followed, Finney "moved beyond pretty," writing clear, uncompromising poems about race and class and family and politics, and about her own sexuality too. Her work was fueled in part by the Civil Rights and Black Arts movements, but it is still very much her own. "I want to be here in my own shoes," she says, "or shoeless, wearing my own clothes . . . and that takes stepping away from the crowd."

In the early '90s, Finney began to teach at the University of Kentucky, where she stayed for almost two decades. From 2007 to 2009, she was poet-in-residence at Smith. She is currently the John H. Bennett, Jr. Chair of Southern Literature and Creative Writing at the University of South Carolina. Her fourth book of poems, *Head Off & Split,* was awarded the 2011 National Book Award for poetry.

He Never Had It Made

These words were read upon the investiture of Ernest A. Finney Jr.
as the first Black Chief Justice of the Supreme Court of the State of
South Carolina, December 1, 1994, Columbia, S.C.

Just a plain brown paper sack boy
from a place and people
who sweet fed him everything in double doses
just in case his man size pockets should ever
wear a hole

An ordinary brown corduroy boy
from folk who never had it made
but still managed to make
whatever they were to be from scratch

A regular little fellow
whose mother never got to bathe or watch him grow
or even gaze him from the farmhouse window
where he loved to sit on a summertime box
of Virginia cured day dreams
unbrellaed by the big oak tree
and inbetween chores
and stare away at the longest dirt road
the only way in or out
to grandpop's farm
the same country road that all country boys
tried to stare down in their day
wondering what or who could ever be
at the end of all that dirt
watching it for signs of life
maybe somebody from the city might visit
some somebody   from one of those shiny ready made
places
who could make magic

of a brown boy's country fried beginnings

Maybe one of those far away places
would take him just as homespun as he was
and grow him up to be something legal
maybe handsome
even dap debonair
and he might just become
the somebody who could easy talk
the most complicated of things
for the regulars

and for all others   be
shiny as new money

From the first he was looking to be
one of those new Black men
who came visiting from the North
to talk pretty at the State College of South Carolina
one of those kinds
with the pocket chains and the shiny grey suits
with a hundred pounds of law books
under their arms
just like some kind of natural growth
stout with the law on their minds
devotees of justice
maybe he could be one of their kind

He never had it made
he only had a proud father and a circle of stubborn
arms and wiggling fingers
to keep his dying mother's promise
to raise the boy up at their sides
and not just anywheres
Don't let no strangers have him

knowing he would never have her there
to see to any of the raising herself

This one
that one there
had it sweetened and sifted
chewed up and spit back on his plate
he for sure had it prayed over
then chicken scratched around
in somebody's kitchen who loved him
through and through
over somebody's fire who pointed first to his
pantslegs
and then maybe a switch
whenever he was off his daily chalk straight line

And from beneath his granddaddy's wagon wheels
and from up under his people's stern tutelage
he was surely begun
but it wasn't nothing guaranteed
you know the ways I mean
all silver and engraved

He might'a had it boiled up every morning
explained and preached and on sunday gospelized
by an early rising grandmother
then a significant Claflin College
And I'm quite sure he soda jerked it back and forth
and baked his dreams in his own high hopes
to try and make sure it could so   maybe happen

The good Lord willing and the creek don't rise

But he never had it brought out on some royal platter
never promised to him at his broken bones of a birth

the making of this man's silk deeds
came straight from polyester dreams
from tears and sea water sweat
from love and dirt   work   and the graciousness of his
God
all following him like a North star

He always loved the law
even in the middle of all those many years
when his own daughter argued history to him
poeting always what wasn't right   fair or true
how he with the calm of a sailor
who had seen the ocean at its worst and then its best
with all the faith two eyes could keep safe for her
how he would always no matter say
"The law works, Girl."

And his own poetry has kept what was right   right
and he has kept her   and the law breathing

A steady drop of water
will wear a hole in a rock, Daughter.
Such are the vicissitudes of life, Son.
If you see me and the bear fighting,
you go and help the bear, my friend.
It's alright Babygirl, you win some and you lose some.
Just do the best you can with what you got everybody.

He is the justice man
and from his waiting tables as a young lawyer
for the white and the privileged
to this day here   he has always believed
back then as boy with only a road
up here as man who never looks back
the law works Girl

Papa
Daddy
The Justice Man
you never had it made
but here you are making it
and all of us cross over with you
proud as peacocks in our brightest polyester
maybe that's what Pop
maybe that's what Mama Carlene
would say

Christian McEwen: Let's begin with the poem you wrote about your grand-mother, Beulah Davenport. Could you say something about that?

Nikky Finney: Folks always ask how I became a poet, when did all that start? Some of the answers I know and some I don't. But my grand-mother was a huge influence. She was a farming woman, a woman who grew things with her hands, and spent a lot of time outdoors—a wom-an who could look at the sky and tell you how the day was going to go, weather wise—deeply rooted in human connectedness to geography and landscape.

I was the oldest granddaughter, and she and I were incredibly close. So many of my own sensibilities—being a human being, being alive, what matters in the world, what doesn't matter, cycles of life and death—all those things come from my grandmother, who could walk into the woods and tell you what leaf would make a good tea and what leaf to avoid forever. She was a very smart, very passionate, no middle-of-the-road kind of woman, and I wanted to write something that would reflect an incredibly powerful life on this earth—99 years. She was born in 1900 and died in 1999. I had the good fortune, the privilege, of holding her hand when she crossed over.

I remember the day I arrived at her door from Kentucky. She'd been diagnosed six months before with ovarian cancer, and my mother said,

"She's waiting on you," and I said, "How can you tell?" and my mother said, "I can tell." So I walked in, and her voice had gone, but I sat down near the bed and her feet were pushing and moving like they wanted to run. I cupped her feet in my hands and I said, "It's all right, it's OK, you can let go," and she leaned back, and three hours later she took her last breath.

So I feel very fortunate to have had my grandmother close in my life for forty-three years, and to still have her in this other configuration of closeness—this closeness going forward. I still see her and talk to her.

CM: That was a big "yes" to her apprenticeship.

NF: Apprenticeship is a great word. She taught me how to be a woman in the world. And I'm forever grateful for having her for so long—her guidance, her counsel—not about metaphor or simile, but about truth. She would accept nothing from you but the truth, the way women of her generation believed in looking you in the eye and telling you. I try to do that in my work.

CM: I felt that in what you wrote about your father. I so much admire the poem you wrote about him. You describe him as just a "regular little fellow," "an ordinary brown corduroy boy," and yet he grew up to be the lawyer, "the justice man," and you grew up to be "the justice man's daughter."

NF: It's interesting that you chose the two people—and my mother won't like this at all—the two people who had the greatest influence in my life. My mother was a huge influence too, but in terms of truth and justice, it was my grandmother for truth, and my father for justice. My father is a quiet soul and even as a lawyer, a lawyer at war, it's as if he's always had a tool belt around his waist. Even in the courtroom, even in the street. He's always, in my mind's eye, hammering away at some door, some illusion, some stereotype. He takes out his little hammer, with his beautiful hands, and tap-taps away at it, and then he might take a swish broom and brush it up without a lot of fanfare, stepping into that new place where those things have now been challenged. That's how I see my father.

He and I were incredibly close—I grew up in his deep light. His name for me is Lovechild—one word. He calls me that to this day. And one of the things he has taught me is that you can knock down barriers in the sweetest way, many times with language, words. That's what I'm trying to do. He wanted me to go to law school and become a lawyer. That was his first dream. But I think he sees the work I do as a kind of artistic justice, because he understands I'm taking on subject matter that means a lot to me. He taught me that, by modeling, there are many ways to change the world.

CM: Am I right in thinking that you're one of three children?

NF: Absolutely. I'm in the middle. There's a brother who is two years older—a lawyer; a brother who is eight years younger—a lawyer; and then the artist/poet/lovechild.

CM: What was your relationship to art and poetry as a child? I'm thinking of your lines about yourself as infant photographer, "not with any eye but with skin did I see this."

NF: I was born a stone's throw from the Atlantic Ocean, in a really tiny town called Conway, South Carolina. And I was born a jaundiced baby. I had to stay in the hospital for a week, which drove my mother crazy, and she doesn't like to talk about it. I stayed in that incubator with that round opening, with somebody's hand coming through to check on me, and that's how I began to see the world. I love circles. I'm using the image of that circular opening as a kind of lens.

My family were farmers, and I grew up on a farm at the top of the state. My mother's brother, my Uncle Billy, came home from Vietnam with trunk-loads of photography equipment and basically abandoned it. My grandmother stored it in the top of the barn, and I discovered it one day when I was just a girl. There I was at the barn door looking out over this hundred acres of land—my grandfather's pride and joy—and I had a telephoto lens, a fisheye lens, an underwater lens, a beautiful Nikon F camera that I had no idea how to use. But I figured it out by messing around with it.

To this day, I use the image of lenses to talk about writing with my students. "When I want to do a closeup, I get the telephoto lens; when I want to get the whole scene, I use the wide angle." It's a very visual language.

So there I am, a girl of twelve, doing these camera shots of cows' heads, butterflies, snakes in the grass, the hay barn. How much the visual world means to me, and how quietly I take them in, these deeply sensory images— the smell of the hay, the rain—they're all coming while I'm standing there, and my eyes, I imagine, clicking the picture. I use the metaphor of the camera to travel back in time to see it.

CM: Wonderful, rich, precise detail. So was this when you began to think of yourself as a poet?

NF: My writing really began at thirteen, fourteen, fifteen. I was just inun-dated with the sensory world of South Carolina. I believe that the wan-dering, contemplative nature I have now was born when I was a girl, from walking across the farm, discovering a snakeskin and picking it up with a stick, climbing a tree, figuring out how I felt about my grandmother yelling at me for having not done something. How I felt about the calf that had been stillborn two days before, or the men who gathered at the farm to slaughter the pigs for the holidays. The sound of the pigs was still in my ear.

So here I was, this tender, tender heart. My mother would describe me as a sensitive girl, and that may be true, but I was also hyper-aware with a deep sensitivity to the sensory world, which is the foundation for my writing.

CM: Looking at your acknowledgments, I find Lucille Clifton, Walter Mosley, Toni Cade Bambara. When did you first encounter their work?

NF: Much later. I was raised in a small town in South Carolina, at the height of integration in the late '60s, early '70s. I started out going to Catholic school in Sumter, South Carolina, and my mom and dad said, "We know you like this school, but there's something bigger going on and we have to be a part of it. So we have to do something we really don't want to do—move you to the public school system."

That was very traumatic for me and for my older brother. But we took it in stride. Most of my teachers in those days were white, Southern teachers who gave me the names that I became familiar with going forward—Walt Whitman, Dickinson, Frost. It wasn't until I left home at eighteen, and went to an historically black school in Alabama, Talladega College, that I really blossomed into understanding the continuum of writers I was stepping into. I took a course with Dr. Gloria Gayles. She introduced me to Toni Cade Bambara, Toni Morrison, the Harlem Renaissance writers, Countee Cullen, Claude McKay, Gwendolyn Brooks.

So there was a connection made in my teens that made everything explode around me. First, loving words and language, then reading of poets and writers—really good stuff—but then rocketing into, *holy cow!* African American culture. Stories about women that I never thought would make it into a book. The permission that that class and that poet-in-her-own-right scholar woman gave me made all the difference in the world.

Nikki Giovanni was coming to campus, and Dr. Gayles said, "Step up and say you're a poet." I was shy. I'd come from a small town. How could I walk up to Nikki Giovanni and say, "I'm a poet, too?" What would she say? Would she laugh at me?

There were levels of falling into the life of a poet. It didn't just come all at once. It was almost like climbing a ladder. That's how I feel about it now. "This is good, this is amazing, this is where I'm supposed to be. Take the rung of the ladder with more confidence."

CM: There's a question you asked Lucille Clifton, which I'd like to ask of you. You asked her to think of a moment in her life so precious that if she could wear it, she would. What might such a moment be for you?

NF: My mother and my father are two amazing people, and they raised us in this womb, this nest of the sweetest love. I feel almost embarrassed to talk about it. I am the child who left home. When I started leaving home, and at an early age—seventeen—my parents would take me to the airport, park the car, walk me in, and they would not leave until the plane was in the air.

I'd say, "Mom, Dad, I can get there, it's all right." "No, we'll take you," and they'd stand there until I was gone. There's a ritual of my leaving them. My father empties out his pockets and hands his money to me. My mother does the same, not with money, but with some other object I might need. Oranges, candy, a peppermint. So there's this exchange that happens.

That's the picture, the image, that I remember to this day. They park, they go as far as they can go, and then they turn around. It's the ritual of releasing me to the universe. We don't do this anymore. Sometimes I wish we'd think more about how we leave each other, and how we might never see each other again. That's my charm.

CM: That's magnificent. It makes me wonder, as the recipient of so much love, where you have been able to give it on.

NF: I think to the page, but I don't know that I really like that. I'm not a hermit poet. I have these amazing relationships with people, friends, partners. But I do feel that the purest sense of it, the purest sense of the love I've been given, does go into the work. That may not be what I wish, but I think it's true.

CM: Through giving it to the page, you're giving it to the universe, to history, the future.

NF: There's also no human personality blocking that love. I think I love fiercely. I love powerfully. But I also have this deep, deep relationship to a pencil and a piece of paper that goes back to my beginnings—my understanding of who I am in the world that never ceases to amaze me. So in that spirit, I'd have to claim my work as the greatest love that has shaped me.

CM: Thank you.

NF: Thank *you.* I didn't know that until you asked me. It's an important question.

CM: I think of your lines about the black skillet sizzling and "pencilfrying / sweet Black alphabets / In an allnight oil." And I wonder whether you're guided to a poem primarily by its music or by its subject matter?

NF: There's a lot of music in my head. There was music before there was language. There was music before there was poetry. There's a play going on in my head right now, music and the visuals that accompany the music. There's Nina Simone and a piano in Paris, 1963, and the writing of *To Be Young, Gifted and Black,* there's the sound of James Brown singing "To Be Black and Proud," and the visual memory of his feet skating across the Ed

Sullivan Show on black-and-white TV. My brow must have been gnarled in amazement, because who had ever seen anybody's feet do that? I have all of my father's jazz albums from the '60s, and I refuse to give them up for the easiness of CDs because album covers are art. There was the large, beautiful shot of the faces I just love to look at. There's this music that's coupled with the visuals—Billie Holliday, the arresting intonations of Sarah Vaughan. All of the memories go into the sound I hope to make as a poet. I don't ever want to lose my connection to that.

Growing up on a farm, sound was critical. Sound traced the day—the rooster crowing, the milk truck stopping half a mile up the road (I can still hear the brakes), the pickup, my grandmother, the postman—everything was situated by sound and sight.

CM: You spoke in an earlier interview of the power of the human voice, how it can make people want to jump and shout.

NF: I listened for a very long time as a girl. I was incredibly quiet. My mother used to check in on me, "Are you OK?" I didn't come out of a quiet family or a quiet time. I had noisy brothers. The '60s were incredibly violent, loud, and noisy. My grandmother would roll me out into the garden—hot, mosquitoes, sun, flies—and she said, "I've never seen a child just sit there and look around like that, notice the storm clouds coming." That was my sensory perception growing bigger and getting fed. Later, when I was in church, I learned to adore a great microphone, because it doesn't destroy the beauty of the human voice. People will come up to me after a reading and ask if I have a CD, because there's something about the sound of my voice. I can't hear it, but I do know that I was raised up in a world where I paid close attention to sound and elocution.

CM: At what point did you cease to be this silent, attentive child and become a voice in your own right?

NF: It had to be in my twenties. I had to decide whether to be this quiet, nice girl who had been writing in her journal books since she was thirteen—I still write in them—or step into the shoes that had been made for me. It was a conscious decision. I remember it clearly. I was writing, but writing very privately. Writing and storing things away in a trunk. Writing and closing them down in a desk drawer. Not sharing them. Two or three absolute things happened that changed the direction of my life. Meeting Toni Cade Bambara when I was twenty-one. She had been teaching at Spellman College, but she wasn't allowed to teach that year, so she began to host a writing workshop in her house the first Sunday of every month. Twelve noon till sometimes twelve at night. Whoever brought work, we stayed with it until it was done. I was in that workshop for two years, and it changed my life. I was always a "pretty" writer. I could write pretty words and I knew how to do that. People would say, "Wow, you can do that." Toni Cade Bambara was the first person to say to me, "OK, Nikky, you can write a pretty poem. So what? What's the plan? What are you going to do next?"

I had to really think about the breath behind the words, what the words would do out in the world and what I wanted them to do. That was a huge moment for me. I had to talk about how I wanted to communicate something—not just move the alphabet around. I wanted to tell a story. I wanted that story to matter. I wanted that story to start a conversation between people who didn't usually talk to each other. "Let me tell you this little scene, this little story. Let me tell you about this person." I grew up a girl who read things that mattered, that changed my life when I read them. Words can change our life. Stories can make you travel around the world. They can bring opposing forces into the same room to have a conversation. I still believe language has that absolute power. And I've believed that all my life.

But at twenty-one, I met Toni Cade Bambara, and I began stepping out to do some readings. I was still a shy Southern girl. But the older I got and the more themes I took on, and got close to and got through, the more clarity and understanding I had, and that encouraged me to write other things.

It's important to remember that I grew up in the '70s, when the Black Arts Movement was huge in the States. There were people standing up and saying, "We have to be responsible for what we say. We have to say very courageous, hard things," and so they were models for me. But I wanted to say the hard things in a tender way. I didn't always see people doing that. I saw some shouting, I saw some harsh words and language. I saw some un-beautiful language. And I didn't want to do that. I knew there was a way to do both, and I just had to figure out how to get there.

So I have to tell you this story. I'm with Toni Cade Bambara and we're walking in Atlanta, and a man approaches. He looks like a bus driver and he says, "Aren't you that writer lady?" I think, oh, he's gonna ask her for an autograph or a book, and she goes, "Yeah, I'm that writer." She was well known around Atlanta. And he says, "Well, I want to buy a house, but I can't figure out this contract." And he pulls out the bank forms and says, "Can you help me?" And I'm stunned, I'm startled. I'm standing there, going, what does he mean asking her about something that's totally disconnected from what she does? And she says, "Be at my house Saturday at four o'clock. What's your name?" He says, "Roy," and she says, "Come by the house, Roy, and I'll help you."

At that moment, what it meant to be a writer was completely transformed for me. You don't sit alone at your desk stowed away from life. You don't become a hermit according to the twisted western stereotype: you must be tragic and you must wear a scarf around your neck, and you must act like nobody understands you, you must act like you don't care. No! She taught me in that moment that there was a human being who worked hard, who'd saved enough money to buy a house—the American dream— and the one thing keeping him from that was that he couldn't write. She said, "I will step into this scenario because I am a writer." Huge moment for me. It shaped everything going forward for me. She was an amazing woman—a writer, an activist, a truth-teller.

CM: Great story.

NF: He got the house.

CM: This connects beautifully to your own passion for justice as manifested in poems like "The Devil is Beating his Wife," "The Butt of the Joke," and "The Girlfriend's Train."

So maybe talk a little bit more about current events.

NF: I'd grown up in this family that was incredibly active and involved in justice issues: the '60s, Malcolm X, Dr. King, Nina Simone. But I began to understand that I had to start educating myself. You have to do this. You have to find where your place is and when you find it, you can't be afraid of what you find. You can run away from it for a little while, but then you have to embrace it, dance with it, feed it, nurture it, give it sunshine and water, because as far as I know, this is my one chance. I don't want to leave wearing somebody else's clothes. I want to be here in my own shoes, or shoeless, wearing my own clothes, doing what I'm supposed to be doing, and that takes stepping away from the crowd and standing on the bank of the river, and realizing that it's gonna be lonely sometimes. I'm gonna be isolated from the community, the people I love, sometimes, but this is the work I have to do.

CM: I'm reminded here of the lesbian issue. And I'm thinking of the poem "Sex," where the narrator is asked, "What do you know about it anyway?" by her beloved mother.

NF: Yes. That poem. . . . I just had to figure out how to write about it. You used the word "beloved" and that is so true. So how do I write this story giving honor to my love for my mother and also honoring the truth of my life? It was the most difficult balancing act I've done as a writer. But my mother really did say that to me. The belief that a woman loving a woman is "less than" the love that a woman and a man shares, that nothing I do can equal what my brothers do in their marriages—it set me on my head.

I knew I had to write about it, because not to write about it would have been a lie, and I teach my students to tell the truth. I had to do what I so often talk about. I came to the beauty and bounty of being a lesbian when I was twenty-five, so maybe a little later in my life than others, perhaps because of having been raised in the South—the very closed-minded, church-infused South.

But I gloriously came to it, both through writing and through paying attention to women's lives and to my own relationships, how they blossomed, when my heart beat fast. Moving out to California when I was twenty-six, being in a different terrain and landscape, able to explore my heart, my feelings, not worrying about breaking my mother's and my father's hearts. Being able to do that from literally a world away and not coming home so often then, because I was exploring who I was, and then realizing I had to go home. That it's not something to run away from, nor should I, and I was very proud of it. Coming out to my mom when I was thirty, having gone out and gotten my words and muscles and language together. She came out to visit me. We'd had a wonderful day with several of my friends, all of whom are gay. When I told her, she broke down and started crying. It was a very emotional time for her, but what I came to understand was how much my family loved me and how I'd always been different and how I had loved being different. How I had nurtured my difference through language, and through the camera's lens, through wandering, through music, through the creation of many different modes of creativity, the love for the sensual world.

I remember reading this essay by Audre Lorde called "Uses of the Erotic." It's the most stunning essay I've ever read about the power of being a lesbian in the world. It gave me such permission. It was so freeing. It was so true to my own life that I wanted to tape every page to my body and never take it off. [Laughter.] But I deal with and handle tough subjects, I hope, quietly but powerfully. I still don't stand on the box on the corner of the street. I still want to go home with my pencil and sharpen it, razor-sharp, and come back fighting on the page with things that are unfair, with anybody who tries to say that my love is not equal to somebody else's love. If I have to fight for the rest of my life putting language together that represents my right to love and to live and be, then I will.

CM: Thank you. My heart is still following your stories down into so many pathways.

In your interview with Lucille Clifton, she talks about students feeling that first tingle as "the end," when in fact it's only the beginning. So how do you figure out when a piece of work is done?

NF: I have a checklist of technical things that I'm trying to do in a piece of work. Things like, "What's the title going to be? What's the end coming to?"

But something I tell my students—something I can't teach them—has to do with writing every day. It has to do with spending time with something up to a point where you know it so well that you begin to see what it means, and begin to back away, because it has begun to live on its own without you. That may happen by passing it to somebody for a reading, or reading it aloud to an audience. I'm always reading things that are unfinished to get them to that end. There's an African saying that the work is never done till somebody hears it, and I truly believe that.

So once I've released it and some commentary comes back, I feel like I've walked around it the five required times to look at it from all sides. I've looked at it in a thunderstorm, by candlelight, by fluorescent light. I stop, I put it away. I've looked at it and it steeps for a while, and I don't read it for a long time. I come back to it, and when I'm reading it the next time, I can tell when it's finished. Does it need something or not? And I can let it go.

CM: Students aren't always so willing to allow time for that period of waiting, of trusting, leaving aside, returning . . .

NF: It's also what's hard about the academic setting. You have these four-teen weeks. It all has to happen then. It's impossible. That's one of the things that always grated against me as a teacher in the academy. This little envelope of time is not right, it's not correct. It sometimes takes two or three years for a poem to grow up into itself in the right light. You can't envelope it into those fourteen weeks. But, you can teach the power of putting something away for fourteen weeks. You can teach the power of writing every day toward something, and letting a student see what hap-pened on the seventh day. The power of sitting with something, steeping it, can be modeled, even in an academic setting.

CM: Whose work do you find yourself admiring now? Who nourishes you?

NF: Toni Morrison always teaches me something. When her novels come out, it's a holiday. I take the day off to begin to read. I take myself out to lunch. I love her work. I also love Edward P. Jones's work. He's a novelist and short story writer. His work is full of poetry, and the specificity of language, of black culture. He keeps alive a language from black culture that is going away. I'm a person who is trying to hold on to something behind her—many things—not everything—I'm an old soul in that way. Jones's work is a mirror for a lot of the things I want to be mindful of in my life.

I'm actually going back and rereading *Leaves of Grass* for the first time in a very long time. My coming to Northampton was a return to books that I'd been reading twenty years ago, and because you change as a reader, the work changes in crazy, wonderful ways that I'd never been able to take in before. So I've been rereading Gabriel Garcia Marquez and Robert Frost. I'm also reading a lot of Canadian short story writers.

I'm also very interested in film. I'm working on a longer story—I won't say a novel because I'm not far enough into it—that has a lot of prose poems and a lot of scenes work. I'm interested in how a longer story is a series of scenes, and how that happens on the screen, and what that has to do with this longer work. So I'm reading a lot of old classics—and I'm reading newspapers. I'm as connected to electronic media as the next person, but I don't want to put all my eggs in that basket. I like getting up in the morning and reading the paper.

CM: Working on this long short story, or short long story—what's the difference between working on a poem and something like that?

NF: Pace. I write long poems. I'm a long-winded poet. Everyone calls me that. When I was a lifeguard, we had to tread water, and I was a great water-treader. I could stay out there for long periods of time. You've got to have really strong arms to do it, but because it was meditative, I got really good at it. So when I'm working on the longer story, I often (and here's my visual) think of myself as treading water, but not standing still. Moving around, looking at things in the middle of the deep blue sea, trying to get to shore. So it is about pace and some sort of longer thread than I usually need with the poetry. When I look at the seventy-five pages I've written, I think that's just a long poem, but that helps me get into it. Poetry is my first breath, and I can't leave that out of whatever this is. But it's not a typical long story. It's still very lyrical because I love the lyrical. But it's something very different that I've never done before.

CM: Stamina.

NF: Exactly.

CM: I wanted to ask you about your walking, because you mentioned that as a source of contemplation.

NF: Walking has always been important, but it was not until I moved to

Northampton that I rediscovered walking. Maybe because I was about to turn fifty, maybe the notion that millions of years ago this area was connected to the African continent—the Pangaea—when all the continents were one. So when I walk across the Connecticut River, I think, "Ah, I'm walking to Africa!" Dinosaur prints—you can go see them. It's connected to when I was a girl and was going to be a paleontologist. I just knew dinosaurs would be what I'd spend my life pursuing. But I love walking, and I've found so much language for what I'm working on now with my every morning or every afternoon walks down to the Connecticut River, up on the levee, through the asparagus fields, through the corn fields, down to the water . . . past where a fox ran by yesterday (beautiful animal that just shot past me) and where a snake was last Tuesday, or where an eagle flew this morning.

But walking, my goodness, it goes back to being a girl on my grandmother's farm, walking in the woods to escape the sound of the slaughter of the pigs, it goes back to walking and wandering to find out what I thought about something. I'm still doing that fifty years later. I always want to take care of my knees because I always want to get around, get somewhere, walk off the beaten path. You climb a tree to discover who you are, you use your arms, you see somebody else's footprints, or something else's footprints and you know our paths cross on this planet.

I taught this class a while back, and one of the assignments was to get on a bus and ride to another part of town and come back and write about the experience. I had a student who had never been on a city bus get out of his red Lamborghini, give the bus driver a $100 bill, and the driver said, "Son, I can't change this. We don't give change." And there was this beautiful essay he wrote about not knowing that bus drivers didn't give change and how he discovered something about himself when he got off his beaten path—a path that he took every day with his windows rolled up and his music blaring. He got to sit next to the little black lady from Ebenezer Baptist Church, who called him son also and invited him to her Sunday service. He actually went, and at first he was fearful because he was walking into a black church and he was the only white person around. But when he saw the arms of Mrs. Jackson open up to him and she sat him down in the front row like her son, it changed his life. He said, "I can never go back to being fearful because of what some TV show or some news channel taught me. I had Mrs. Jackson. I had a real person to associate my feelings with." So walking, or touching each other's garment, or touching our knees on the bus, brings us back to humanity and brings us back to what's important in the world, which is: maybe we're different, but maybe we're not different, and that's a conversation we've got to keep having.

Walking is sacred. I tell my mother that it's church, and she doesn't quite agree, but it's very much the most sacred moment of my day.

CM: That moment when you began, essentially, to talk about the community of the universe reminded me of your poem "My Old Kentucky Home," about the white bones snuggling up next to the black bones.

NF: Does it matter? You know there used to be these laws that if you were black, you had to be buried here, if you were white, you had to be buried there. Really? That's ridiculous! At that point are we all not, finally, the same? [Laughs.]

CM: You've been poet-in-residence at Smith for two years now, and you're about to leave, you've got twenty-eight days . . .

NF: Yes, twenty-eight days. The countdown has begun. I want to say that I will never be the same. My life has changed, deepened. I cannot leave here the same woman I was when I arrived. I am joyous about every memory I have here—about the grandmother in the wheelchair with the Obama sign or the "Impeach Bush" sign, the two women I saw my second day here, holding hands and pushing a baby carriage, the two men who were across the street with the three dogs, the woman police officer with the almost bald head, the black man who owns the typewriter shop in Amherst—all against the grain of what is the stereotype or what is expected. I want to say that I will be back, that I've found a home here. I want to say that my students have taught me so much about being a poet and being a teacher. I take them with me wherever I go. I want to say I've rediscovered four-leaf clovers—you'll find me on my hands and knees in the low grass by the river looking for them.

And I want to thank every person who smiled and said hello. There are so many places in the world where people walk by each other and they don't smile or recognize each other, or pretend they don't see somebody who looks a little different or has on something they don't agree with. And I've found so many people who simply smiled and said good morning. So thank you.

ARACELIS GIRMAY

Interviewed April 9, 2013

Aracelis Girmay was born in 1977 in Santa Ana, California, of Eritrean, Puerto Rican, and African American descent. Neither of her parents read poetry. But an aunt gave her a typewriter in junior high school, and she loved "the machine of it, the sound of it." In ninth grade, she was assigned Toni Morrison's *The Bluest Eye.* "Oh," she thought, *"we're allowed to write like that!"* Lucille Clifton, Joy Harjo, and Adrienne Rich were all strong influences too. "I was acquiring life-lines," she says now. "The spirit of their books was part of my parade in high school and early college."

Girmay moved to New York City to attend college, and later taught for a number of community programs, including the Teachers & Writers Collaborative and ACTION, an arts activism workshop in the South Bronx. Meanwhile, she kept writing. She won the GLCA New Writers Award for her first book, *Teeth,* and the Isabella Gardner Poetry Award for her second, *Kingdom Animalia,* and was a finalist for the National Book Critics Circle Award. She currently teaches poetry in Drew University's low-residency MFA program and at the School for Interdisciplinary Arts at Hampshire College.

A woman of intense and haunting beauty, with huge eyes, high cheekbones, and a perfect smile, she writes poems (tender, complex, and original) that seem, more than usually, like a faithful sounding of her most private truth.

Praise Song for the Donkey

*for Lama & Haya & the donkey, killed by an
Israeli missile in Beit Lahiya, northern Gaza*

*"It was not possible to identify which parts
belonged to the donkey & to the girls."
Witness, Gaza, Palestine, 2009*

Praise the Mohawk roof
of the donkey's good & gray head, praise
its dangerous mane hollering out. Beneath
her soft & mournful gray, still beneath
the skull, where it is dusk, praise
the rooms of the donkey's eye & brain,
its pulley & clang, this sound
of hooves & the girls still saying words.
Praise the girls still saying words,
praise the girls, their hands, the hooves
of their hearts hoofing against their opened chests
opened on the open road plainly, praise
the plain day, praise the donkey in it, praise
the fat tongue's memory of grass or hay,
the hundred nights of animal sleep
flung far from bodies, the sturdy house of bones, all over
the decimated road where every thing is flying, praise
the deep, dark machine of the donkey's eye,
the girl's eye, like a movie-house crumbling
in a field outside of town—,
praise the houses & rocks it held once, the sky
before & after the missile, praise the dark
& donkey soul crossing over, every one,
every hill & girl it ever saw, crossing over
in the red suitcase of its blood, into the earth,
praise the donkey earth, earth of girls,
earth of funerals & girls, praise the small,

black luggage of the donkey's eye
in a field, flung far,
filling the ants & birds
with what
it saw.

Christian McEwen: We spoke together back in 2009, but since that time a great deal has happened, including the publication of *Kingdom Animalia*.

Aracelis Girmay: *Kingdom Animalia* came out in the fall of 2011. It was kind of wild. In July, I got a call from BOA saying Laure-Anne Bosselar had received my manuscript submission for the Isabella Gardner Award and they wanted to publish it. So quite a lot changed over the span of maybe three or four months. Many things . . .

CM: I've been reading over the transcript from our last interview and noticing again the richness of your heritage. Your mother played the congas and your grandmother was an anthropologist, and actually did her PhD on salsa lyrics. There was always music around. And I wondered if you'd talk about how that music has influenced your writing.

AG: It is such a gift to get to be with you in conversation again. To hear those things back feels as if I'm meeting another self again.

Music. . . . I've been reading Gwendolyn Brooks with my students at Hampshire. It's a small, sweet, sharp, sharp group. And I've been thinking about how, in Brooks's work, there's a layer of narrative that you can understand, pushed along by the words and the meanings of the words, and then a kind of sonic narrative that happens underneath, even if you just beat out her beats and her meter, without letting people know what the words are. The kind of "sonic narrative" that happens underneath a poem is something I've been really, really interested in.

When I think about the music on my mom's side of the family, part of what I think about is that I don't speak Tigrigna. That's one of my dad's languages. There's a kind of music in Tigrigna that feels very similar to the sonic narrative in Brooks, when you don't quite know what the words are meaning, but you hear the pattern of speech.

And so, in some of the poems in *Kingdom Animalia* and a few in *Teeth* there's an attempt to try to follow what I think of as the Tigrigna music in English. That's something I want to think of more, especially my own intimidation. How intimidated I can get when it comes to scanning! I sometimes worry that my ear is mishearing the accent or stress, though now, more and more, this is less worrisome and more interesting. There's a lot of information in meter.

CM: I was wondering too, whether music had helped give you courage in terms of technique, and perhaps also a certain readiness to listen. You write in one of your poems about "ordinary sounds clanging like miracles," as if you were moving out from music as itself to the sounds of the world as themselves being music. So, how do you get the sounds of the world into poetry? How do you think about that aspect of listening to the world?

AG: I'm struck by that idea of music as giving someone, me, a poet, anyone, courage. Could you say more about what that could mean?

CM: I suppose for myself when I listened to my uncles playing Scottish folk songs, there was a way that music entered the blood and straightened the spine and enlarged the sense of possibility. And did it all in a magnificently non-verbal way.

AG: Mm-hmm.

CM: I don't have too much language for it, but I can feel it in your poems. I'm being given a lot more than the verbal surface meaning, magical as that is.

AG: I've not heard music articulated in that exact way. Maybe in a cousin way. That's interesting, really interesting to me. Right away, I think of a few things. One is, I think there's a kind of pulse in some of the poems. And I guess I'm thinking literally of the music of them: a kind of litany-like pulsing or engine behind the poem. It can sometimes feel like that, like a motor that is so pulsing that you have to keep digging and investigating further. Scaffolding is not the right word—but there's some way that music feels like a thing to hold on to, or a thing that propels me forward into the new discovery of a poem.

Part of your question makes me think about reading Darwin and the fact that we're all somehow related. The fact of our inter-connectedness helps me—how do I say it? To rethink who I imagine might speak to music. Or what I imagine music might come from. The fact of the drill clanging outside. Or the daffodil, seemingly still in a field. So—what might the drill help me to see about the daffodil? What might the daffodil help me to ask about the giraffe?

I'm imagining that the senses I attribute to one place or one body might be carried over—and those very same questions might help me to ask questions of a totally different body. And this connects too with the question of silence—not political questions about who is silenced, but the silences I'm loyal to, and why. And then there are the silences that come from imagining that X, whatever X is, doesn't have language or can't speak. And so, the poem's asking me to think about these things, and helping me to listen more deeply, thoughtfully, whether they're human words or not.

CM: There is a magnificent book by David Abram, called *Becoming Animal,* where he engages in conversation with the non-human world. I think you'd like it.

AG: Thank you.

CM: *Kingdom Animalia* has a powerful undertow, having to do with mortality. As if the fact of death were a lesson you were impressing on yourself over and over again. I think particularly of your lines, "Oh, body, be held now by whom you love. / Whole years will be spent, underneath these impossible stars, / when dirt's the only animal who will sleep with you / & touch you with / its mouth." And I wondered if you'd comment on that theme. Did it have to do with your grandparents' deaths particularly?

AG: My grandparents on my father's side died quite a while ago, and I never met them. But the last time I went back to Eritrea, I spent a lot of time with my grandfather's brother. When it was time to leave, I remember crossing the tarmac to get to the airplane, and how deep and black that night was, and is in my mind right now. Everything just seemed so beautifully, densely, black. And also, every step leaving felt so full of distance, as if each step was like a thousand miles, you know, just getting on the airplane and realizing I probably wouldn't see him again. He was ninety-six, the last time I saw him, and he has died since.

And my grandmother's sister, who was a beautiful, beautiful spirit, she also died. That was the last time I saw her. Being in Eritrea itself feels to me very much about trying to remember or see something, some kind of history or family. And also, being aware of my own timeline, my own lifeline, in relation to it. Moments I'm there are so short and fleeting. And so I think that these poems are very much informed by those deaths.

But they're also thinking about a relationship to a place, you know. Going back after six years, and the generational changes that can happen in such a short time. Somehow that forces me to be aware of how small I am, we are, and how small a human life is up against the vastness of universe. Different things happening in the family. Different changes happening in the family. That asked me to look as much as I can, to think about how short this time is, and to try to be present in it.

CM: Patrick Rosal has a line about "the story of a city composing a man," and I wondered whether you felt you yourself had been "composed" by one particular place.

AG: My mother's from Chicago, and my father was born in Ethiopia, and his family is from Eritrea and went back and forth. But even Chicago felt far away when I was a child. It felt so far from California, where I was raised. So Santa Ana, I feel very much of that place.

But there was also a lot of moving. So there was always this sense of holding many places in my imagination, or in my experience of the world. Also a great sense of displacement. So an orange tree or a color, a specific color of the sky. Or the smell of sweat and a color of the skin. Those things felt like a home I could move with, more than any one specific city. I definitely feel made up of a patchwork of cities or places. A patchwork of cities that I imagined and didn't get to experience.

So when I look at the mud, any mud, no matter where I am, I feel "OK, I know you. You know me. I'm somehow of you." Or crows. Sometimes walking from the library to my office at Hampshire, and *crow!* There are crows everywhere, so I think, "OK, I'm home in this crow sound." I guess the places that feel like home can actually be found in many places. The smell of frankincense and coffee, no matter where I am, becomes a kind of mother.

But there's the home that I move with, and then there's something that happens when I go to a place my family has lived before—a house or a village or a city. I'm always looking and imagining, *"What was here? The tree was probably here. What must you have seen? What are the things with history that hold a history of a place whose language maybe I can't speak?"* And what does it mean to consider two generations ago, my so-and-so crossed with this tree in one of its incarnations? I think those mothers and fathers are in many places.

CM: I love the idea of finding home in the sound of the crow, or home in the scent of frankincense or coffee. And I know what you mean about making the acquaintance of those older presences. Something I think about on the Smith campus, walking under the trees, is that Sylvia Plath walked under those trees. The trees are old enough to have witnessed her. I saw a movie about Gabriela Mistral. And among her books and papers, there was a little folded envelope holding earth from the place where she was born in northern Chile. There it was. Old earth from fifty years ago.

AG: Oh my goodness! Did she mark it?

CM: Yes. There was the name of her village. She'd been carrying it around with her wherever she went.

AG: It makes me think of this writer, Tiphanie Yanique. She's from the Virgin Islands, and she was talking about her first child, and how panicked she felt that her child was not going to be born in the Virgin Islands. She was trying to wait, to figure out a way to give birth back at her home, but the baby was born in New York. And she said that she kept his umbilical cord and took it back and buried it in the Virgin Islands.

So I think about that too. Like, what does it mean? What are the hopes of a family? What do they imagine, who do they imagine will come next?

The small details, or the great big details: I don't know if they're small or big. Of a birth. And the umbilical cord. I think about my mom, who kept ours. I don't know where they are, if they are, any more. I want to ask my mother what she thought she'd do with them. If she thought she'd travel with them wherever she went.

CM: In our last interview you spoke about the presence of the natural world and the constancy of the sky, and the grass, and the trees. How when a seagull flew across your path, maybe there was a message there. You wrote about the language of crows, and what the hawk might be "spelling" as it moved across the sky. Does the natural world still talk to you in that way?

AG: Yes. Although this is a moment in my life where I'm having to really push to make time. Which I do. Yesterday I was out walking for three hours, which was really so good. That's a balance that I need to prioritize and work toward. But it's a struggle.

CM: I understand that teaching at Hampshire is tremendously demanding for the professors, in part because it's so flexible and generous for students. And that must be quite a challenge: to protect your private soul against what the students need and would love to have from you.

AG: I think that's true. Because so much of the work is one-on-one, I think I'm growing immensely; my mind is constantly being stretched into new territory. So I feel the vastness of the world, and possibility, and this excitement, which is beautiful. But I'm also someone who needs a lot of quiet time. I *love love love* that feeling of just being lost in a thought, or waking up early and watching the sky change, and the city just start to come alive. So I guess I'm meeting myself in this new place and under these new circumstances, and I'm realizing how thirsty I am, how essential that quiet is to me. Maybe even more than other people. I don't know. But I definitely need a lot of quiet.

CM: You have these lines in a poem to your grandfather, "Wear a body I can see with my slowest eye," and I had a question about the issue of pace in your own writing, and I think you just answered it. The need to slow down. Time to take things in and be fed by what surrounds you, not always through the verbal channel.

AG: Yes. Alberto Ríos has this poem "Gray Dogs," where he's writing about the dogs running in the distance. He describes the dogs almost like birds. He doesn't describe their feet. And someone asked him in an interview, "Why that description?" And Ríos said what was important was getting to articulate what he was actually seeing—and when the dogs were running in the distance, he couldn't see their four legs. He was trying to write away from the assumption that because they're dogs, you imagine they're going to have four legs. He talked about "slowing down" or "backing up"—not filling in the gaps, but allowing them to be, for the world to be as you see it. Which also feels to me like a rejection of the quick summary, you know: "the slow eye."

CM: The French poet Paul Valéry says he "wants to give the feeling without the boredom of its conveyance."

AG: Ah. Ah-ha.

CM: When I interviewed Patrick Rosal, he spoke of you with great affection and admiration. And I wondered if you'd speak about Patrick as a poet friend.

AG: Patrick is such a dear, dear friend. We met maybe in 2005. And really quickly Patrick felt like a kind of brother to me. We share our manuscripts and say, "What do you think about this poem?" We'll have tea or coffee, and talk about a million things. He's an incredible teacher with just a huge, huge mind and huge heart. And there's such a sharpness there that I respect and admire so much. It's been amazing to have him to talk to about teaching. "How do you carve out time? What do you do in this situation in a classroom?" I feel like he helps me all the time to suss things out. I taught his *Boneshepherds* last year. And the way that he is able in those poems to walk with big history, and the complication of history, is just such a model to me.

In the work I imagine he's one of the people I might be writing to, among other people I have or haven't met before. He's very, very, very, very dear. But also, I think of his work, how deeply interdisciplinary it is: his sound projects, his essays. He does some dee-jaying with poems. There's an energy in terms of what might be possible. He's someone to dream with. Yeah.

CM: And are there any new names you'd like to praise?

AG: Yeah! There's a poet I just love. Shane McCrae. He has a poem that starts, "Dear Once-Incarnate-/Silence dear/Lord if I leave Your table full/ Who hungers in my place . . . Can't-We-All/Just-Get-Along dear Every-King" And it goes on. It's about eight lines. And in this poem the way he's using syntax to both mean and resist resolution, ah, is just genius, brilliant. He's looking at Rodney King, the beating of Rodney King, but it could be any king. It could be Dr. King, it could be God king. So there are these seemingly simple poems, but deeply complicated and elliptical lyrics. I've been teaching his poems lately, 'cause he reminds me of what might be possible, and how a craft element like syntax can be utterly mind-blowing, and carry gorgeous music, but also a kind of origami meaning.

Who else have I been reading? Kamilah Aisha Moon also has a book coming out. It's called *She Has a Name,* and she's thinking about her sister's autism, and family love, among other things. The cover is from a painting by her sister. And these are poems thinking about silence and family. And autism, but also mental health. Can I say one more?

CM: Of course.

AG: Eduardo Corral has a book, *Slow Lightning.* And again, he's someone like Patrick, who walks with this acute awareness of how history is involved in everything we are doing. The poems are deeply lyrical, imagistic, and gorgeous to listen to. And yet you go and you go and you go, and you find the complications are always there.

Anyway, those are the three I would say.

CM: When we spoke last, you mentioned your teacher Mrs. Robinson, who was your English teacher in high school, and you said she was one of your "necessaries." You felt seen by her. And I wondered if you'd talk about what it's meant to be seen like that, and who else you might have felt seen by. And indeed, how you try to give that kind of seeing to your own students.

AG: Mmm. I had a ballet teacher who gave free lessons to the kids in Santa Ana, mostly girls. She'd give ballet classes in the basement of this church. The church was called Saint Joseph's, so it became St. Joseph's Ballet, and now it's a kind of institution. Her name was Sister Beth. My mom ran into her years later and she said, "I dropped the habit." A great joke! So now it's just Beth.

But, those afternoons and sometimes weekend Saturdays of dancing in a room, and not having to use my voice to say what I wanted to say, but getting to dance as my way of being, were so special. I know I felt really seen by her, and also scared and intimidated. I was very shy. But the kind of looking that a dance teacher does, talking about expression and articulation of every part—your hand, or your feet—and the work of practicing again and again . . . you know, I might think, "My toe is pointed." But then there'd be that little shift she'd help me make in my foot or in my leg, and seeing that that small shift meant everything. And I can see the ways that that connects to poem making. That kind of rigor, and dedication, and love, and also that excitement for beauty and effort—trying. She was a beautiful, beautiful model. I should think more about that.

With my own students, I have a colleague now, Nell Arnold [N.S. Koenings], who writes fiction. And I'm so taught by her way of paying attention and her active asking of questions and listening. And her excitement and hunger for ideas. Like Patrick, things feel possible with Nell.

So those are some of the people I think of at this moment. Part of what I hope to do with students is to help create a space where the students feel comfortable experimenting, playing, finding, making big messes. And then also struggling: helping to cause the struggle maybe, and also support it, because so much discovery is born out of that, the work of playing, experimenting, but also of flailing through the mess of an experiment, whether emotional or conceptual.

CM: There's beauty on the other side of the struggle, or there's order, or however one wants to put it.

AG: Yeah.

CM: There's such potency in your references to your childhood. It seemed to me that the terror and the beauty and the loss of childhood had been something of a touchstone in your writing. I wondered how it was to become fully adult when childhood was so still so mesmerizing, so potent.

AG: I don't know if this answers your question. But I do know that sewn into my relationship with childhood and my memory of being young, which feels very clear and potent to me—sewn into that has been a loss always. I'm very happy to be an adult. And I was very happy in many ways as a child. But one of the themes of childhood for me was feeling as if I'd been born prematurely, not being ready. . . .

I went to boarding school when I was thirteen. I just remember how I clearly didn't want to go. My mother drove me in a borrowed car, three hours up to school, and the gate was closed. We could have called someone, or figured out how to get in, but neither of us was ready. She said, "OK, I'll just bring you back tomorrow." So we drove all the way home, slept, and then the next day left.

I didn't feel ready the next day either.

There were other instances, like my parents' divorce—many instances where it felt like there was a backward looking or a desire to stay somewhere just a little longer. So in my relationship to childhood in the poems—there's a longing and a melancholy there. I feel very joyful and alive in my life now. But alongside that, there's an understanding of the death of something. Maybe the death of family in the way I knew it. Maybe that's the heart of it. More than longing for youth, it's a kind of longing for what I understood the family was. And then its taking a different shape, and then longing again. That's there still, now that I'm older, but there's a different kind of peace. I am thrilled that I get to decide many things, like if I want to move to a place where I can have a garden. These are things I can choose on my own, which feels like a giant and glorious gift that I don't take for granted.

CM: Thank you. You said that so beautifully.

I love your poem to the ampersand. It's so inventive and witty and tender and unexpected.

AG: Anne Sexton. Her legs, have you seen the way she crosses her knees, but then pulls the one foot behind the other ankle? A kind of double-cross-ing.

CM: Yes.

AG: In the photos?

CM: Yes. And the name Sexton is also a kind of doubling.

This is one of your chances to pontificate—but I wondered if you'd talk about how you conceive of your task as a poet. You have a wonderful poem about a young man making love to himself under a tree. You write, "And only the sky to call you husband/ and only the air to suck you clean." And in that poem, you transform something that could easily have been voyeuristic, salacious, uncomfortable, into something very beautiful and almost sacred. This stays with me as one of your achievements as a poet. But I wondered: What do you most want to do with this tremendous gift you have?

AG: Thank you for calling it a gift.

For myself, I hope that the poems are chances to ask new—or not necessarily new—questions, to discover something. But also, they're all striving in various ways, especially in the difficult conversation, the engagement with a specific problem or violence, even, to try to articulate something, to speak into a silence, or through a silence. To work something serious out. And when I say "serious," I guess I mean—*high stakes*. To call attention to that high stakes thing, whatever it is, and in the struggle of talking or articulating or discovering, to also look for some generosity or kindness. Not that the poems do that, but that's what the world can do, and I'm trying to find that in the poems, even in really difficult, difficult places.

I was thinking about this great moment with the poet Thomas Sayers Ellis. A few of us read in a movie theater. And there was a documentary I absolutely hated. It just violently spoke of women, of young women, especially black women. "What's so wrong with the black woman today?" That was its premise. The director was there for Q&A. And half of the audience was cheering, and the other half, I think, we all felt appalled.

And at the end of the film, people started asking questions. Thomas had his hand up and he just yelled, "Who do you love?" It was very loud, and people were raising their hands to talk, but Thomas just wouldn't stop. "WHO DO YOU LOVE?" Yelling!

I just had chills, because I thought, what a beautiful question, and what a hard question too, for this director to engage with. And probably for Thomas or me or any one of us to truly engage with—but especially, especially, a man growing up in an utterly racist and utterly patriarchal, capitalist system. The director kind of stumbled through, and didn't really say much. And I thought of June Jordan's question, "Where is the love here?"

People say that was one of the questions she held. Elizabeth Alexander has a wonderful essay on the work and life of June Jordan, and Alexander quotes this question, "Where is the love here?" and how that question becomes the question you hold in any situation.

And I feel really taught by that, and by Thomas Sayers Ellis's question, "Who do you love?" 'Cause my poems—they want to hold, they want to move toward that kind of work.

CM: One of the things that strikes me in your work is its tremendous tenderness and delicacy. For example, when you address the goats, "Were you my children once? Do I know your names?" And perhaps because I come from Britain, from an older and more ironical culture, I wondered whether your work had ever been mistreated because of that open-heartedness, whether you'd ever encountered cynicism or irony or unwelcome among readers or even fellow writers.

AG: The first thing I think of is giving a reading where I read that poem. And tearing up—more than tearing up—I started crying, which has only happened to me this once ever at a reading, and it was that very part you just read. Many dear people, dear to me people, were there. But there was a kind of confusion. "Why did that happen? Why did that move you so?" I felt misunderstood. People think sometimes I'm being funny. Or that I couldn't possibly have had this moment with the goats. The other poem, with the man under the tree making love to himself, was the same. I imagine that the work could be held in many ways, so I don't necessarily feel heartbroken by somebody not holding it in the way I intended. But I do sometimes feel I have to say strongly, "No, that wasn't being cute. This is serious to me." The poem hasn't done its work enough if the person reading it doesn't know. But I've definitely had to clarify a few times—and I'm sure it's happened again and again without me being present. But, that said, I'm in the world and used to being misread or misunderstood quite a lot, and so while sometimes this hurts more than other times, having gone to school at mainly white institutions, with my particular parents and my particular friends, I've been trained in this work of having to really fight and struggle to hear my voice through the voices others have imagined for me, and the identities others have imagined were mine.

CM: I wonder if you'd describe a couple of assignments you might give your students.

AG: Most recently we've been reading *Maud Martha* in my Gwendolyn Brooks class. You can find it in *Blacks,* but it was published on its own. It's got these snippets of prose, numbered prose: moments when the protagonist, Maud Martha, will be in the kitchen chopping up the chicken for dinner, and talking about the fact that the chicken had a family once, and maybe the chicken is a kind of person too. Then, later on, you see her struggling through the birth of a child, and her relationship to her mother, and she feels entirely powerless. Things are constantly changing. Maud Martha as a character defies simplification.

So I ask my students to create two short prose pieces in the vein of Gwendolyn Brooks—memoir pieces where they are dealing with an element of their own subject position, be it class, race, or gender, showing how it might look in one piece, and then totally debunking that in the next piece, based on their own life stories.

'Cause I think we get these ideas about each other, and certainly about ourselves, based on a fixed identify or a fixed subject position, and I want them to really wrestle with that, which Brooks is doing throughout her work.

Another assignment was to interview someone of their choosing about "home," and then to transcribe the interview. And from there, to write a poem using only words from that interview, and another poem in which they could use any words, but where they tried to copy the speech patterns of that character, that persona.

So those are some things we did in the Brooks class.

CM: That's lovely.

If you had one piece of advice to give to those young writers, what would you like them to know, that you now know, from the slight advantage of your years?

AG: This connects to the question of seeing in my students, and also to the issue of voice and of mistreatment. I hope any young person, whether they think of themselves as a poet or not, will remember how absolutely valuable each voice is, and how particular to every second it has had on earth.

I think of rocks forming over thousands of years. Human time is different from geological time, but we've been forged by so many things, and to think that you or I exist at all totally blows my mind! So how lucky there's a person writing a poem, and to not ever feel discouraged, even if that poem is misunderstood, to really work to write in the voice or voices that are yours, as opposed to what you think your voice should be. Imitation, of course, is important, maybe part of the learning. But really working to find and give space to the particularities and idiosyncrasies of your voice—the way you speak, the music you listen to, your favorite flower—whatever it is. All that is rich, rich gold, and totally miraculous to me.

EDWARD HIRSCH

Interviewed April 12, 2011

Edward Hirsch was born in Chicago in 1950. In one of his poems, he describes himself as a "skinny, long-beaked boy" perching "in the branches of the old branch library" all Sabbath long. A decade later, he would slip into the college library just before it closed at midnight, and have two hours to himself until the cleaning crew discovered him. Even now, he says, he likes walking, thinking, making notes, then finding a café, and working for a couple of hours. "I'm a lifelong insomniac."

That diligent reading, writing (and insomnia) has helped to fuel a tremendously productive career. Now in his mid-sixties, Hirsch has published nine books of poems and six collections of prose, including the surprise bestseller, *How to Read a Poem and Fall in Love with Poetry*. He has taught at Wayne State University and at the University of Houston, Texas, and has become a well-known advocate for poetry. He has also received numerous fellowships and awards, among them a five-year MacArthur "genius" award. In 2002, he was appointed president of the John Simon Guggenheim Foundation.

Such professional successes have their satisfactions. But Hirsch has had to endure tremendous sorrow too. In August, 2011, several months after our interview, his only son, Gabriel, died at the age of twenty-two. Hirsch's book-length elegy was long-listed for the National Book Award. As he told me, "You don't write poetry out of 'literary culture' or prizes or external things. You write them out of a deep well of obsessiveness. And I try to do that."

The Widening Sky

I am so small walking on the beach
at night under the widening sky.
The wet sand quickens beneath my feet
and the waves thunder against the shore.

I am moving away from the boardwalk
with its colorful streamers of people
and the hotels with their blinking lights.
The wind sighs for hundreds of miles.

I am disappearing so far into the dark
I have vanished from sight.
I am a tiny seashell
that has secretly drifted ashore

and carries the sound of the ocean
surging through its body.
I am so small now no one can see me.
How can I be filled with such a vast love?

Christian McEwen: I especially love your poem "The Widening Sky," its modesty, its specificity, and, I guess, its tenderness. And I wondered if you'd speak about what's involved in preserving that kind of tenderness in a not-so-tender world.

Edward Hirsch: I don't think we should underestimate the capacity for tenderness that poetry opens up inside of us, as human beings. I think this is especially striking to Americans—maybe to all people—but especially to Americans, because there's a very strong stoic, pragmatic, materialist side of American culture. Maybe it has something to do with our Puritan ancestors—*their* Puritan ancestors I should say.

But, in any case, I think poetry can open up something very deep and fundamental, very affectionate, very tender inside of us toward each other.

CM: I read that you were a good friend of William Maxwell, and I wondered if you'd speak a little bit about him. I think of him as a man who was able to do his public work, and yet was also able to be tremendously tender and affectionate and open.

EH: I adored William Maxwell. He was already an old man by the time I came to know him, but I think I can say it was love at first sight for me. Many people felt that way about him. I attached myself to him and we spent a lot of time together near the end of his life. I was always very moved by him. And I was always deeply grateful to be in his presence.

He could be very steely in daily life, but he had enormous wells of feeling inside of him. He had a great capacity for wonder, which showed in his face. His childhood was very close to him even as an old man.

When Bill liked someone, when he was interested in you, the first thing he wanted to find out was about your childhood. He got in touch with you through your childhood. That was very close to him, because his own childhood was so terribly sundered by the death of his mother from influenza when he was ten years old. He had a strong sense of a before and an after—of a paradisiacal early realm, an early life, and then it being cut off from him. Everything was fixed in his memory very, very deeply. I think that *So Long, See You Tomorrow* is one of the great American books. It is his masterpiece. His childhood is very close to him in that book. But it's there in all of his work really.

CM: You rarely read books where you feel the presence of the author quite so fully, quite so tenderly.

EH: I think it's that he remembers so clearly, and is trying so clearly to evoke the world of small-town Illinois that he grew up in: what that atmosphere was like, and what the feeling was like, and the description of the houses with their open porches and the wide streets and elm trees and so forth.

He once told me that the house where he'd been happy as a child came up for sale and he was offered it. He had thought, all those years, that he would buy it. And then he realized he couldn't move back there. That world was lost.

Two of my friends, Michael Collier and Charlie Baxter, and I edited a book about William Maxwell called *A William Maxwell Portrait*. And one of the striking things about that book is that almost everyone that writes about Bill has a strong feeling for him. People who just read him and never knew him have a powerful feeling about him. There's something about the understated quality of his work, its modesty, and its deep reserves of feeling, and the boy in that work, that make you feel very close to it. I'm just thrilled that you care about it so much.

CM: Oh, hugely.

EH: He's a wonderful writer.

CM: For me, he's one of those writers whose books you just read and read once you discover them, and in a way, gorge on his presence.

EH: He also turned out to be a very great letter writer. I highly recommend his letters back and forth with Sylvia Townsend Warner and Frank O'Connor and now Eudora Welty. He's a terrific correspondent. One of the things that is just wonderful about his correspondence, say with Sylvia Townsend Warner, is first he's her editor and then she begins to recognize that he's a writer too. And then they start to become friends. They become family members, practically. Their friendship really becomes a very substantial, deep, lifelong friendship. You can see it progressing through the letters.

CM: They only met four times.

EH: Yeah, they were almost never together.

CM: I love that book.

EH: One of the funniest moments is when Sylvia Townsend Warner is sending Maxwell a story for *The New Yorker* where he'd been an editor for so long. And she says, "But I know Mr. Shawn doesn't really like my work."

And then there's a little footnote saying that at that point they had published 114 pieces of hers, which is just so revealing about what it means to be a writer: the anxiety of the author.

CM: Thank you for reminding me of that.

And thank you, too, for what you said about Maxwell connecting with adult friends through their childhoods. Perhaps you could talk about your own childhood, and the poem "Branch Library," which has you in it as a boy. "A skinny, long-beaked boy."

EH: That poem evokes the feeling I first had when I was writing poetry in high school. The whole poem turns on the idea of the branch library. I'd go back and forth between the stacks where I was reading and the tables where I was writing. I think the poem came about because I felt I was losing touch with that boy, and with the feeling I first had for poetry. And, as it says in the poem, I'd give anything to get it back. So the poem is really a kind of prayer, an impossible prayer, an impossible quest—*"Give me back that boy!"* Get that boy back for me, because I want to be in touch with what I first felt for poetry when I'd just started, when I was beginning to write.

CM: I love that poem.

EH: I had a funny experience recently: a teacher asked me to read it at a very sophisticated high school. I read it. And there was dead silence. I was just looking at the students. And I said, "Do you know what a branch library is?" And no one knew. Someone said, "Is that a library where they just have poetry?" And I said, "Well no, it's not." It had never occurred to me that they wouldn't know what a branch library is. They actually had experienced a smaller side library. It just hadn't been called that. There's a main library. And then there are smaller branches of the larger library.

And of course the poem turns on something that's accidental in English: that the branch library suggests both a provincial library and the branches of a tree. The whole poem develops that metaphor of the boy being like a bird in the stacks. This came home to me very strikingly because a friend of mine was translating the poem into Polish, and, of course, the pun there doesn't work at all. In Polish, the branches of a tree are one thing, and the branch of the library is another, and they're just not connected. But by some accident of English, they are, and that's what allows my central metaphor—which I push—of the boy being like a bird.

CM: Oh, I love that. "The skinny long-beaked boy."

You write in *How to Read a Poem* that you feel that reading is itself endangered these days. And I wondered if you'd expand on that.

EH: There are a lot of indications: the literacy rates, the dropout rates, the tremendous success of mass media, the twenty-four-hour news span, eight hundred cable channels. The constant din and buzz of the culture seems to obliterate a certain kind of attentiveness that is crucial for reading. It's not that people don't read at all, although I think their attention spans are so short now that when they do read, it's often in very short bursts or on the Internet. They don't concentrate enough for sustained reading.

You can get something from reading poetry that way. But I feel that a certain kind of sustained reading puts us in touch with our interior lives. And that's endangered in our culture because you need to be alone with yourself, you need some presence, and you need to be able to give yourself up to the experience of absorption. And that is at risk. To me it's a tremendous loss because some of the great joys of my life, some of the great experiences that I've had, have been through reading, which delivers you up to yourself in another kind of way.

So I proselytize a little bit on behalf of that experience.

CM: I thought you proselytized magnificently in *How to Read a Poem*. Also, as I was reading your poems, I realized how many had been shaped by your adult reading. I'm thinking of poems like "Wild Gratitude," which has its roots in Christopher Smart and his poem to his cat Jeoffry, or the memorial poem to Simone Weil. Or the times you take on the voices of other writers—the voices of Diderot or Baudelaire or whomever. I wondered if you'd talk a little bit about how it was to do that.

EH: First of all, I think most people make a very sharp distinction between writing about your personal life and writing from another voice or about a literary figure. And I don't make that distinction. The writers I've read have meant so much to me, and have been so much a part of my life, that I just had a strong feeling from the time I was setting out that part of my project was to write about them—to bring them into my personal life.

They were already part of my personal life.

I do think there's something different about writing *about* someone else, and writing *from their point of view*. In my poem "Wild Gratitude," I parallel playing with my own cat Zooey, sort of maniacally and playfully, absurdly in a way, with Christopher Smart playing with his cat Jeoffry, as I imagine it through his extraordinary eighteenth-century poem "Jubilate Agno." I go back and forth between Christopher Smart and my own experience, to push it and see what that will yield, what it has to teach. It's an experiment, as all poems are.

Now, the experience of writing from another point of view is something else, especially if you are writing from the point of view of someone who actually existed. I think there's something abject and beautiful about taking on a viewpoint of someone who already existed because—as the dramatic monologue does—it suggests a kind of dependency. When you're writing about just your own experience, you're relying on your own experience. When you're writing about yourself and a relationship to a writer, you're relying on your experience and what you've read. When you take on the voice of Diderot or the voice of Charles Baudelaire, you're dependent upon that previous writer's experience. And the irony of it or, I think, the playfulness of it, is that you're writing something they did not write.

And it's something you have to make your own. If you can't make it your own, there's really no point in doing it, because Baudelaire was already a great writer and you don't need to write the poems that Baudelaire wrote. But if you can see Baudelaire as a vehicle for something of your own, and you can merge your own voice with Baudelaire's voice, then you've got something interesting: a kind of hybrid.

But we don't really know how to think about this. The dramatic monologue really exists for creating speakers. T. S. Eliot creates the speaker of "The Love Song of J. Alfred Prufrock" and pretends he's speaking from the point of view of Prufrock, who isn't really a character. Hugh Kenner calls him "a name plus a voice." When you're taking on the name of a pre-existing writer, you're taking on the style of that writer as well. And you're sort of filtering your own style through the style of this pre-existing writer.

What's liberating about it, if it works, is that it enables you to speak in a way that you couldn't speak in your own person, and to say things that you couldn't ordinarily say. The limitation is: Is it so much like Baudelaire that it's not your own? Or—even more painfully—Baudelaire was such a great writer, can your poem live up to his? Can you be convincing when you speak as Baudelaire? My entire sequence of poems, "The Lectures on Love," takes known speakers from the past, literary figures, and presents their so-called lectures on love. The form of those poems is all pretty much the same. They work in a certain way. I merge my own form with the style of the writer who is supposedly speaking, and I end up with a kind of symposium on love.

CM: My favorite of all was the one where you take on the voice of Gertrude Stein. What a poem! And what a pleasure it must have been to write it.

EH: Oh, it was so much fun! It was hard, but it was fun to try to think like Gertrude Stein. There's a plot in the poem. There's a drama that takes place. And I was a little wary about what I was up to. But when I wrote "I like it when we eat on moving trains. / The food slides a little under our manners," I felt I actually could do it. That just seemed weird and funny and worthy of Gertrude Stein. So that was it.

Also, writers don't know how to write about happiness very well. A lot of people think it's impossible to write about. And Gertrude Stein has a joy—it's quite a fulfilled poetry, quite a fulfilled fiction at times. It's got the joy of astonishment. I wanted to try and capture that sense of astonishment through the language and through taking apart the language. How it just keeps breaking itself down and deconstructing itself in the way she does. I find an odd poetry in the way she writes—close to nonsense at times.

CM: "Alice had lice, and the lice had Alice." My God, that's wonderful.

EH: Thank you.

CM: Was it you who quoted, "Happiness writes white"?

EH: Yes. I quote that as the title of a poem in *Special Orders* because I've heard it said many times that all poetry is elegiac. "All poetry is melancholy. All poetry is about loss." And it's not that there's not some truth in that. But it's also true that poetry is about saving something. It's about rescuing something. It's about fulfillment. There's a tremendous amount of love poetry of love lost, but there's also sometimes a poetry of love attained. And I don't think we know how to talk about that.

Now, it's not that there's a sustained happiness, or that happiness is something that lasts for a long time. But there are moments of joy, and poems can capture that. And it's not true that "happiness writes white," which is something that Philip Larkin liked to quote, meaning it can't be written. That it just goes blank. That's not actually true. There are poems that do try to capture the state with some precision.

CM: I'm very fond of your poem written for Gerald Stern, "The Swimmers," and I wondered if you'd talk about other contemporary writer friends, perhaps especially those who have been an inspiration in your own work. I was looking at your texts and thinking, "Who's behind this? Who are the great elders here? Brodsky? Milosz? Philip Levine?"

EH: Well, you're doing very well. Are you thinking about my personal relations or my reading or both?

CM: I think both.

EH: Well, let's start with "The Swimmers." When I was in my early twenties, I guess twenty-five or so, I went to graduate school at the University of Pennsylvania, and I applied for a job in Poets in the Schools. You go around and teach poetry writing to small children. And the director of the program called me and said, "We like your application, but there's a poet you have to interview with. His name is Gerald Stern." And that's how I came to meet Jerry. He interviewed me for the job. I had to pay for the coffee, but he gave me the job.

He was marvelous at treating me like an equal, he has a gift for that. And he has a gift for friendship. So we began talking about poetry, and we've been talking about poetry for nearly forty years. Thirty-five, anyway. He was never my teacher, but he helped get me started. He has some terrific swimming poems, so "The Swimmers" is about swimming with him and talking about poetry. The structure of the poem is that I basically ransack all the poets who are swimmers and look at how swimming works in their poems. Or not swimming so much as drowning, sometimes.

And through Jerry I met Philip Levine when I started my first teaching job at Wayne State University in Detroit. That's Phil's alma mater. He came to Detroit in 1982 or '83 to visit his twin brother. They invited me over, and we became fast friends. They're great older friends for me, and they mean a lot to me along with several other poets of that generation—W. S. Merwin is also a great model for me, and Richard Howard is a dear friend. They just helped show me what a life in poetry could look like.

Jerry and Phil, in particular, are very strongly urban poets and so that helped me think through what it meant to be a city poet.

When I was in my early twenties, my teachers were modernists, and I began to feel some dissatisfaction with what I was reading. I love modernism. I'm a child of modernism. I grew up on Eliot and Pound and Williams and Wallace Stevens and Marianne Moore. I might not have been able to phrase it very exactly, but I began to feel that something was lacking in this great poetry that meant so much to me. I began to feel that it was cold. And that coldness was an ideal of modernist poetry. It wasn't something I was just projecting. I mean, Pound wanted his poetry to be sculptural. Pound and Eliot treated anything that was too heated as sentimental. But I think I was looking for something else. And I discovered Eastern European poetry.

That's when I came across the Polish poets: Czeslaw Milosz, Zbigniew Herbert, and Tadeusz Rózewicz. And I discovered the Russian poets: Osip Mandelstam, Anna Akhmatova, Marina Tsvetaeva, and Boris Pasternak. I discovered Hungarian poets like Attila József, Miklós Radnóti, and others. And so I began to forge for myself a model of what I could do, because these poets had a kind of tenderness and a well of feeling without any loss of intellectual power. They're intellectuals—there's no question about that—but they don't banish tenderness from their own work. They don't consider it "womanly," the way a lot of modernists did. And this is what I think I was looking for. And this is why these models were so important to me.

Later I became friends with Czeslaw Milosz. He liked what I wrote about him. I can't say I was an intimate of his. But I just cherished his work, and I cherished him as a model. And the same with Joseph Brodsky. Brodsky and I really did become friends because I spent a year at the American

Academy in Rome, and he was there for a couple of months. And while he was there we had coffee every day and got a chance to talk about poetry. The way they talked about poetry was galvanizing to me because it was really a matter of life and death. When I was in my twenties, I just wanted to make a life as a poet. And by the time I was in my thirties, I was trying to figure out what that life could look like. What I wanted it to be. How I wanted to start thinking about poetry in American culture. And finding these writers from Poland and from Russia and other places where poetry has such a deep place in the culture helped me think through my own ideas about poetry, and what the place of poetry should be or could be in American life.

CM: That makes a lot of sense. Thank you.

I wonder if you've come across that lovely book of interviews with Seamus Heaney called *Stepping Stones*. He also talks about Brodsky with great affection, and Milosz.

EH: I'm crazy about that book. I wish we had a book like that for every major poet. Dennis O'Driscoll does a terrific job at getting Heaney to talk about every stage of his life. The part I loved most, actually, was about Heaney's childhood. Because there he describes what the walk to school was like, and what you saw from his backyard, and his experience in the family with so many other siblings, and the death of his brother. I found it a wonderful evocation of his rural Northern Irish childhood.

He was also friends with Brodsky and he admired Milosz, and I think we have many of the same tastes. I really enjoyed that. But I already knew that. What I really love about that book is the part about his childhood and the way it's delivered up for us.

CM: I'm with you.

This is a delicate question, but you've had such success in your life. All those prizes and awards and accolades. And yet, many of the poems you write about yourself are filled with pain and self-recrimination. And I wondered if you'd talk about that discrepancy.

EH: Well, prizes are a very nice thing. I'm happy for them, and I'm happy to have a certain success in the world, but that's not exactly where you live.

The place you live in is the childhood you had, and your early adulthood, and the life you actually lead day-to-day. And where you come from and who you are and what your experience is. I don't know anyone who's escaped tragedy. I don't think I'm special in this, but I've had my share. And every poet I know has been deeply shaped by traumatic things that happened, especially in his or her childhood. Some really traumatic things happened in my childhood. And I guess one doesn't exactly recover.

I think you're lucky if you're a poet, if you have a career that can enable your vocation and you can have a professional life that goes hand-in-hand with that. But they're not the same thing. The main thing is that you have a life, which you inhabit. And that you try to write your poems out of that life. You don't write your poems out of "literary culture" or prizes or external things. You write them out of a deep well of obsessiveness. Theodore Roethke says you have to get down to where your own obsessions are. And I try to do that. As I've gotten older I've been very determined to write a poetry of relentless self-scrutiny.

I've always admired a poetry that is willing to implicate the poet, not just point fingers at other people. This is one of the problems I have with a lot of explicitly political poetry. I know we need it. Sometimes you need to protest. But political poetry really sees the enemy as external. And it's usually a somewhat simplified enemy. The kind of poetry I want to write, even if it's political, implicates the self. Dostoevsky has a poetic that suggests, "Convict thyself." And that's close to my own heart. I try to counsel myself to obey that. To let the external things fall away, and to be in touch with something that's resonant and powerful in relationship to my own life and to how I see human life.

CM: Who else do you think writes that self-scrutinizing poetry with integrity?

EH: I would say early Milosz—the poem "Voices of Poor People," the poem "Dedication," the moment when he calls himself an "uncircumcised Jew," the moment he acknowledges "those he could not save." The reason those early poems are important to me is because so much is at stake in the way he writes them, so much is at stake in poetry itself. He is responsible to those he could not rescue. He is responsible to the dead.

Joseph Brodsky was also like this, which is why he called himself a

"Calvinist." He believed in relentless self-scrutiny. This is something Brodsky helped me see in Robert Frost and Thomas Hardy. People often say that Frost was a terrible person. Brodsky responded by pointing out that there was nothing one could say against Frost that Frost hadn't already said against himself. I've always been moved by the darker side of Frost, who is very self-incriminating. He really takes a ruthless look at his own experience.

Thomas Hardy is the same. Think of the great elegies he wrote in the early teens—*Poems of 1912–13*. There's a lot of self-recrimination in his relationship to his wife, his now dead wife. There's tremendous remorse there. He falls in love with his wife again, but she's already dead. And he's very aware of his neglect while she was alive. I think that's one of the things that give those poems their deep resonance.

CM: And as I'm listening, I'm thinking, well of course, Hopkins too. The desolate sonnets.

EH: Those terrible sonnets are extraordinary. They were one of my first models in poetry. I discovered Hopkins when I was a freshman in college. I write about this in *How to Read a Poem*. I didn't know those desolate sonnets and I began to read them. I remember reading "I wake and feel the fell of dark, not day," and it just took the top of my head off. It took me a while to realize that it was even a sonnet. I just was so moved by the desolation. And I identified so strongly with it. I felt that Hopkins was delivering to me a feeling of desolation that I'd had but I couldn't name. I was very grateful to him for that. Then when I realized it was actually a sonnet, that he'd constructed it as a sonnet, that he'd made that desolation into something, it became all that much more moving to me.

CM: Yes, absolutely.

There are so many things I want to ask and our time, I know, is running short. You have a poem in *Lay Back the Darkness* that is itself called "Lay Back the Darkness," about your father's Alzheimer's. And I wondered if you would talk about the satisfactions, the anxieties, the complications of giving form to such intimate family stories.

EH: In a way it can't be defended. You're violating something. You're taking moments in your family's life that most people would prefer to have kept secret. And you're making them known. What I would say is, I never exactly set out to write about my father's Alzheimer's. It was never a plan. If you'd told me as a young poet that someday I'd be writing about this, I would have laughed at you as an impossibility. But my father was very dear to me, and his Alzheimer's lasted for ten years. It was a long, painful, awful way of dying. And it was just something that we were going through. The poem "Lay Back the Darkness" is, I guess, a kind of prayer to ease his pain, because I didn't have a way to do it. There's something very deep and warm in that poem about the feeling for my father—but there's also something cold about the act of writing poetry: you are committing something to paper, and looking hard at it. My father was a salesman by profession and he had the salesman's charm, and the gift for charming people. And he couldn't charm his way out of this one. And so, "Lay Back the Darkness" became a kind of prayer for my father pacing back and forth and being unable to rest.

I've gotten some comfort from that poem in that it seems to have spoken to a lot of other people who have had parents who've had Alzheimer's. It's had a kind of life that way, and that's made me feel a little better about writing it, because it's given some consolation to other people. There's a little bit of betrayal in it, I think. But there's a little bit of betrayal in all poetry, that is if we're going to get down to dark things. If you're going to use your own experience, then other people are going to be involved, and they're going to be implicated. You try to treat them with as much care and as much thoughtfulness as you can. But nonetheless, you are trying to write the life you've really lived. And my father figures into it.

CM: It's a tremendous poem.

EH: Thank you very much. The idea is that something social falls away, and my father in the shuffling—this endless walking back and forth—loses the social role of being a father or being a husband or even being a son. He returns to this primitive state of being a boy in Germany at the edge of a forest, listening to something out there very wild that's coming for him.

It felt like that to me. But the original plan of the poem was really, "Help me, spirits."

CM: I think it's true that you can't write a poem like that without betrayal. And yet it can't be consoling unless you tell the full truth.

EH: Well, that's the ruthlessness of poetry. I don't think it's easy for poets to own up to it. People like to pretend that everything about their enterprise is noble. I don't think it all is. But, if poetry is going to be helpful, then it has to tell the truth. And that means you're going to have to say some unpleasant things. And I don't think the poet should exempt himself or herself from saying those things. Other people are going to be involved and you try to tell the truth as you see it. It's part of the job description.

CM: You have a poem called "The Poet at Seven," which has the lines "He has the typical / blood of the exile, the refugee, the victim." And I was wondering if you'd say something about what it has meant to be Jewish in America in this last half century, and at the same time, how that intersects with what you were talking about earlier—carrying an American identity and a poet's identity, all those three together.

EH: That's a very astute reading. You've identified the poem in which I try to think through something. I'm trying in "The Poet at Seven" to think through how, on the one hand, you could be living an ordinary, middle-class American childhood, and, on the other, you could have something else coursing through you, something older and more ancient.

I have the idea that American Judaism is a very seemingly natural and fluid thing, but there's something very contradictory in it. American life takes you in one direction, and Jewish life takes you in another. I'm not saying that no Americans have a sense of history. But in American culture itself we don't have a very strong sense of history. We don't have a strong sense of where we come from. Henry Ford famously said, "History is bunk." One of the geniuses of the American character is how we continually remake ourselves. How we live in the present and go forward with this tremendous vitality and optimism.

But Judaism is a historical religion, and Jews are people of the book. Judaism goes back a long way. And Judaism is also related to suffering. And so, here I'm trying to work out what it means to be an American and a Jew and, therefore, to be an American-Jewish writer. What it means to be a Jewish poet. And I think I'm partially forged out of this conflict. I mean, I'm not a European Jew and I'm not a European-Jewish poet. I'm not a Russian-Jewish poet. I'm not a Hebrew poet. I'm an American-Jewish poet. So that means that I try to be in touch with something very deep and resonant in Judaism, which has a long history, and also in touch with what it means to be American. And these two things—these two incompatibles that somehow go together—forge my character. And I continually try to work it out in different poems: "The Poet at Seven," "My First Theology Lesson," the poems about my Jewish forebears, and then seemingly unrelated poems like, "American Summer."

CM: I'm wondering if your draw toward Polish and Russian poetry is the Jewish self reaching toward a culture with more recognition of history and tragedy.

EH: Completely. You know, my grandfather wrote poetry and he died when I was eight years old. And I later found myself looking for something that was familiar to me, but unfamiliar in my American experience. And when I began to find Eastern European poetry—some of it by Jewish poets, but a lot of it not by Jewish poets—I feel I recognized something I identified with that was actually closer to me than Anglo-American modernism. In a literary way, American literature derived from English literature. The history of American literature is in relationship to English literature. And so all of us who write in English think of ourselves in some way in relationship to English poetry.

But I don't have any family in England. My family had nothing to do with England. And the sort of Anglicanism that came to us in a religious way had nothing to do with my own experience. A lot of the English poetry I read—no matter how great—was a little foreign to me. As a Jew, especially, when you read the history of English poetry, you're continually othered. I mean, my first great love was the metaphysical poets. But, you know, Jews were referred to in metaphysical poetry as alien creatures. And so when I discovered Eastern European poetry in my early twenties, I found something I recognized. And part of my goal became to find the tonalities of that poetry and bring it back to American poetry.

When I first went to Eastern Europe when I was in my early twenties, when I first went to Poland and Russia, to what was then Czechoslovakia, a lot of things I'd thought of as Jewish turned out just to be Polish or Russian. I thought they were Jewish because that was my experience, but it turns out, you know, a lot of Polish Jews were really acculturated into Poland, and a lot of the Polish experience was familiar to me. That's one of the reasons anti-Semitism in these countries is so painful to me, because I recognize those places. I'm not a Polish poet. I'm not a Hungarian poet. I'm not a Russian poet. But I feel very great kinship with some of the figures in that poetry.

One aspect of this has to do with the suffering of people who've come before us, and a determination not to forget and to remember. And these poets are in touch with something not just in themselves, but in the cultures from which they come. I admire that about them. They are not collectivist poets. They're not protest poets. But they are aware that they come from a country where things have happened. And that's important.

CM: When you teach, how do you engage with what one might call "American amnesia" in your students? There are so many young people who may not have that sense of the past and of the potency of poetry, and for whom words are disappearing things on a screen.

EH: Well, lecturing doesn't work very well. I don't think lecturing them or hectoring them about what they don't know is very successful. My own experience is that what works is when you bring in poems that you care about. The poems themselves, the naked poems, often do communicate. And when the poems communicate, then my experience is that students want to know more about them. They want to know more about the people who wrote them. They want to know more about the circumstances out of which they're written. Once you're engaged by the poems, then I think you might want to know more about the history. I don't think you start with a lecture about the history or what we don't know or how ignorant we are, *et cetera*. You're a teacher. Your job is to teach. And I think the way to teach in poetry is through the poems. My experience is that when students care about the poems, they're just much more open to wanting to know about the experience.

Sometimes now, you find that we just have higher mountains to climb than we used to have. A couple months ago, I was saying something about a Russian poet and someone said, "What was communism?" And then you realize you have a little more work to do.

CM: I myself have been thinking a lot about attention and slowing down. I just completed a book about all that. And I wondered if you'd speak about finding room for attention in a world that seems increasingly distracted and fragmented. I'm thinking of your lines from "Earthly Light," "that February day I looked directly / into a wintry, invisible world / and that was when I turned away."

EH: Those lines come at the very end of my poem "Earthly Light," which is a kind of homage to seventeenth-century Dutch art. It's the last poem in my book *Earthly Measures*. Much of that book has to do with a longing for transcendence. The poems embody a quest for something beyond. And at the end of that poem, I critique my own longing for transcendence. It's kind of an argument with myself. That's where I say, "that was when I turned away / from the God or gods I had wanted / so long and so much to believe in." I give up the hope of a transcendental force, saying that this world too needs our complete attention. I'm riffing off something that Simone Weil said, "Absolutely unmixed attention is prayer." I think it's a wonderful thing to say, and I recognize what she means, that there's a kind of full attention, unmixed by anything worldly, and she called that prayer toward the beyond, toward God.

I'm taking her idea of "absolutely unmixed attention" and saying maybe we should direct it not just toward God, but toward Earth itself, toward the world we're actually living in. Political, social, natural. This world too needs our attention, and our full presence. Our unmixed attention doesn't need only to look at something atemporal and divine. We can also look at something that is fleeting and transient and, in fact, we need to. We need to cherish the world we have as it's disappearing in front of us. This is part of our project. Here, particularly, it's the project of poetry, but not only of poetry, also of paying attention. We need to pay attention to the world, which is in our keeping. That's the sort of prayer there. But it's a prayer not toward the other world, but toward this one. We're here right now and we need to give our full attention to the world we're actually living in.

JANE HIRSHFIELD

Interviewed October 4, 2011

Jane Hirshfield was born in New York City in 1953, and now lives in the San Francisco Bay area. From early on, she understood that she wanted to become a writer. The first book she ever bought—at eight years old—was a collection of Japanese haiku. She wrote steadily, if privately, throughout her childhood. "I was writing to find a self," she says. "To explore who I was, what I felt, what I thought. To fill in the missing."

Hirshfield published her first poem in 1973, then set aside her work for a number of years in order to study Zen. "Poetry and Zen feel to me like the left foot and the right foot of my walking forwards," she explains. But as a poet, she prefers what is called "tea-house practice." I don't want my poems walking around in Buddhist robes, or hung on a Buddhist coat peg. I want them available to anybody."

Now in her early sixties, Hirshfield has published seven books of poetry, as well as several anthologies and the classic book of essays *Nine Gates: Entering the Mind of Poetry*. Her poems appear regularly in *The New Yorker*, *The Atlantic*, and *Poetry*, and have been included in six editions of *Best American Poetry*. She has received numerous fellowships and awards. Yet most of her poems still focus on the quiet illuminations to be found in ordinary domestic life: ways of "opening the eyes more, opening the ears more, having the skin be more permeable."

"I work with what is at hand," she says. "There is probably not a tree in my garden that hasn't called forth its poem."

The Door

A note waterfalls steadily
through us,
just below hearing.

Or this early light
streaming through dusty glass:
what enters, enters like that,
unstoppable gift.

And yet there is also the other,
the breath-space held between any call
and its answer—

In the querying
first scuff of footstep,
the wood owl's repeating,
the two-counting heart:

A little sabbath
minnow whose brightness silvers past time.

The rest-note,
unwritten,
hinged between worlds,
that precedes change and allows it.

Christian McEwen: I'd like to start by asking you about your childhood in relation to poetry: whom you read, whom you admired, how you came to write.

Jane Hirshfield: I was taught to write by a public school teacher called Mrs. Barlow.

She must've done something wizardly, because by the time I left her care, there was a large piece of brown paper, the kind with the big blue lines on it, that said, "I want to be a writer when I grow up." I have no memory of this. But after my first, small press, book came out in 1982, my mother pulled it from a dresser drawer, and I was entirely startled.

I do remember the first book I ever bought: a one-dollar Peter Pauper Press hardback of Japanese haiku. I was eight years old. So, quite inexplicably, my attraction to and love for Japanese poetry goes back to the very beginning. I grew up on East 20th Street in New York—what did I see in these natural-world poems? I suppose I saw something that was missing and that I knew I wanted. I wrote throughout my childhood, mostly hiding my poems under the bed. I was not writing for other people. I was writing to find a self, in a deeply protected way. To explore who I was, what I felt, what I thought. To fill in the missing.

CM: Thank you. That's a wonderful story. And the haiku book, too. I love these pre-foreshadowings, or whatever one might call them.

JH: My love of poetry is a mystery. My family was entirely unliterary, so I can't figure out where any of it came from. But, sometimes if you're lucky you know what you want, what you love, from the beginning, and if you're very lucky you're able to go forward with that into a life.

CM: I wanted to ask about your relationship to Buddhism, and also to art, to painting, to looking. In your poem "Autumn," you write about "the gold leaf flaking from the trees." Would you say more about the place where Buddhism and close-looking intersect for you?

JH: I think Buddhism, poetry, the attention of art, and the attention of contemplation (in whatever vocabulary that appears) all share a single tap-root—which is the deep desire for a greater intimacy with experience. Each of these things is a way of opening the eyes more, opening the ears more, having the skin be more permeable.

Again, this desire is something that pulled me forward from the beginning. I always wanted and pursued it, in whatever way was available to me. As a young person it was primarily poetry, and then as I read poetry, I encountered the ideas of Buddhism in certain poems. In college, I designed my own major, creative writing and literature in translation, because I wanted to read in languages I didn't know. I began taking courses in Chinese poetry in translation, Japanese poetry in translation, Japanese Noh drama. And of course, this is a body of work that is filled with Buddhist reference.

After I graduated from college, I worked on a farm for a year and then, it being the early '70s, got into a red Dodge van with tie-dyed curtains heading off to look for my future. I thought that would be waitressing and writing poems. But I knew there was one Zen monastery in America, the only one at the time. It was Tassajara Zen Mountain Center, in the Ventana wilderness, inland from Big Sur. And because I knew it was there, I went, and because it was summer and outsiders can visit in the summer, I went in, and was a guest student for a week. I thought I'd stay for a few months till I found out what this Buddhism business was all about.

But after a few months, what you find out is that you know nothing, and so I stayed in full-time Zen practice for eight years.

CM: I believe you were lay ordained in the lineage of Soto Zen back in '79. What has that meant for your life?

JH: I was lay ordained after three years of monastic practice. Lay ordination, priest ordination, marriage, funerals—in Buddhism, the core set of vows is exactly the same. To take these vows as a lay practitioner is both a sign that your teacher is recognizing your practice, and also a rather simple, formal statement of your commitment to live in accordance with that awareness. Each person's expression of that awareness will be his or her own, and unique. Still, one of mine that seems to have gone out into the public world is something I said to Bill Moyers in a PBS interview. All Buddhism in seven words: "Everything changes, everything is connected. Pay attention."

CM: I love that.

JH: Thank you. I truly do believe that if you notice that everything changes and that everything is connected, all of Buddhism's views and vows emerge from that. If you don't cling to the world and you understand that self and other are not separate, then what in Buddhism is called the Paramitas— right livelihood, right meditation, right understanding, right effort, right generosity—all will follow.

I'm committed to the path of lay practice. I remain thrilled that I had the opportunity as a lay person to do monastic practice. Still, I also think that in America, for the life of Buddhism here and now, it's important that people be able to practice with full respect while leading an ordinary life. This for me is part of the essence of Zen. It has to do with awareness, not circumstance: the taste of your own tongue in your own mouth, something always available. In one well-known traditional story, a teacher is asked, "What is your special practice?" The answer: "Chopping wood, carrying water." If Zen practice is not able to inhabit a regular life in regular clothes, I'm not sure what good it can do us as a species. We of course need those who can teach and who are able to devote their entire lives to living in a certain way, but we also want teaching to happen in very ordinary and invisible ways. One name for this is "tea-house practice."

Traditionally, there are said to be four paths: priest practice, monastic practice, lay practice, and tea-house practice. Tea-house practice is the little old lady by the side of the road who runs a tea house, and nobody knows why they like to go there so much, or why her tea tastes a little different than anybody else's. It has something to do with the way she wipes the counter, it has something to do with the way she pours the water. It's too late for me to keep my Buddhist practice completely hidden in my knapsack. But as a poet, I want to do tea-house practice. I don't want my poems walking around in Buddhist robes, or hung on a Buddhist coat peg. I want them available to anybody. It's important to me that I not be using a specialized or different vocabulary.

CM: Thank you for explaining it so fully.

I want to go back to the question about looking in relation to art and art history. Say more on that, if you would.

JH: As human beings, and as artists, we all draw from the gifts given us by millennia of culture-makers before us. If I refer to a Byzantine icon or a painting by Watteau, to a Sumerian epic or a Shakespeare play, this is simply a way to include some of that accumulated body of wisdom in my poem. It's a technique that is very pervasive, to speak as a craft mechanic for a moment. Japanese poetry uses allusive reference all the time, because Japanese poetic forms are so very brief. The only way you can expand a seventeen-syllable haiku or thirty-one syllable tanka is by using phrases that call to mind other haiku, other tanka, other histories of relationship to certain images. To me this just feels a very natural way of speaking. There is no separation for me between the world of myth, the world of art, the world of observing the natural, the world of science. My own poems don't only allude to works of art or historical figures, they use scientific references as well. In recent years, especially, biology and geology and physics have become as much a part of my vocabulary as "apple" or "pear."

CM: In your poem "Not-Yet," you write about the "not yet dead, not yet lost, not yet taken." And I wondered if you'd comment on that piercing recognition of mortality, of transience.

JH: That poem was written after the man I then lived with almost died in a quite abrupt event—an aortic dissection. Death almost happened, then didn't. That poem is the shaken aftermath of that. And of course, as with any poem, what emerges from one particular circumstance can speak to all the varieties of that same event. "Not-Yet" holds the simple blessing and gratitude of, "Oh, that did not happen!" And just under the spoken words, the complete awareness that someday it will.

CM: I think of Jane Kenyon's poem "Otherwise."

JH: A marvelous poem.

CM: Before we began the interview, we were talking about some of your poems—which you've described as "pebbles" or, in one case, "sentencings." Would you talk a little bit about form?

JH: The very short poem has been part of my vocabulary from the beginning. I should say that, though I've loved them from the start, I never wanted to write actual haiku or tanka. I've written two haiku in my life as a poet; one was written in the 1970s, and one appears in the most recent book, *Come, Thief.* And I've never written in the tanka form myself, although I translated many tanka, with huge joy, for *The Ink Dark Moon,* back in the mid 1980s. The experience of working so closely with five-line poems helped shape and confirm my sense of the lyric, my exhilaration at the way large meaning can reside in the smallest of cups. But I'm not Japanese, I'm American. As a poet and as a person, I'm a hybrid of many world traditions. I've been shaped by very short poems from many different sources. The riddle, the Chinese quatrain, the short poems of Pessoa and Brecht, the fragments of Sappho. I have always wanted to find a way of speaking that found my own music for my own thoughts, my own feelings. Denise Levertov called this, beautifully, "organic form." I wanted to find my way to my own organic short-form poem.

The idea of calling these "pebble" poems came when I was asked to write an essay for a book that had to do with influence and mastery. I was writing about the influence of short poems on my own short poems, and that's when I coined the word "pebbles"— not at first to describe my own work, but to describe those other poems. For instance, there are some very short poems by Bertolt Brecht which I just adore. I named the form in a small bow of homage to Zbigniew Herbert's poem, "Pebble," because this particular subset of poetry feels to me a little recalcitrant. Herbert's pebble is warmed only by the human hand that holds it, that changes its nature. And in the same way, my own short poems work only when the person reading or listening has a response, when they hold them in their hands and lives and bring to them their own human responsiveness.

After writing about this, I became more conscious of it, of practicing that form. In my next book, *After,* there's a series of seventeen "pebbles," and in *Come, Thief,* a series of fifteen.

And then there are even shorter "poems": lines I put together in a brief fragment poem called "Sentencings." Those are so brief they don't even qualify as "pebbles," they are shooting stars of thought across the horizon.

There is a part of me that is a staunch defender of the very small. We in the West have a bias toward the large. If a work of literature is "important," we seem to think, it's going to look like Homer or Dante or

Shakespeare or Milton. And I do of course love Homer and Dante and Shakespeare and Milton, but I equally love and revere the tiny shard that cuts deep into the heart. Often what we remember from the great epics is a phrase, a line: the power of that brief comprehension that holds feeling, that holds idea, that holds music, and that operates as if you were living inside of a black sheet, and had cut the tiniest hole in it, and could look out and see a universe.

The shortest free-standing poem I've written is simply called "Sentence." It reads, "The body of a starving horse does not forget the size it was born to." That poem is a grammatical sentence. It's also referring to "sentence" in the judicial meaning of the word. What is says is literally true of a starving horse: in terms of the bones, a seventeen-hand horse will be seventeen hands till the day he dies. But it's also attempting to say something almost unsayable about what is resonant in us—that no matter what happens to a person in this life, no matter how severely he or she is diminished by the always accidental circumstances of birth and culture and history, there is something of enormous magnitude that cannot be taken away.

CM: The largeness remains of the spirit of possibility.

Among your "Sentencings" are the lines about the stone that is first wet and then dry. I wonder if you'd mind reading them.

JH: "A thing too perfect to be remembered: / stone beautiful only when wet."

CM: I love that. It's one of those things one has experienced many times, and never seen before in a poem.

JH: Ah, thank you.

CM: You've named the universe. A corner of the universe.

JH: I'm going to meander on, and say that what this poem holds is not only true of many experiences in a life, it's also true of poetry itself. A poem needs to re-enact itself in you in order to live. It needs to be wetted by your full life, its tears, its minutes and hours, its history. You have to have the full experience to have the experience at all. Does this make any sense? We've all lifted lovely stones out of a river, stones that were so colorful and jewel-like, and then put them on the shelf, where they dry . . . and then we wonder, "Why did I bring that plain rock home?"

CM: Yes, absolutely.

One of my own preoccupations is the real, material world, as opposed to the cyberspace world: the difference between walking through a wonderful landscape and seeing its image on the screen. And the power of the pause in an increasingly speedy world. You have a lovely poem called "The Door." I wondered if you'd comment on the pause and the breath space you mention there, the little sabbath tucked inside the poem.

[JH reads "The Door." See page 158.]

JH: I feel such moments in so many ways. It is an experience that anyone who has done zazen meditation knows well. There's the in-breath, there's the out-breath, and between them, the moment of transition, which you can fall into, and not leave, as you breathe in, as you breathe out. All possibility comes in the moment when *what is* vanishes and *what is next* or *what is not* has not yet appeared. This is how we change, by letting go of the past, by letting go of the status quo, the reified thought. I think this is why we require sabbath in our lives, and silence in our words: because nothing new can come unless there's a space for it to enter.

CM: You said that so beautifully. Is that something you try to help your students see?

JH: There's one place where I teach both poetry and Zen, and that's when I teach at my old monastery. When I speak of it in the poetry world, when I'm not being overly Buddhist, I find I will praise silence rather frequently. I praise what happens within silence and the unsaid. And I praise not knowing, abiding in question rather than leaping to what may be a too-easy answer. I also often speak about transition in poetry. In fiction or playwriting, that is absolutely common. But in poetry workshops, it's relatively rare. I asked my friends about this when I began teaching it, and no one had ever said a word to them about transitions in poetry. For a transition to happen, you need a gap, a little sabbath. I sometimes feel that all wisdom, all newness of insight and experience, lives in the hinges—of poems, of a life.

CM: Thank you, thank you.

In your prose book, *Nine Gates: Entering the Mind of Poetry,* you say that art is a neighbor to artifice, and you talk about enhancement and exaggeration and rearrangement. You talk about playfulness, and you talk about passion and rebellion. For the most part, your own poems are very plain. I wondered why they are so free of the enhancements you mention in *Nine Gates.*

JH: Oh, but they're not! They offer deceptive simplicities and quiet ornateness. When I read "simple" poems by others closely, if they are good and effective at all, I always find in them hidden drawers, language-acts of sleight of hand, undercurrents doing the work beneath the plain surface. Any poem that is working as a poem will have in it the articulation, the movability of our deepest being. And occasionally I do kick up my heels and write ornately. There's the poem "The Stone of Heaven" at the end of *The October Palace.* I don't think I'm so bare of ornaments as you're describing. I'm not generally Whitmanesque in my work, but for me, one feather of the peacock tail goes a long way. In a quiet room, a small sound is large.

CM: I didn't mean to—

JH: Dismiss my poems!

CM: I don't. I see them as tremendously resonant. But I also see them as choosing clarity and a certain kind of plainness over a certain kind of ornateness.

JH: Often the case, I have to agree. Some of that is just temperament. Every once in a while, I'll put on a great big glorious pair of earrings, but mostly I don't wear them at all. People come to their art with certain innate flavors of flamboyance or preferences for simplicity. I'm not in general a creature comfortable with self-display. I love clarity—but only if there is something genuine to be clear about. I rarely find pleasure in pure obfuscation. For me, one reason poetry and art exist is to give me some experience that is clearly able to be felt, even if not clearly able to be said. The most direct sentence (as in the poem "Sentence") can have many meanings beyond those of the straightforward words, and it's the tension between the two levels that, for me, awakens. But truly, I'm glad there's a broad range of styles and approaches in the world. I read many things quite different from what I write, and take enormous pleasure in the full panoply.

Narrative poetry is much the same, for me, or what's still called "confessional poetry." I rarely tell anything like the direct autobiographical story in my poems. I can think of two poems, perhaps, in which I do that. Yet I can read narrative and autobiographical poetry with great pleasure.

CM: I remember "1973," which is a tale of first love, first poems, first homemaking.

JH: That is one of the two. Yes.

CM: And did writing that tell you that you didn't need to do it again?

JH: No, no, it's not like that at all. I write the poems that ask me to write them, and if that kind of poem were to come to me again I would write it gladly. I don't direct what comes. I try, if anything, to behave like a petri dish in a tenth-grade biology class. You just expose the petri dish to the air and see what takes root in it. That's my relationship to the kinds of poems I write, whether they're short or long.

The opposite of the "pebbles" in the recent books are the poems called "assays," which tend to be longer, more meditative, more full of thinking. They are much more extended meditations on their subjects, and yet they're related to the "pebbles" in some way. I am always hoping to surprise myself. To surprise myself formally, to surprise myself in subject matter, to find what it is in me that has not found its expression, and to let the poem itself tell me what its expression is going to be.

CM: So the poems in your last book, which are playing with rhyme and repetition, weren't made from your decision to pursue rhyme and repetition?

JH: Oh, no, no, no, it's quite the opposite. They are the voice that came. Also, if you look carefully through my work, there are poems in what I think of as wandering rhyme going all the way back. I've always done it. It's more noticeable in the recent book, perhaps, because the more sound-based poems are mostly together, near the end of the book.

But you can find rhyme throughout my work. These are poems that feel to me as if the horses pulling the wagon are language itself. The music is writing the poem as much as and more than the mind is, and one speaks differently when that happens. Though I'll add that every poem must have some quotient of music in it or fall into dust motes. I do want every possible tool in the writerly tool chest. There's a villanelle in *Come, Thief,* for instance. I've never written another, but have wondered for a long time if I would, after noticing that Bishop's "One Art," Thomas's "Do Not Go Gentle," and Roethke's "The Waking" were each the only villanelles those poets wrote. Still, I couldn't *try* to write one. "A Hand Is Made by What It Holds and Makes" came when it needed to come, and I found myself writing it. The villanelle's change and recurrence offered the only possible shape for that particular experience and set of feelings.

CM: One of my pleasures in reading your work is the way you return to the specificities of the natural or the material world. Buttons and scissors and spoons and hairbrushes and mugs and towels. I wondered if you'd comment on that.

JH: I think two things are at play here—both a love of the actual/ordinary, and also a deep fidelity to the possibilities of anything, anything at all, be-coming a gate. That is, I want poems to register a sense of intimacy with what already is, and I want them to lead me into some additional measures of experience, comprehension, and feeling.

I write with what is at hand. A cracked blue coffee cup shows up in many of my books, because I had my morning coffee for many years in that cup. It was, literally, what was at hand. There's probably not a tree in my garden that hasn't called forth its poem. The mountain out my window has called forth its poems. The use of the ordinary image is found in every poetic tradition, as central to poems as nouns and verbs, tongues and elbows. We think with what is here, and we are prehensile in our thinking—that intimacy of hold and touch is part of why one way to say "understand" is to say "grasp." There's a marvelous book by George Lakoff and Mark Johnson, *Metaphors We Live By.* It makes the case that every thought we have is rooted in the physical world. The word "abstract" has in its root etymology the concept of "pulling," of "traction." We pull abstract meaning out of the ground where it has its roots. The word "language" has in its etymology the concept of "tongue." We can't speak without drawing on the physical because we are animals in a physical world. What else is there?

CM: You probably know David Abram's recent book, *Becoming Animal.*

JH: Yes, yes, and I know David.

CM: I love that book.

I wondered if you'd talk about the number of selves we each contain. You have a poem called "Red Berries" where you talk about one woman washing her face and another picking up the hairbrush and another stepping out of her slippers. It reminded me of Milosz's lines about poetry being there to remind us how difficult it is to remain just one person.

JH: What a perfect association.

CM: The multitude of selves. Could you remark on that in your own work?

JH: It's an idea that has always appealed to me, anywhere I've met it. In Zen, for instance, one of the central teachings is that if you are not bound to the idea of a single continuous self, then every moment the self is changed and the world is new. But no idea found in Buddhism is only Buddhist—these are human perceptions, available to anyone. Neruda has a marvelous poem, "We Are Many," which has been translated by Alastair Reid. It's been a favorite poem of mine for decades now. If we think of ourselves as singular, we limit who we might be, and I want to find out who else I could be, what other lives I might be able to recognize, if only for a moment, as also mine. What I want is something more intimate: empathy for all the beings of the world, and for all the possible ways of being in it. So, what you find in my poems is often an exploration forward and an invitation toward greater largeness, greater possibility, greater permeability of border and being.

CM: Lovely. In fact that swerves back to David Abram, and the letting in of the non-human world.

JH: Yes, and I think all poetry does this. If you say, "The moon is a white cat," you have to let in "moon" and you have to let in "cat." You have to let the objects and animals into your own psyche, where they will prowl around in the middle of the night and do what they're going to do, and you have to allow your own psyche to know itself as existing in the objects, animals it doesn't ordinarily think of as itself. This is how we feel more fully, this is how we know more widely and wildly. If there is a mountain in a poem, you feel *mountain-ness,* you feel its inhumanness and its longevity. You feel the enormous biological and geological life the mountain houses. You feel what it does to your legs to walk on a mountain, how it feels in your eyes to gaze at a mountain and to look out from the top of one. The word "mountain" in a poem is a thread, and if you pull on the thread, all those experiences and knowledges are tugged into presence.

CM: Yes.

By the way, I'm so glad that you love Alastair Reid's translations. He's a dear friend of mine.

JH: Oh, please tell him he's an extraordinary writer and an extraordinary man. I've never met him.

CM: We were talking about the mountain, and so I just want to say that I particularly love your poem "The Mountain" with its reference to Tu Fu.

I wonder what you are reading these days and what you see as your own growing edge.

JH: For new reading, I'll name two younger poets, as vastly different as two younger poets could be. One is Christina Davis, who has a first book out from Alice James Books, *Forth a Raven.* And the other is Matthew Zapruder, and his *Come On All You Ghosts,* from Copper Canyon. Both books are tremendously exciting finds for me. Then there's another younger poet, Bridget Lowe, who's writing a series of "pilgrim" poems I think are very exciting.

For what I might see as my growing edge, I'm not sure I can answer, or would want to be able to answer. I think the very nature of that experience is that it hasn't yet formed into anything identifiable or nameable. A root tendril doesn't know yet what direction it will be drawn toward, and those decisions must happen protected from awareness and will, hidden in under-earth darkness.

But if what I turn to to read gives some hint of where the root finds sustenance. . . . At this point I am reading long loves. Some of them are still alive and giving me new poems to read, for example, Wislawa Szymborska. But also all the great twentieth-century Polish poets. Milosz and Zbigniew Herbert I reread frequently. Then, to change continents, Borges. And then Horace and Catullus. Every once in a while, I go back and reread *The Odyssey,* probably in a new translation.

Revisiting the classics has become increasingly fertile for me. There are some references to Tolstoy in *Come, Thief,* because while writing the book I reread both *Anna Karenina* and *War and Peace.* There is so much to take in, and when you read something when you're in your later fifties, it's very different from the book you read when you were seventeen. *Anna Karenina,* for instance, became a completely different book for me. It was no longer a book about a love affair or adultery, it became a book almost entirely about people's spiritual lives. The weight of the book moved, not completely off Anna of course, because Anna is a tremendous and haunting character, but much more into Levin than I'd remembered—and even the most minor characters are always given us with some sense of their spiritual concerns and center.

I was, during this rereading, fascinated by Levin. I especially love the section at the end where he's had his great spiritual experience of opening, and he's walking down the road with his visitors and family, feeling and discovering who he now is: "Oh, I can still feel irritable, how interesting!" That made me laugh with delight, because it's so true. "Oh sure, sure, I've understood God, I've had a great experience of oneness and, look, I still get angry! Look, I still am petty." Tolstoy captures something so very accurate and humane in this description, humane because it gives people permission to be fully themselves. We tend to hold in our minds an image of "spiritual" people as fully enlightened saints. But if you read the actual stories of even those we call saints—I discovered this when I was researching *Women In Praise of the Sacred*—you find out that every one of them has a dark night of the soul not only before their great realization, but again, afterwards. Yet we forget this, and we feel like failures if we don't live up to this imaginary ideal of perfected character. Perhaps that's why I find so very helpful something the thirteenth-century Zen teacher Dogen famously said, "A Zen master's life is one long mistake."

CM: That's wonderful. I'm with you on rereading Tolstoy. I myself reread *War and Peace* and *Anna Karenina* this past long, cold winter, and was amazed by what was hiding there that was invisible to me as a teenager.

JH: Exactly, and how so many things that used to be boring become fascinating.

CM: The war, which I just galloped through when I read it first.

JH: The war, and also Tolstoy's sense of the causes of history. To me it's fascinating; it all seems so contemporary until the very end, the appendix, in which he says, "Because we can't comprehend these things, the only explanation has to be the existence of God." Until the moment he says that, he presents such a postmodern, multifaceted, multi-threaded view of history. It's tremendously sophisticated.

CM: Yes, and the way he offers us grief. The little peasant boy sitting on the top of the stove listening to the soldiers talking.

JH: And the dog running into the battlefield.

CM: Extraordinary moments. I think it's easy to believe that the classics are somehow false classics because you've been told to admire them from too young.

JH: Yes, yes!

CM: It's wonderful to return to them and love them for real.

JH: Yes, we've been clubbed by reputation.

CM: That's right.
   Well, we're coming toward the end, so I just wanted to ask you a few more things. There were a couple of poems in your most recent book where I thought you were moving into entirely new territory. Among those I particularly admired were "When Your Life Looks Back" and "I Ran Out

Naked in the Sun." I wondered if you'd pick one of those to read and then comment on it.

JH: Do you have a preference?

CM: I love them both.

JH: So do I, and they're completely different!

CM: Let's do, "I Ran Out Naked in the Sun." That's—

JH: More unusual, especially for me?

CM: More unusual, yes.

[JH reads "I Ran Out Naked in the Sun."]

JH: I've never written anything quite like this in my life, both in what it's saying and in how it says it. This poem is probably the closest I'll ever come to writing an Irish ballad. The rhymes of course bow toward Emily Dickinson, in rhythm a bit and in that they're slant rhyme. "Warm" and "storm." "Sun" and "then." It's—I'm sorry, I'm stuttering around a bit here because it's so hard for me to talk about this poem. It arrived in its own voice and I will, I suppose, nakedly confess, it happened. I did run out naked in the sun and I did run out naked in the rain and it did thunder and I did shout "more." How embarrassing is that! I had just turned fifty-five, so was, as the poem describes it, "leaning toward sixty." An age when you can't help but see how your life is changing and that there are certain things that, if you're not saying goodbye to them yet, you know you will. And yet, you love. You want. Passion does not abate. The nakedness before the elements does not abate.

The thing that surprises me about the poem isn't that I wrote it, it's that I published it. I rarely show my poems to anyone, but a friend came by and asked to see my new work and—just very unlike me—I just gave her the whole sheaf. She adored this poem and I thought, *"She does?"* Then I gave it at a little reading and they really liked it, and then the third time I read it, I read it to 2,000 people at the Dodge Poetry Festival, and they seemed to really like it, too. I'd have been terribly embarrassed to say these things about longing and naked desire and aging in straightforward statements. I am here. But somehow the singing of poetry, the way longing is set into forms, made it bearable for me to let that poem be public.

CM: It's a wonderful poem.

JH: Thank you. I'll probably shorten that answer up a lot when it's in transcript!

CM: No!

SOUND ENGINEER: No!

CM: I think because it's risky it gives a truth that other people are perhaps also feeling and also afraid to say.

JH: Yes. And because it is risky, it needed the rhyme and the sound to hold it. This is one thing rhyme and meter exist for, one thing that repetition exists for. To make vessels that give intimacy a bearably shareable life.

CM: One of the reasons I like this poem so much is the sense of transgression: that you, the good gray poet who loves the world in its ordinariness, and loves its beauty, should demand "More!" There's a greed there I adore.

JH: Thank you, thank you, yes. Admitting to an unseemly greed is indeed at the heart of it.

CM: The first people to read this interview will be the young apprentice writers at Smith College. They are on the cusp of taking their own work seriously, and they're not always quite sure where to go. Is there anything you would like to say to them, particularly?

JH: What I would say is that the best thing a writer can do is throw open your windows several inches wider than feels comfortable, unlock your doors, be willing to write horribly badly. You can always throw what you've written into the woodstove later, if you need to. But, take the risk of embarrassing yourself and not knowing if you have or not. Also, read furiously and widely. Read beyond your own zone of preference and comfort, but don't abandon your own sense of what's good. Don't let anybody tell you something is good poetry if it does not speak to you. You might find five years from now that it does speak to you. Finally, I would say: be permeable. Be aware and permeable. Know what you are seeing and feeling and what you are saying, allow these things their fullness, and that fierceness and courage will serve you well.

YUSEF KOMUNYAKAA

Interviewed September 17, 2013

Yusef Komunyakaa was born in Bogalusa, Louisiana, in 1947, the eldest of six children. His father was a carpenter who could read and write only his name. His great grandmother had been a slave. Komunyakaa was named for his father, James William Brown, and later renamed himself after his Trinidadian grandfather. He started working in the fields when he was still a child. But from early on, he was entranced by the landscape that surrounded him and wanted to learn the names of things. "It was a way of seeing," he says now, "and also of discovering language."

Komunyakaa served in Vietnam in his early twenties, and was awarded a Bronze Star. He began to write seriously soon afterwards, inspired by contemporary poets like Langston Hughes. In the years that followed, he published more than a dozen books of poetry, along with several plays, performance literature, and libretti. He received both the Pulitzer Prize and the Kingsley Tufts Poetry Award for *Neon Vernacular* in 1994, and has also been honored with a number of other awards, including the Ruth Lilly Poetry Prize, the Shelley Memorial Award, and the 2011 Wallace Stevens Award.

Komunyakaa has been writing now for more than forty years, but still delights in the moments of surprise. "I like writing poems and coming to a phrase where I laugh out loud and say, 'Gosh, where did that come from?' Those moments are gifts."

Black Figs

Because they tasted so damn good, I swore
   I'd never eat another one, but three seedy little hearts
beckoned tonight from a green leaf-shaped saucer
   swollen with ripeness, ready to spill a gutty
sacrament on my tongue. Their skins too smooth
   to trust or believe. Shall I play Nat King Cole's
"Nature Boy" or Cassandra's "Death Letter"
   this Gypsy hour? I have a few words to steal
back the taste of earth. I know laughter can rip
   stitches, & deeds come undone in the middle of a dance.
Socrates talked himself into raising the cup to his lips
   to toast the avenging oracle, but I told the gods no
false kisses, they could keep their ambrosia & nectar,
   & let me live my days & nights. I nibble each globe,
each succulent bud down to its broken-off stem
   like a boy trying to make a candy bar last
the whole day, & laughter unlocks my throat
   when a light falls across Bleecker Street
against the ugly fire escape.

Christian McEwen: I know that you were born in Louisiana, the eldest of six children. You said, "I grew up with some strange characters around me, storytellers and sorcerers," and I wondered if you'd say something about that life and that landscape.

Yusef Komunyakaa: I believe one internalizes a landscape, and the reflection of that landscape is carried within. Especially, I'm thinking particularly about Bogalusa, Louisiana, a place of some very old rituals. One learned to gaze up at the sky and know the time of day, how to bake sweet potatoes in the hot ashes of a potbellied, wood-burning stove on wintry evenings, and to welcome the voice of Cousin Rosabel talking about hoo-doo, sassafras candy, and money-conjuring powder sprinkled on the back doorsteps. Yes, Bogalusa was a place where many rituals took place and, also a landscape I could lose myself; it was a place of great meditation. In retrospect, it was a good place to be from, yet when growing up I was told it was a good place to be a long ways from.

There were storytellers, the oral tradition was alive. I remember Mr. Yake, who told ghost stories, and I would always be at the edge of my chair. And there were other storytellers closer to the folk tradition, who told animal stories about the fox and the rabbit, the bear and the turtle. And also there were teenage boys who were great at playing "the Dozens" —a survival game. One couldn't get angry, but had to sharpen one's skill in creating a biting wit of verbal dexterity. Boys insinuated about each other's mothers and sisters—those most sacred individuals—and one lost if he punched the signifying speaker. Perhaps such a ritual of innuendo journeys back to West Africa.

CM: You say in the book *Blue Notes,* "Many times I'd read poetry in order to establish a moment of contemplation. And other times I'd go out to the wooded areas around my house to allow myself solitude." I wonder if you'd talk about your own relationship to words, to poetry, as a child.

YK: I came to poetry in grade school, I think it was during so-called "Negro History Week," and I discovered Langston Hughes, Paul Laurence Dunbar, Phyllis Wheatley, James Weldon Johnson, and Gwendolyn Brooks. But later in junior high I discovered other poets such as William Blake, Edgar Allan Poe, and Emily Dickinson. The first two poems I memorized were James Weldon Johnson's "The Creation" and "Annabel Lee" by Poe.

But of course I also read the Bible, we all did at that time in the South, and I was drawn to the language throughout the Scriptures. Those grand metaphors still seem surrealistic to me. However, I didn't realize biblical text as poetry when I was reading it, and didn't realize how many other poets it probably influenced as well, including Walt Whitman.

CM: When you're in high school I understand you wrote a poem that was a hundred lines long in rhymed quatrains.

YK: Right.

CM: So clearly you were reading sonnets, ballads, couplets, *et cetera*. Did you experience your teachers, your family as encouraging? Or was it really a long, solitary row to hoe?

YK: Yes, but when I attempted that series of twenty-five quatrains, I hadn't even dreamt of writing a poem. I was very shy. I didn't trust my voice. So finally I wrote those hundred lines, and I was too shy to read it, and the student who read it, years later she promised to keep it a secret. It was that bad. There were very trite rhymes—a good example would be "success" and "progress." It was written for my fellow students—a moment when I attempted to propel myself, as well as them, out into that scary future.

I didn't attempt to write poetry for a long time after that, but I kept reading it. And I did keep a notebook of sorts, and so poetry was there, still tugging at my psyche. But I didn't realize I would actually end up writing poetry. So I surprised myself.

CM: That's great.

One of the things I noticed when I read your work was the extraordinary specificity of the language—in your childhood memories, but also in present-day poems. I'm thinking, for example, of your description of the armadillo, "two quicksilver eyes / peer out from under a coral helmet / color of fossil." You've got a brilliant phrase-making eye.

YK: I think from early on, I wanted to learn the names of things. It's not so much that in naming things we control them, but more that we attempt to experience what those things are experiencing. So naming things was very important to me. It was a way of seeing and also discovering language. I love the sounds associated with names—the names of trees, the names of flowers, the scientific names as well as the vernacular. How they clash sometimes with each other, and other times how they embrace each other. So that's important for me. It's a process of discovery, and that's what nature became for me. It was a guide. I think Seamus Heaney talks about nature in a similar way: meta-language and such, that essentially the poem is informed by nature. I believe, at times, his work conveys a rural certainty that expands time and place.

CM: Seamus Heaney, of course, died just last month [August 2013], and I happened to be reading your work when that news came over the radio. Did you ever cross paths with him?

YK: Yes. A few times.

CM: Can you speak a little about your memories of him?

YK: Well, I'd been reading him early on, and I think it was "Digging" that led me to his books—*Death of a Naturalist, North, Station Island, Seeing Things,* his translation of *Beowulf*—and I finally crossed paths with him, I think it was around 2001 or 2002, at Paul Muldoon's house. And I was too in awe to actually discuss anything reverential, but just being in his presence was informative. A year or two later, I was reading in Ireland, and our paths crossed again, a "Hello," you know, that kind of thing. He was such a genuine person, a great poet of the world. I was invited in 2011 to St. Lucia to celebrate Derek Walcott's eighty-first birthday, and Seamus and his wife, Marie, were there as well, and there I had time to converse with him, to be in his presence.

CM: That was a good experience.

YK: That was a great experience.

CM: What a lovely, warm, genial man he was.

In many of your poems, you pay tribute to jazz, and you said that it wasn't so much what you listened to, but how you listened. And I wondered if you'd say a bit more about listening.

YK: Well, essentially, I like the idea of listening with the whole body— that's more what it is than anything else. Not just listening with the head, with the mind, because if one listens in that way, the music is abstracted. Listening with the whole body, it's very tangible, it's a part of oneself, becomes a part of oneself. I think maybe listening to music may parallel listening to the deep silence of nature as well.

CM: Lovely.

YK: I think there's a singing underneath things, and one doesn't know if one's being beckoned, or if one is—if it's the opposite of that—being challenged. Because I believe in nature, and perhaps in art as well, beauty and terror live side by side, coexisting, influencing each other, and creating an element of tension.

I suppose I wish I were a musician. I love listening to music, being challenged by the colors of sound.

CM: Has it given you courage in terms of your own writing?

YK: I hope so, just the idea of the musician knowing his or her instrument so well that he or she can risk traveling through oneself out into the future. Maybe that's what poetry is as well—learning the instrument—and trusting, or entrusting oneself to the instrument of language until there's poetry. In that sense, sound is always part of poetry, and we come to trust language, taking a risk, going someplace we hadn't even thought of before, projecting ourselves into a future as well as back into a past, and arriving at a place where one finds a certain foundation, a belief in possibility. It is a place where we risk discovering an unsayable that holds us accountable.

CM: I understand that you first began to write seriously as a student at a poetry workshop in Colorado Springs and you enjoyed—and I think this was your phrase—"how the work radiated with a number of surprises."

YK: That was an interesting time because I thought I knew what poetry was or is, but it became a place of discovery. I'd been drawn early on to very formalized poetry, and the poetry I was reading in Colorado Springs for the most part was actually modernist, and in a way it brought me back to Langston Hughes. I do see Langston Hughes as influenced by the blues tradition, and I grew up with the blues without even knowing it was the blues; everything around me was the blues. And I realized in Colorado Springs that embracing free verse, or blank verse, I could sing in a different way and maybe one that was truer to my experiences, to my observations and risky dreams.

And still the poem was made, a made thing. And in that way it relates to growing up the son of a carpenter. I admired the precision, but I also admired moments of surprise, the twists and turns within a crafted object, the same way a poem embraces what it is made of. I like writing a phrase where I laugh out loud and I say, *"Damn, where did that come from?"* Those moments are gifts.

CM: One of the things I marveled at was your use of persona. You have so many poems written in voices that are not your own, and as a female reader I was tremendously impressed by your ability to take on the voice of a woman. Or the voice of the universe. And I wondered when you discovered that as a way to write.

YK: I don't think I was ever really conscious of it. However, I grew up aware of the thoughts and concerns of the women around me, especially my grandmothers, since they were my prime caretakers. And I'm talking not just caretakers of body, but caretakers of the psyche. I think perhaps they taught me how to dream. I really trusted them, and I learned many things from them, and much of it was unconscious, such as the fact I didn't know I knew how to cook, you know, but somehow I always knew the right ingredients, mixtures, and temperatures. They'd never really taught me, it was just my observation, watching every move and just taking that all in, listening and seeing. I knew the rhythm.

I was back in Louisiana in May of 1982 and I heard my maternal grandmother talking in the next room, and I said to myself, "Oh that's why, that's why I have certain expressions in my poems." It was amazing really. I thought—I had the ego to believe—I self-invented myself. But that wasn't the case at all. I had borrowed from and attemped to reshape what was around me. I had internalized the voices of women: singers, seers, workers. I trusted them.

CM: You mentioned dreams just now; would you say a little more about dreams in terms of your work?

YK: With dreams I realized, growing up in Bogalusa, I was also dreaming myself away from that place. And at the same time, now, I find myself dreaming myself back, or realizing I have never left. One could do impossible things in dreams, but also one could become very humble in dreams. Flying in dreams was very intriguing and foreboding to me. I don't know how many men actually fly in dreams, but early on, especially when I was a teenager, I could fly in dreams. And up until recently I suppose I thought

I could even levitate, you know, in dreams, with my eyes open. I had very few frightening dreams. Some people tell me about horrifying dreams, but I've had hardly any of those, knock on wood.

CM: I'm sitting here and thinking about you and Seamus Heaney: Seamus being the eldest of nine children and you the oldest of six, and how you both had tremendous access to your childhood landscape, and a great loyalty to it, and yet also this huge brain. And how you both managed not to abandon that childhood whilst at the same time going forward into the radiant adulthood. I don't mean to idealize this, but you have pulled together a very wide range of lives.

YK: Well, one does travel!

CM: One does travel, clearly. As you say yourself, "I am a black man, I am a poet, a bohemian, / & there isn't a road my mind doesn't travel."
   So I guess my question has to do with your task as a poet of turning the world into the word and vice versa.

YK: I suppose we are responsible for what we witness, what we observe, not that we attempt to let what we have observed dictate the direction of the poem, but at least it has some deep residence there. What I'm getting at is—I still want the poem to surprise me. I don't want answers as much as I need questions. I think questions are what really humanize us. And I suppose I want mystery to still reside there as well. I think that's how poetry became and remains so human, it's that questioning, almost like a begging or summoning that takes us to the elemental or the brink.
   I can imagine early-early human beings not even having the faculties to pose the questions, but some mechanics locked into the brain, still posing questions, even though they were not articulated. Mmm, and so maybe that has something to do with the poem as well. You know, there have been so many nails driven into the coffin of poetry, and yet poetry is still with us. And I think it will continue to be with us—even in an over-technological society, it still resides here. Because poetry is capable of doing some shape-shifting of its own.

CM: Do you see one of those nails in the coffin of poetry as being the plethora of technologies nowadays, the inundation of information?

YK: I think so. I attempted to resist technology. For a long time, I didn't have a computer. But finally students demanded that I have a computer, that I come into the modern age. But poems are not built out of information. That's what I mean about surprises; that's how images dovetail. I cannot see how a poem exists without images, without imagination. I believe, if anything, a poem is really a composite of images, sometimes moved by tropes of insinuation.

CM: I guess one of the books that might have tilted you toward more information and less toward mystery was your Vietnam book, *Dien Cai Dau,* which means "crazy man," right?

YK: Yeah, crazy in the head.

CM: Because being there was crazy for really everyone.

YK: Also, we American GIs heard *"beaucoup dien cai dau"* as "boocoo dinky dau."

CM: "Very crazy. Very much crazy."

YK: Right.
    But when I heard it, it was not what it meant as much as the sound, the music of the phrase. And later on I understood what it meant, and much later heard an echo of French colonialism.

CM: You had an amazing description of working on those poems while you were renovating an old house in New Orleans. Every time you got a line in your head, you'd have to descend the ladder in order to write it down. Those poems were written twelve, fourteen years after your experience in Vietnam. Would you talk about that long gestation, and how it was finally to find words for that experience?

YK: Well, I'd been writing poems that I thought came closer to Surrealism. Those were the poems I loved reading as well, especially some of the so-called American Surrealists published in George Hitchcock's *Kayak* magazine, but also going back to Bretón, some of the Negritude poets too,

Aimé Césaire. I didn't think my experience in Vietnam would be poetry. I thought I would write an essay or a book of essays about that experience. But working on the house on Piety Street in New Orleans in August, the heat, the dust, and all that, momentarily I was back in Vietnam. I just found myself writing lines down, and before I knew it, I'd written a poem. Then I'd written three poems, you know! And I kept writing them.

There are other poems about Vietnam as well, but I told myself that I wouldn't write about Vietnam anymore. I wanted to write about other things, other feelings, and yet perhaps Vietnam interconnects with those other moments, other times, other histories. Because of growing up in Bogalusa, I wasn't afraid of the Vietnam landscape when I arrived there. I embraced that landscape, because it was almost like embracing home, with all the tall grass, animals, snakes, and all of that. Nature was very busy, very vibrant, and it embraced my psyche. But at the same time, the opposite of that was true as well. Death was always around the next corner, right? I think if I had grown up in a city, in New York City, Chicago, or in Denver, I would have been very afraid in Vietnam, and the landscape itself would have been an enemy.

CM: So the fact that you weren't afraid of the landscape freed you to see the story differently.

YK: To see and feel it differently, yes.

CM: Thank you.

I'm not sure how to ask this question, but clearly one of the things you've had to wrestle with as an African-American poet is the issue of racism, and you've managed to do it without becoming enthralled to what you call at one point "service literature." Your poems are way larger than that; you've managed to tell very uncomfortable, very painful truths without starting always from a place of bitterness, and I wondered if you'd speak a little bit about that journey.

YK: Right.

I think language itself is political. Where the problem exists for me is this: when what is spoken destroys the speaker. I have great problems with that, and that can happen in so many ways, in so many degrees. We are responsible for what we utter, for what we say and believe—I have always believed that, and perhaps that came from instructions from my grandmothers as well, that I had to be responsible for what I said. I couldn't just speak out of anger. Not that what I said had to be measured in every way, not that it wasn't informed with abrupt moments of passion, which has perhaps also edged into my poetry in some way.

There's this idea of being responsible for what we say, and at the same time being surprised.

CM: Lovely. So the immediate knee-jerk response is not necessarily permitted, or one notices it and does something else, makes it into a dance, or takes on someone else's voice, or moves on sideways.

YK: Well, it's interesting, because at times, now, I wish had been writing plays through the years.

I think it was Amiri Baraka who said that every poet should be a playwright. I had started reading plays early on; now finally I'm writing some plays. That probably would have given me a larger canvas, because I love reading plays, I love seeing plays, you know, I love August Wilson, I love Shakespeare, Derek Walcott, Harold Pinter. There are so many playwrights I see as poets. Adrienne Kennedy, it's amazing what she does with her characters through language. I really see her as a poet who writes plays. It's interesting when a character comes alive and speaks, sometimes, just basic unembellished truths. And at the same time another character comes in and says something that is completely out of this world, slightly opposite, very ornate, and both tones are working side by side, existing within the same frame of human experience through dialogue and action.

I wish poems could house those varied moments as well, side by side, and maybe create a certain tension where the levels of diction shift.

CM: You said somewhere that you didn't want all the poems in your book to be like a little line-up of paper dolls, each one the exact same kind of poem. I certainly feel your poems have an amazingly wide range of dictions, each of them with equal felicity and authority. So you're doing it, you're doing it!

YK: I try to!

CM: Absolutely, my God. In *Talking Dirty to the Dogs,* or—"to the Gods," rather. In *Talking Dirty to the Gods* . . .

YK: That's interesting.

CM: Thanks, Mr. Freud! I was aware of the ways in which those ancient Greek and Roman myths were intertwined in each of your poems. And I wondered what those classical references gave you that you couldn't have achieved without them, and whether you ever felt at all hamstrung by them—a little bit too taut with all that high classical reference.

YK: Well, the structure of those poems—each one is sixteen lines with four lines per stanza—when I was writing some of those poems, they would actually go beyond the frame, and I would not torture the language but . . . but—

CM: The carpenter's son came out.

YK: Right, and I think it had a lot to do with how I was actually writing the poems. Sometimes they'd emerge complete in sixteen lines, because I was composing some of the poems as I walked to work. It was probably a mile and a half, or two miles, and it was instructive in that way.

It was when I first got to Princeton, I wanted to create a terrain where the high and the low lived side by side within the same frame, where the poems would, I should say, expand. They were tortured, I shouldn't say "torture," but they were controlled, and at the same time I wanted them to break out and expand like those flowers, those little Japanese paper flowers that are dropped into a glass of water and grow out.

CM: Yeah, wonderful.

You said in *Blue Notes* that it was difficult for you to write about very private things, but that you were constantly moving closer to that personal terrain. And I guess I felt a greater openness and maybe one could say integration in *The Chameleon Couch.* And I wondered how it was to be the writer behind that book, what the experience was.

YK: Hmm. I had some fun with that book. I like to think I always have fun when I'm writing, and yet I know that isn't the case. But I was surprised by some of the poems, where they actually went. It was framed, well, by the title, *Chameleon Couch*. I had that title for some time, and I knew the poems coming under that title would appear different, that's what I felt. So the title was making some demands on the subject matter, and consequently it created a certain freedom for me. I believe that's what happened. And I hope there's a dialogue between the poems in that book.

CM: Thank you. Yes, those poems, the poems in *Warhorses* and in *The Chameleon Couch*, all have that amazing syntax, that oblique vision. Do you have *Warhorses* with you? Because there's a poem written from the woman's point of view, and I'd love you to read that.

YK: [Reads "My Wide Hips Raise to Warriors."]

CM: There are so many layers to those later poems. There's the wisdom, there's the human experience, there's the personal voice, there's the mythical quality to it. It's the sound of you coming into your inheritance of your whole working life. It's magnificent stuff.

YK: Thank you.

CM: Thank you, thank *you*.

You say somewhere, I think in *Blue Notes,* "I keep a mental notebook," and "I might write down an image that's recurred for four, five, six years." You talk about writing every day. You said just now that when you were at Princeton you would compose poems on your daily walk. Could you talk a little bit about your work habits?

YK: I attempt to write every day still, and now I'm writing plays, some essays, and poems. I'm working on a very interesting, strange, challenging project about astronauts, with three other librettists. Just thinking about the life of an astronaut is very rewarding to me.

How do I go about writing? I still keep notebooks. I also keep many torn out pages, scraps of paper, things of the sort. At one time I wanted to create a kind of visual chaos, where it wasn't just neatly controlled. I wanted to be able to pick up a sheet of paper from a stack, early in the morning, and finish a poem I thought I would never finish, or that I thought I had completely forgotten. I still love working that way. I wrote notes in the margins of books and magazines. I was all over the map, and yet I felt when I was doing that I had great control. If someone else looked, perhaps they saw complete chaos, but I seemed to have known where everything was. And it was strange; I don't know if I have that today. I don't think so. I suppose it has something to do with time.

CM: Have you gotten more orderly?

YK: Well, maybe out of necessity, because I used to keep my monthly calendar in my head, things like that, you know. I can't do that any longer.

I wish I could. It's like wearing glasses, right? I've tricked myself to believe that I don't need them, but no, I do.

CM: This goes back to what you were saying earlier, but I wondered if you'd talk about the relationship between poetry and healing, both for the poet and his audience. You say in *Blue Notes,* "I try to encourage a space into which a reader can come and participate in the meaning." So you're giving over some of the power to the reader, him or herself.

YK: What I actually mean by that is: I don't want the poem to be completely tied up neatly. And a poem can mean many different things; it depends on the reader or the listener, what he or she brings to the poem. And for the poet often it is what he or she can risk discovering. Perhaps for the reader it's the same thing: what one can risk discovering. I want to write poems that don't take us on epic journeys, but on some journey that goes within the terrain that's inside. It doesn't have to be complicated; it can be very simple and what's needed at that moment.

I like the idea of praising things as well. That's what I really took from Neruda, I think, his ability to praise things.

CM: Yes, those marvelous odes.

YK: Yes, yes. And sometimes they're so simple and yet they're not. It depends on how the light slants through the window, what we see.

CM: You say in *Blue Notes* that you try to convince your students to write about the things that are very close to them—it doesn't have to be some trip to Italy or Japan—and you emphasize reading and observation. I wondered what else you find yourself saying consistently to your own students.

YK: I find myself saying, "Read everything." And what I mean is that one should read philosophy, history, folklore, one should read science texts. I used to assign *Scientific American.* At first my students were a little baffled—why *Scientific American,* right? But we often got some wonderful poems, and sometimes there's just the intensity of an image. And also I would say, "Well, science can often point us to where terror and beauty communicate."

I tell them not to sit at the computer and write, to write everything in longhand if possible, and then use the computer as a tool, because I think technology can sometimes trick us. What I mean by this is that it creates the illusion the poem is finished. And I say that time should always be part of the equation.

CM: I'm thinking of your saying that your father never rushed his work, and that you like to think of the precision with which he crafted tables and shelves and houses as the same kind of process you employ in your own work.

YK: I hope so. That was my dialogue with him, yes.

CM: It's been magnificent talking to you, a real joy.

YK: Thank you. Great, great questions.

MAXINE KUMIN

Interviewed March 28, 2011

Maxine Kumin was born Maxine Winokur in 1925, the only girl in a family of three boys. She wrote her first poem at the age of eight. Her high school English teacher taught her prosody, so that by the time she went to college, "I knew how to scan a line. I knew the names of the feet, and I knew caesura, metonymy, anaphora." But her college instructor, Wallace Stegner, advised her to give up writing poems, and Kumin didn't write for seven years.

By the late '50s, Kumin was married, with three young children, and had begun to write again. When she met Anne Sexton at a local poetry workshop, the two became firm friends and literary allies. Each one installed a dedicated phone on which to call the other. "We were restless mothers with small children, trying to break into the domain of the male Pooh-Bahs," Kumin said.

When Kumin died in 2014, she had published almost twenty books of poetry, as well as essays, novels, short stories and children's books. She had won the Pulitzer Prize for her fourth collection, *Up Country,* and had received numerous other honors and awards. In the early '80s, she was appointed Consultant in Poetry to the Library of Congress (aka the Poet Laureate of the United States), and later, New Hampshire Poet Laureate. The Pooh-Bahs were long since vanquished. As she wrote in one of her poems, "Poetry is like farming. It's a calling. It needs constancy and a long life."

Nurture

From a documentary on marsupials I learn
that a pillowcase makes a fine
substitute pouch for an orphaned kangaroo.

I am drawn to such dramas of animal rescue.
They are warm in the throat. I suffer, the critic proclaims,
from an overabundance of maternal genes.

Bring me your fallen fledgling, your bummer lamb,
lead the abused, the starvelings, into my barn.
Advise the hunted deer to leap into my corn.

And had there been a wild child—
filthy and fierce as a ferret, he is called
in one nineteenth-century account—

a wild child to love, it is safe to assume,
given my fireside inked with paw prints,
there would have been room.

Think of the language we two, same and not-same,
might have constructed from sign,
scratch, grimace, grunt, vowel:

Laughter our first noun, and our long verb, howl.

Christian McEwen: I wanted to start by praising your poem "Six Weeks After" with its "bright wheel of healing colors" and "the strobic lozenges of the goldfinches." And I wondered if you'd speak about the healing that can sometimes come from looking.

Maxine Kumin: There are times when the only resource you have is observation. That poem is about a relatively minor accident. In 1998, I had a much more serious accident. In that case I don't think the healing came very much from looking. It was the presence of my daughter who took leave from her job and actually pushed me into recording every day something about the day before and the day to come. We thought, "Well, we'll get an article out of it." And then, of course, it turned into a book, a memoir titled *Inside the Halo and Beyond: Anatomy of a Recovery*.

But, in "Six Weeks After," the viewer is grateful just to be able to watch the simple progression of the seasons. I'm a keen watcher, especially of birds. And the goldfinches that were mentioned in the poem are once again now just beginning very, very slightly to change color. I always enjoy watching that. And I love watching the dogs, and for forty years I loved watching our horses. I think the things that heal me are the live things around me.

CM: I loved the advice you quoted from Robert Frost in *Still to Mow*: "Look up from the page. Pause between poems. Say something about the next one." And also the section in *The Long Marriage* where you were engaging with your various friends and mentors, some only existent through books. In that book you mention Gorky, and Rukeyser, and Gerard Manley Hopkins, and Marianne Moore, and Rilke, and Carolyn Kizer. I wondered whose work you were reading now and whether any new names had been added to that pantheon.

MK: Well, I do go back to that old pantheon. I still reread Auden with enjoyment. And I still have my little breviary-shaped *A Shropshire Lad* of Housman's that I take everywhere with me. I find now that I'm old-old I have to fight to retain the poems that are in my memory bank. I slip a line here or a word there. So, you know, I keep it with me. My husband and I each work out on what we call the "dreadmill" on the front porch every other day. It's an old-fashioned treadmill, not really designed to hold a book, but you can just barely balance *The Shropshire Lad* there. So, that helps me get through my horrible ten minutes.

Hopkins is very dear to my heart. So is May Swenson, a name that I don't think got mentioned before. Then, of course, I read all my contemporaries.

Those are what a friend calls my "trade books." They come across my desk at a huge rate. So I have to look at them closely.

CM: There's a line in *The Long Marriage* where you refer to yourself as a "girl-child parched with my own small longings." And then in another poem you describe Rukeyser as "the first woman poet I knew who was willing to say the unsaid." And I wondered if you'd be willing to trace the ways in which simply being female had impacted your own writing.

MK: It's interesting that you should ask because I am, at the moment, working on a piece for the Folger Shakespeare Library. They're going to have a program on women writers, and they're bringing out a chapbook on women writers over five centuries. They asked me to contribute something. I couldn't bear to write another article. So I started a sonnet and then another—so far I have nine of them, basically Elizabethan, but I've taken certain liberties and am using quite a lot of slant rhyme. What a challenge! I didn't know what I was letting myself in for.

Part of these "Sonnets Uncorseted" is about Margaret Cavendish, but part is about my own experience. I write about going to college in the '40s, during the Second World War. When I was a student at Radcliffe, I never saw a single woman faculty member, nor a woman instructor, not even a teaching assistant. Certainly no women full professors. All of the faculty were male. Eventually, I earned my master's degree, which was my ticket to a teaching job at Tufts University. Alberta Arthurs—she went on to become director for arts and humanities at the Rockefeller Foundation—and I were the only women in the English Department. And because we were women, we were only considered fit to teach Freshmen Composition to the phys. ed. majors and the dental technicians. And there was no ladies' room. We had to fight to get a ladies' room installed in the building.

To get published was such a struggle at the time. Anne Sexton and I were restless mothers with small children trying to break into the domain of the male Pooh-Bahs. Eventually, one of us sold a poem to *The New Yorker* and the other one sold a poem to *Harper's*. That was the beginning. But it was really inch by inch. One of my "Sonnets Uncorseted" deals with how we were regarded by the male poets. We met their planes. We took them to their gigs. At the last minute, we drove frantically through traffic so that they could catch their planes for the next gig, and they would say to us admiringly, "You drive like a man." And if we wrote a poem that they perchance found worthy, they would say, "You write like a man." It was a long, hard fight. I think that students today have no real concept of what the women's movement consisted of, or how personal the struggle was.

But that's just a one-minute capsule of a long and complicated experience.

CM: In those years what women were you reading? Whose lives were inspiring to you?

MK: Of course we read Friedan and of course we read Simone de Beauvoir, although I hated her relationship with Sartre. The women poets that I read were certainly Muriel Rukeyser, Denise Levertov, and Adrienne Rich. We were pretty much all of an age, though Muriel was quite a bit older. I was slow to come to Bogan, Bishop, and Marianne Moore; Moore felt exotic to me. When I was poet laureate in 1981–82, I had the prerogative of choosing poets to come to give readings each month. Because of the dearth of women poets in my own experience, I was determined to make a broad selection of women representing a variety of ethnic groups and opinions. Two of the most notable were Audre Lorde and Adrienne Rich. Rich had turned down invitations from male laureates in the past, so I was delighted that she accepted mine. The line for entry to her reading stretched around the block and the overflow crowd had to watch on closed circuit television in an extra room.

Let me digress and go back to the luncheon where they announced that I was to be the laureate—at the time the position was called "Poetry Consultant to the Library of Congress." There was a long table around which the press were seated, along with the librarian and the assistant librarian, among others. I was asked how I felt about receiving this honor. Of course I said I was humbled and gratified, especially since I was only the fifth woman to hold the position since its inception in 1936. Daniel Boorstin who was then the chief librarian grabbed the microphone and said, "We don't count." I took it back and said, "But we do!" So the lines were clearly drawn. Today I think the playing field is still not quite level, but we're at a juncture where there are women with important roles in the literary arena. Paula Deitz, for example, is now editor of the *Hudson*

Review. She's doing a wonderful job. Hilda Raz recently retired from being editor of *Prairie Schooner.* She was replaced by a man. But I think we are going to see more and more women moving into senior editorships, and that will be a good thing.

CM: I'm jumping way back. But I wondered if you'd speak a little bit about your childhood reading, and what books you read when you were very small.

MK: When I was very small, I read or had read to me, I can't really distinguish, A. A. Milne and Robert Louis Stevenson. At one point I was given a book that I really, really loved, called *Silver Snaffles,* written by a young British woman named Primrose Cumming. It's about a little girl who becomes friends with an assortment of chatty ponies, and she's invited to walk through the wall of the dark corner of the back stall. She enters this other land where the ponies educate her in good stable management and good horse manners and so on. They have a mock hunt in which I think the foxes hunt the ponies. It's a charming book. I found it again in the stacks at the Library of Congress and sat down on the floor then and there to reread it and wept. I don't know whether I was crying for my lost childhood or with relief that I had finally found the book again. I still felt that it was very well written. At the end of the story the little girl is given a pony of her own, which means she can never go through the dark corner at the back of the stall into that other world again. I thought that was the saddest ending of any book I'd ever known. I also loved all of the books about the Bastable children. I don't know why I got hooked on these British authors, but for years I favored British spellings over American ones and was constantly being marked down by my teachers for spelling "honour," "favour," and so on.

CM: Thank you for telling me about Primrose Cumming.

MK: Had you heard of her before?

CM: No. I'm touched.

MK: There's one copy of the original version of *Silver Snaffles* available through Amazon, for five hundred and some odd dollars.

CM: I'm afraid I'm going to pass on that one, but I'm glad to know it's in existence!

Is there anything you know deeply now as a poet that you wish you'd recognized as a young person? There's a moment in *House, Bridge, Fountain, Gate* where you say, "Well, the firm old fathers are dead and I didn't come to grief. I came to words instead." And I was wondering what it meant to have "come to words" as the young woman you were then.

MK: They say that behind every writer there is an unhappy childhood. So I would start there. I had three older brothers, but I was very isolated as the only girl in the family. Two of my brothers were away at college, and one was in high school while I was still in grammar school. To make matters worse, I spent my junior high and high school years in a different school district, not the one where my brothers had gone. My father didn't approve of private schools, but he relented to the extent of letting me go out of the district to another public school where one paid $200 a year for the privilege. But it meant I had to travel an hour and a half each way by trolley and train. That enhanced my loneliness. I never really made close friends at school, and that made me more of a bookworm. Which was useful in getting me started as a writer.

I had two remarkable teachers in high school to whom I owe a great debt, one a Latin teacher, the other an English teacher. Because I was in the last year of a pilot program called "The Columbia Study Group," we kept the same teachers all the way from eighth grade to graduation. I had five years of Latin. In my senior year, I was translating Ovid's *Metamorphoses* into matching hexameters in English. My English teacher was an extraordinary woman. She taught prosody to willing and unwilling students, but even the unwilling ones shaped up for her. She had a remarkable skill for guiding kids. By the time I went to college I knew how to scan a line, I knew the names of the feet, and I knew caesura, metonymy, anaphora. I didn't know how to write a poem, but I knew how to read and appreciate one.

What appalled me teaching graduate students many, many years later was that a lot of them couldn't tell a trochee from a tree limb! They had no idea how to scan a line. They didn't know blank verse from free verse. I tried to rectify this—to fill in some of those gaps, but I don't think I was very successful. The resistance was enormous; it was as though we lived on different planets. In my view it's important for students and would-be poets to have a good grounding in prosody and in form. Not that I think everyone should write in form. I think people should write exactly what they're comfortable with. But I think if you've never written a sonnet, if you don't know what a villanelle is, if you've never tried to write a sestina, then you're missing out on how to read poetry.

CM: Yes, absolutely. Blessings on that teacher. Do you remember her name?

MK: Yes, I do. Dorothy Lambert.

CM: Thank you.
There's a line in *House, Bridge, Fountain, Gate*—"that a man may be free of his ghosts / he must return to them like a garden." And I wondered if you still felt that was true, or whether your ghosts—your family ghosts especially—have been in some way companions. You might not even want to be free of them.

MK: You never are, anyway. I find, even at my advanced age, that I have ever-stronger memories of my mother and my father, memories that amaze me. You can't really leave them behind. They're there.

CM: And that's a blessing.

MK: I think it is.

CM: You've covered so much poetic territory, especially, of course, your immediate family, the larger family of the animals, the surrounding countryside, as well as climate change, torture. I'm thinking of poems like "Extraordinary Rendition," "What You Do," "The Beheadings." Are there any subjects that still remain unbroached?

MK: I don't think so. I think I've pretty much plowed the garden, and I don't see anything very new coming along. When a project like the Folger Library cropped up—yes, that was interesting to me, and so I plunged in. I'm still quite ferocious about the role of women. That's why I was excited about the prospect of choosing a woman from the seventeenth century and then finding a parallel in my own life. But that's not new.

CM: That must be very satisfying—to feel you've made your garden flourish so thoroughly.

MK: Well, I've been writing for how many years? My first book came out in 1961.

CM: That's wonderful. So, fifty years of poetry.

MK: Yes.

CM: Are you working on prose now too? Or is most of your effort going toward those Folger Library poems?

MK: Last year I had a book of essays published called *The Roots of Things*—that's a line from May Swenson. It's a little paperback potpourri. Many of the essays are about poets, some are about horses, others about the landscape we inhabit. You might want to look that up.

CM: I will. Thank you. There's a poem called "Saga" in *Looking for Luck* that you chose not to reprint in *Where I Live*. And it's a bold poem. It's a little uncomfortable. It says some potent things about class in this country. I wondered if you'd be willing to talk about it a little, and maybe even read it.

MK: I'd be happy to. Where we live there is a classic case of rural poverty nearby, a family reminiscent of the Snopeses. The family has always had a very mysterious relationship with the town. We elect a board of three aldermen. We also have one full-time police officer and a couple of part-timers. When it comes to this household, none of them dares to try to enforce any of the laws. The yard is littered with dead cars and trash of every description and the inside is littered with animal feces. "Saga" is my retelling of this sad story.

[MK reads "Saga."]

CM: Whew. Thank you. You invented the family's name, I imagine?

MK: I did.

CM: Could you talk a bit about your connection with animals? I saw an interview where you spoke about the nonverbal communication that can take place between humans and animals. And I wondered if you'd say more about that.

MK: We've always had at least two dogs. Rescues. When I came home from the rehab hospital after my nearly fatal accident in 1998, they came up on either side of me, and I just sank my hands in their fur. That was a healing moment, not visual, but tactile. Of course, we complain about them all the time. They're such a nuisance. They're always on the wrong side of the door. Our hound dog goes out around 6:15 in the morning and you can hear him *bark, bark, bark, barking* a huge circle around the property. In good weather, he might stay out for two hours barking. If it's cold he might come in after thirty minutes. He used to be just a hellion around the horses. He would try desperately to spook them. Get them to run. To pay attention. Come right up close, barking in their faces. My chestnut gelding would put up with it for a while. Finally he would put his nose down and go right for him. The dog would beat it out of there, dive between the fence boards.

When we first came to the farm, we had a very special, mostly Dalmatian, dog from a local family. He was not a shelter dog. He was incredible with the horses, the only dog we ever had that established a relationship with the horses. He came with us whenever we rode. There was no body of water he couldn't cross. He could keep up no matter how many miles we rode. He formed a very close bond with one of our mares and spent a lot of time lying down in the stall with her. We could always find Gus curled up with Jenny. When she foaled she wouldn't let him in her stall anymore. And he was the epitome of a hangdog. *What did I do? Why is she rejecting me?* I remember that very well.

We do have a problem with porcupines. I haven't personally shot one, but I admit I have encouraged others to come and shoot them. We had a caretaker who was a former state cop and owned a lot of guns. I think he killed seven porkies in one year, which sounds cruel, but porcupines and dogs just do not go together. We took in one little part-Dachshund that my horse vet brought to us. Four hundred and fifty dollars later we gave her back. I cannot tell you how many times we had to trot off to the vet to have quills removed from her snout. Not just one or two, but fifty at a time. We have moose that like our woods pond. It's fun to see their tracks across the shallows. Their scat is very identifiable. We also have deer, fox, coyote, raccoon, and bear.

CM: I so much enjoyed your poem "Recycling," from *Looking for Luck*. You provide the most amazing information and out of it comes something beautiful, something shapely. And it made me curious about your reading habits. Whether you listen to NPR or read *Harper's*. I wondered where you gathered this information.

MK: I'm an omnivorous reader, of magazines, literary journals, essays, novels. The information just comes.

CM: Just comes. And you receive it and make order out of it. Thank you for that work, the work of making those things into poetry. I wanted to ask if you'd read, perhaps, some of those early poems. I very much enjoyed, for example, that early poem "Widow" and then some later poems, like the pantoum "What You Do." Would you do that?

MK: Sure.

CM: In fact, if you wouldn't mind reading both "Widow" and "Hearth."

MK: I'd forgotten this poem.

CM: It's very beautifully put together.

MK: You know, "Widow" sat in my bone pile of discarded poems for several years. I couldn't complete it. And then, one of those days I was going through the discards, up it came and the ending just wrote itself.

CM: That's a good story.

[MK reads "Widow."]

MK: I know where I stopped.

CM: Where did you stop?

MK: "I stuff the noisy door." And then years later the rest just came. I like to think you earn it eventually.

Oh, I don't like this poem "Hearth." It's a sexist poem now. At the time that I wrote it, of course, I didn't realize that.

CM: Let's let it go. Let's read "What You Do."

MK: Just a word about these torture poems: Dick Wilbur, who is a dear friend of mine, criticized these. He didn't think that politics and poetry belong together. Which, of course, I dispute. I feel very strongly that they do, and that we have to bear witness. I didn't set out to write a group of torture poems. Truly, these were wrung from me. And now, I've just got four more, all sonnets. "The Pre-trial Confinement of Bradley Manning" is the most recent one. I'm outraged by these things. And then I can't let them go.

[MK reads "What You Do."]

CM: Wow. It's an extraordinary poem.

MK: But you see, I had to pound it into form or I couldn't write it. Thank you, Dorothy Lambert! But I don't always write in form.

CM: It gives you the pincers to hold the hot coal, I guess.

MK: I really like that image. It's as I say to students all the time—it's much easier to work in form because here's your outline. You've got fourteen lines. You've got a rhyme scheme. Now all you have to do is pour in the lines.

CM: Congratulations. That's an extraordinary set of poems. I guess there is a question connecting to that, which is—what tends to come first for you? Is it the subject matter? Is it the form? Does that change?

MK: It's almost always the subject matter. I might get started on a poem—not necessarily one of these—and the form simply announces itself early on. And then I just follow and do what I'm told. Other times a phrase or a pleasing alliteration gets stuck in my head and may work itself out as a poem.

CM: I'm assuming that if it hadn't been for modern technology, that terrible accident—you wouldn't have made it through.

MK: I shouldn't have made it. It was a miracle that I made it.

The accident happened at a carriage-driving clinic. We had a group called "The Wheelrunners," and we met along with our horses once a month in Vermont. My horse spooked. I won't go into all the details. But one of my driving buddies was there that day, because her mare was pregnant, and she came just to watch. She happened to be an emergency room nurse, and she ran out onto the field and didn't let anyone move me. If they had, I wouldn't be talking to you today. So I was airlifted to Dartmouth-Hitchcock hospital. I had broken my neck in two places. I was in a halo for three months. A halo is an unspeakable device fastened to the skull with four screws. It was truly terrible. My daughter Judith came from overseas and stayed for a month. She urged me to tell the story, so I dictated a little bit to her every day and she kept it on her laptop. By the time she had to go back to work, we saw that it was going to be a book. My wonderful editor at Norton, Carol Houck Smith, just drove me and drove me. She kept saying, "Make it more intimate! Put conversation in it! Put dialogue in it! Tell more! You're too reticent!" She yanked that book out of me. When I finally turned in the manuscript, I said to her, "Here it is, Carol, your goddamn novel."

CM: Congratulations. I love that your daughter pushed you to record a little more each day. Such a simple and powerful tactic.

MK: And looking back on it in, she agrees that she thought it was the only thing that might pull me through. I was really depressed, needless to say.

CM: I'm interested in the question of technology, as something that saved you and that is at the same time utterly aggravating. The new communication technologies create distraction over and over again. And I wondered what you made of cell phones and computers and BlackBerries.

MK: Well, I was slow to get on a computer, but I did finally. My son is very adept and he set me up with a Mac. I do write on the computer now, and I've learned to keep all my drafts and to number them, and call them up every time I sit down. I have email because everything operates by email. My right hand is very bad, so it would be hard for me if I couldn't use email to answer letters. I started out on an old Remington typewriter that had belonged to one of my brothers. I covered the keys with adhesive tape to teach myself how to type. And then eventually I acquired a used IBM Selectric. It had a correcting key, which was wonderful. After that, I moved on to a Macintosh computer. I don't do anything but write on it. It has all these other capabilities that I don't explore. I do have a cell phone. But I'm pretty primitive. One has to go along to some extent. The whole social networking business pretty much horrifies me.

CM: Say more.

MK: I find that all this texting and tweeting is making people semi-literate. They can't write a proper sentence. They don't know how to spell. They don't understand grammar. Grammar is hardly taught anymore. Doctors ask patients to "lay down." It took me a long time to accept the salutation on emails—"Hi so-and-so" without a comma. "Hi Joe." But I do it now like everyone else. And I also write without apostrophes: "havent" and "shouldnt" and so on. It's as though we're in a great hurry. I don't understand where we're going in such a hurry.

CM: I've been thinking a lot about slowness in the past few years, the pleasures of slowness. And the use of slowness as the basis for creativity, how anything you care about, you need to do with some nimbus of slowness around you. Perhaps you could say just a bit more about speed and slowness in your own life.

MK: Because we're quite old now, our lives are a lot more circumscribed than they once were. We no longer travel. I used to teach in Florida in the winter. For many years, we drove down and drove back. We can't do that anymore. So we have slowed down a lot. Victor [MK's husband] is a great reader. We have such different tastes. He devours biography and political science and contemporary affairs. I read novels voraciously; I'm always in the middle of a novel. But I read everything else, too.

I sit at the computer for hours. I pick away at poems. I usually have a couple of things going at a time. Don Hall is a good friend and we exchange worksheets. We have to do it by fax because Don is a Luddite. He won't have a computer in the house. But he has a dedicated fax machine that he's very proud of.

My study is on the ground floor of our old house and it overlooks what we call the sheep pen even though we no longer raise sheep. I'm just surrounded by greenery on three sides. When the snow melts, we begin to walk—Victor and I have always taken the dogs along a certain route. We go out through the bottom pastures and then uphill to the woods road, and then over to the vegetable garden and the pond, and farther uphill to the driving ring, and through the upper pasture and then on down. It's about a thirty-five minute walk. I hope we'll both continue to be able to do that. When it's cold out we walk in the warmest part of the day, and the rest of the time I'm at my desk.

CM: It sounds like a good life to me.

MK: I like it.

CM: I especially loved your lines in "Nurture": "Nothing too small to remember, nothing too slight to stand in awe of." And again, "Poetry is like farming. It's a calling. It needs constancy and long life." We've been talking about this obliquely—but I wondered if you'd talk more directly about the pleasures, the terrors, the responsibilities of that "long life."

MK: Terrors, yes, because there is the overwhelming knowledge that one of us is going to die first. We don't talk about it very much. We just know it's there. The pleasures of a long life are mixed, because I have a lot of arthritis now. It's hard for me to get around. That's only going to go in one direction. But it's nice to be able to look back over all those good years together. And all of the adventures we've had. You know, Victor and I were both competitive trail riders for about twelve years. We used to get a young person to live in for the summer, because we were gone almost every weekend on those rides. Over the years we bred and raised ten of our own horses. The thing I miss most in my life is having a foal in the spring. I always used to say, "A foal in the oven shortens the winter." It's such a wonderful thing to look forward to.

We raised some absolutely wonderful horses.

GWYNETH LEWIS

Interviewed February 11, 2009

Gwyneth Lewis was born in 1959, into a Welsh-speaking family in Cardiff. As a child, she was given a traditional poetic education and won numerous prizes. "The pressure was to produce, to be creative, but in a Welsh way, a Welsh-speaking way."

At eighteen, Lewis moved to England to study at Girton College, Cambridge. The transition wasn't easy. "Cambridge is pretty crushing if you're not a confident person. And why would women from the cultural margins be confident?" But after she graduated (with a double first in English literature) she moved again, this time to the States, to study at Harvard and Columbia. "Coming to the States really saved my life creatively," she says. "I don't think I'd be a writer if I hadn't come here."

In the mid '80s Lewis returned home to the U.K. She has since published eight books of poetry, as well as several non-fiction books; she also writes plays and libretti. She is now an award-winning poet in both English and Welsh. In 2005, she was appointed National Poet of Wales. Among her many honors are the Society of Authors Cholmondeley Award for a distinguished body of work, and the Mary Amelia Cummins Harvey Visiting Fellowship at her old alma mater, Girton College. She won the Crown at the Welsh National Eisteddfod in 2012.

from Chaotic Angels

The smallest angel of which we're aware
is a 'spinning nothing.' Angel of dust,
angel of stem cells, of pollen grains,
angel of branches which divide to a blur
as they're ready to bud, becoming more
than their sum was even an hour before.
Angel of dog smells, angel of stairs,

of gardening, marriage. Cherubim
of rotting rubbish, of seeing far,
of rain's paste diamonds after a shower.
Radiation angels, angels of mud,
angels of slowing and of changing gear,
angels of roundabouts, and of being here
all say: 'You were made for this—prayer.'

Christian McEwen: I read that you were born in Cardiff. Does that mean you grew up in Wales?

Gwyneth Lewis: Yes. I grew up in Cardiff in a Welsh-speaking family, but Cardiff is predominantly English-speaking, so we were at odds with the environment from the beginning. But you know, it worked quite well. I see arguments these days about multilingualism in schools in the U.K. because of immigration, and I think, well, what's the big deal? You know to speak one language at home and another at school, I don't see that it's anything but an enrichment, given that the children are given the appropriate support at home—that's the caveat. It seems to me just wonderful to have access to two cultures through language.

CM: So your mother was the Welsh speaker and your father the English, as in the poem "Mother Tongue"?

GL: No, no. The poem is fictional. I made the father an English speaker to exaggerate the contrast. No, both parents are Welsh speakers. But it is true that I learned English at my father's knee, when my mother was in hospital having my sister, so that part of the poem is true.

CM: And did you speak Welsh in school all those years?

GL: Yes. I was part of the Welsh language education movement, so I had my education in Welsh right up to the age of eighteen, and then went to university—Cambridge, which was very strange. Suddenly, instead of having to translate French into Welsh, I had to translate it into English, which proved my French was good, but my English wasn't always as elastic as it might be, even though I was technically bilingual and had been studying English in English for a long time. But there was very little in my life that required speaking English before I went to university, so that was a big change.

CM: Boy, I can imagine.

GL: I remember reading Eva Hoffman's wonderful book *Lost in Translation,* and being so grateful that somebody had thought through the implications of changing from one culture to another. It's a beautiful book, a very important book.

CM: Have there been other poets or writers who've engaged with the issue of bilingualism or multilingualism in ways that have been useful to you?

GL: No, I think I felt very lonely in that way, because people kept on telling me it was impossible to write in Welsh, and impossible, politically, to write in English if you were Welsh-speaking, so I felt hedged around by prohibitions, which is not a good frame of mind to start working creatively, because you need the opposite, a generous permissiveness, if you're going to get anything done creatively. What encouraged me most was coming to the United States as a graduate student. I lived here for three years, and that gave me the neutral cultural space to have the courage to experiment, and also I had people like Derek Walcott saying, "You've got to start in English. You can do it. It's not an act of betrayal," and people like Joseph Brodsky saying, "Gwyn, you're lucky to have the English language; I envy you," and that clarified issues for me. I don't think anything else—anything less—would have pushed me. Simply because cultural loyalties are complex. So I think coming to the U.S. really saved my life creatively. I don't think I would be a writer if I hadn't come here.

CM: That's impressive. I hadn't realized—I saw your poem to Joseph Brodsky, which I thought was a beautiful memorial poem, and I wondered where he'd entered your life. So was that at Harvard?

GL: No, I got to know Seamus Heaney at Harvard, and went to his workshop, and that was great, and then by a series of accidents I ended up in the Creative Writing Division—the Graduate Writing Division in Columbia University. I shouldn't have been there at all. I only managed to get enrolled there because I started talking to the administrator in passing. It was a great period of poetry-teaching there: we had Derek Walcott, Joseph Brodsky, and C. K. Williams teaching. I owe Joseph Brodsky a lot. He was very kind to me, because, I think, he understood what it was to be abroad, alone; he had been in the same situation. Not everybody else understood that it was quite rough. That was a tremendous education. To have had nothing, and then that, was amazing.

CM: So what was the "nothing"? I was wondering about your relationship with poetry as a child in Wales and then at Cambridge, having done a parallel journey myself from Scotland to England; then I also went to Cambridge. I didn't find Cambridge particularly welcoming for the creative writer. I wondered how that was for you.

GL. That was the nothing. In fact, worse than nothing. Cambridge is pretty crushing if you're not a confident person. And why would women from the cultural margins be confident? I certainly wasn't. Although I was not willing to be put down because of where I came from. I mean I did have a kind of egalitarian confidence, which was not disappointed in Cambridge, but the whole idea of the Canon, of the Greats: you're reading Milton, Shakespeare, all these people, and I think the overriding feeling is of being crushed, creatively. But it does teach you to be a very good reader, which is important. And it also teaches you not to be afraid to launch into anything. I read an enormous amount—almost all of Melville, for example. I did the

American paper for the English tripos, and I read the mad bits of Melville and an awful lot else beside of American literature, so I think while it didn't help the production of creative work, it gave me the critical equipment to not be daunted by anything. I think that's more than half the battle.

Now as for the Welsh background, that was very different. In fact, the pressure was the other way. The pressure was to produce, to be creative, but in a Welsh way, a Welsh-speaking way. And being a slightly perverse person, I bridle at pressures one way or another, and I did have a good poetic education. I mean there is a Welsh-language strict meter system of consonantal correspondence. It's like alliteration, it's a bit like the Anglo-Saxon meters in *Beowulf,* for example, but far more strict, and it also adds rhyme as part of the scheme. I was taught how to do that. I had a teacher who used to teach me it in break-time, and this was a great thing to learn, the craft side of poetry, so I appreciate that in the upbringing. And also the sense that poetry was nothing special; it didn't make you a special person, it was a social activity. I think that gives me a pragmatism in relation to poems that I value.

CM: So were you recognized as a child-poet, or a child who could become a poet, from fairly early on?

GL: Yes. I found that rather embarrassing. But because of Wales's system of competitions, run from the schools and the National Youth Movement, I kept on winning prizes. I wasn't too pleased about that: it makes you visible in a way you don't want to be as a teenager, but I also recognized, pretty early, that my job was to write as best I could, and toward the end of my school days I did rebel against that, because I found it too painful to be so visible; so I stopped writing. That led to a silence for a long time. Do I regret it? No, but I paid a price for it. Periods of not writing for me have been pretty disastrous.

CM: When you went up to Cambridge then, did you come as "the Welsh girl poet," or was that very private and invisible?

GL: I think it was totally invisible. I remember driving up to Cambridge to the interview. My father drove me up, four and a half hours from Cardiff. I always speak Welsh to my father, and he said, "No I think we'd better start speaking English, so that you can have a practice." So I spoke English all the way up with my father, Welsh all the way back! And it was never an impediment, but I was aware of switching codes, and switching modes— but I was interested in poetry all the way through, and heard poets read, and I always knew, it was always nagging me that *I must start again*, but I hadn't realized how much it was a matter of life and death for me. Until later. And once you've lost so much ground, it takes a long, long time to get it back. But I think in some ways it was a wise thing to have stopped then. Because it protected me from being crushed by Cambridge clever intellectual criticism, which people did very well. I think Elizabeth Jennings writes about this, doesn't she, in her autobiography? Have you read it?

CM: I haven't.

GL: I read some quotes by her, saying what a devastating period it was for her to be in Cambridge as a female poet. When I read that, I thought, "Oh, that's great, it wasn't just me."

CM: What years were you there?

GL: '78 to '82.

CM: And what years were you in the States?

GL: I went in '82 and stayed till '85. I thought of staying on. I was looking into the matter, but was persuaded not to. . . . What persuaded me was that if I had stayed I would have become an American poet. I felt that I needed to be closer to my own rhythms at home. I don't know if that was right. Because I admire American poetry a lot. But the rhythm is different, and I think perhaps you do a violence to your own brain waves by taking another rhythm.

CM: So essentially you were a Welsh poet as a young person, and then you became an English-writing poet in the States, and after that you were able to shift back and forth between or to braid the two?

GL: No: I started writing in Welsh in the States. It was the only thing I knew how to do. And the way I got into Columbia was odd. Somebody had sent me to say hello to a friend of his, somebody I'd stayed with on the West Coast, and I was waiting to convey my greetings to the mutual friend, and the administrator of the program said to me—I was saying I was a poet and so on—"I don't know who you are, but I think you should be in this program, not in the English Department. Give me some poems and I'll show the chair them over the weekend."

Well, I didn't have any poems! So I rushed home, wrote a few, translated them in time, and got into the program on the strength of those. I wasn't able to sit in the workshops, because they weren't able to see how they could cope with the translations, but I got to do the seminars, which was perfect for me, because I didn't have the confidence to sit in a workshop. So, gradually I would write more in Welsh, more in Welsh, translate—and then there was a breakthrough poem. I took my courage in both hands and wrote a long English poem, a very gloomy English poem! That set me on my way. The heavens didn't fall in, and I thought, maybe I could survive, writing in English.

So what I've allowed myself to do is to not make any prohibitions but to say, "Right, I can write in both. I don't know anybody else who does, but I will." Since then, it's been all right, creatively. I sometimes get mixed up, and rhyme between languages, but on the whole it's an economy that works for me, creatively, and I have noticed that younger Welsh poets are writing more in English. I think they maybe let me go over the top first and see what the reaction was.

CM: Congratulations! That's a wonderful story. "I'll just go home and write a few poems and that will get me into the program."

GL: Well, terror is a great spur. I knew it was one of the pivotal points. A make-or-break-your-whole-life point, that. Sometimes you know. So it had to be done. One of the poems, I remember, was about the Alamogordo Sands, in Nevada. I don't know where that poem is now, but a strange thing to write about. The white sands.

CM: Wow! Speak a little more about Joseph Brodsky, because clearly he was so important. What was it that he gave you?

GL: I don't believe I knew who he was, first of all. The first thing that struck me was the relief of finding somebody for whom poetry was just as important—I had always felt myself a bit of a freak. To find somebody of his stature who took it seriously, in fact more seriously, was a huge relief. And the intelligence of the man! If you have been bright, well, you pay a price for it. But suddenly to be in company where that was prized, and in fact, if you could answer back, that it was enjoyed, was a tremendous boost for me. I think he's simply the most intelligent man I've ever met. His intelligence was extraordinary. You can see it in the poems, but even in his jokes and things. And his sense of poetic tradition. That was a tremendous addition for me because I had felt very lonely as a poet, very idiosyncratic. Whereas he taught us to put ourselves in relation to Auden, to Frost, and behind Brodsky himself was Akhmatova, so to realize that you weren't on your own with the spoken word, this was a revelation for me. So I've had a sense of poetry as a communal activity ever since. And I think those are the three things that were life-changing for me, and have colored my attitude to poetry ever since. And he was just tremendously genial; he treated me like some kind of hopeless niece. And that I really appreciated, because New York in the '80s was a very tough place. It was quite dangerous, and it was a rough place to be on your own, abroad, because people were struggling enough with their own lives, there wasn't much of the milk of human kindness around. So I really appreciated that. And that it would come from him of all people, I didn't expect.

CM: You had an aunt out in Illinois. Were you able to visit her?

GL: Yes, I did. Yes. I used to go for Christmas. I had been going to see her since I was sixteen. I spent a summer with her and so every chance I got I would go and visit. And in fact when I drove across the States, I'd call by, and I spent a lot of time there over the years.

CM: I was struck as I was reading by some of the earlier poems, where you had words like "sassafras" and "hickory" and "sumac" and such—and I thought, "This is an American vocabulary; where was it learned?"

GL: Largely in Illinois! Because I love plants and I like to know the names of birds and things. So, traveling's always a vocabulary adventure for a poet. *What is that thing there?* Oh, *sassafras,* I like that. So I'm an inveterate buyer of reference books and *The Insects of the Central States of America.* I've got a lot of that kind of a book. Because you need to know in detail what things are. And you learn that from other people who love the birds, or the plants.

CM: Yeah. So you came back to Britain fueled with Brodsky and Seamus Heaney and C. K. Williams and the rest, and you became a television producer in Cardiff?

GL: Yes, not straight away. I went to Oxford then, and came across the poets there. Because I'd had a big scene. And I got lost for a while, doing a doctorate, which probably was a mistake. But it was a transition period between America and making my own way. And I then started writing seriously, and started sending work to poetry magazines. People started knowing my name, and that was really where I started. It's very humbling, poetry, because it takes a long, long time to get any momentum going. I remember when I was in the States, trying to learn to write as an adult as opposed to as a child, having a stomachache, a knot in my stomach. Because if you're built to need this outlet, if you're not expressing yourself as well as you could, simply because you're not skillful enough, or you don't know enough about yourself emotionally—it's very painful. I still had that knot in my stomach in Oxford, but it was getting better, and then when I went back eventually to Cardiff, to Wales, that was a tremendous liberation; I was back on familiar ground. I felt as if I came back to myself. I was able to really start enjoying writing again.

CM: That's a good story: often people have the enthusiasm and enterprise of the States, and then they come back to Britain, and something gets squashed because of a certain unwelcome, and you made your way through that. . . .

GL: You're right about the lack of welcome in England. One of the things I love about the States is the way many people are committed to self improvement. This takes the form of a willingness to self-educate, which I find really admirable. Americans don't regard the self as a finished product. The English are too embarrassed to do this openly, and they should. They do covertly, but there's an embarrassment about it. Embarrassment is very paralyzing; it's a waste of time and effort, emotionally. The lack of that in the U.S. I really enjoy. Whereas in Wales, if you're a poet, well, it's no big deal. I mean, *so?* It's a very matter-of-fact thing. I like that.

In fact, a couple of years ago, when I had been doing things in public as a national poet in Wales, I remember going on a train the day after opening the new Senate building. A lady came up to me, and she said, "Are you the poet?" I said, "Yes." "Oh! Oh, I liked the poem." "Oh," I said, "thank you." But I like that, "Are you the poet?" Just a normal conversation. Things are slightly different in England. I think most poets tend to go incognito about their business every day, so there's a slightly different color in the attitude toward the role of the poet in all three countries. I think perhaps England is the most hostile, although there is a tremendous amount of good writing going on at the moment in Britain.

CM: Who, in Britain do you especially admire?

GL: Well, there are many. There's a whole generation of good writers—and better than good. People like Sean O'Brien, Kathleen Jamie, Alice Oswald, John Burnside, Michael Roberts, Don Paterson, oh, there are many good poets. I could go on. . . .

In the '80s, I felt that American writing was stronger than British writing, and I think at the moment it's slightly the reverse. It doesn't matter. It just means that there's a depth of talent that arranges it differently from time to time. It's important that you come across good poetry to raise one's own game. It's not a comfortable feeling. But if you're interested in writing the best you can, you have to be prepared to reckon with the best in the field. And that requires humility.

CM: Do you have poet friends with whom you trade work, or is it rather that you meet them through their books?

GL: I know my contemporaries through their books. I do have friends who are poets. But the only person I show poems to is Les Murray. I trust his opinion, for my work. I met him at a festival where he was running a master class, and we just understood each other. He has been a tremendous help to me. Like him, I suffer from depression, and see myself as a religious poet. He's quite an extraordinary figure, and has had to come to terms with that himself. And I think that I'm not a person who's always easy for people to cope with. Being sensitive, I feel it tremendously. So he's been a great ally in that. Because you don't just harden yourself to it. You have to find your way around in different ways that don't knock the edge off your sympathies.

CM: What do you think it is that makes people find you hard? Is it the work, the subject matter, or the Welsh tradition?

GL: I think within the Welsh tradition I'm anomalous. You always want to fit into your home background; I'm old enough to have made my peace with the fact that I don't. This doesn't mean that you're not of value. I think being a woman, seeing through some things, not being a joiner of groups, are all essential things to me. But it's painful socially. I can see, now that I'm older, that people also value that. Fitting in is not the main thing; the main thing is to tell the truth. Oddly enough, suffering from depression and having written a book about it has helped me very much, because I went out on a limb to do that. It's not something that one feels proud of, but the reaction has been so great. So many people have said, "I'm so glad you wrote that book, thank you." It's not a question of artistic pride; it's a question of human solidarity. You think, "Ah, I'm not alone," even though I might feel like it. That has had a knock-on effect on how I feel about my poetry. I don't feel so lonely as I did.

CM: Yeah, I was going to ask you about the difference between working in prose in a very open way and working in a more crafted way in poetry, and also, in relation to Britain, "coming out" as somebody who suffers with depression. Again, the culture is, I think, in some ways more open to those stories now, but on the other hand, there is that same old British embarrassment. It's interesting to hear that people in general have just been very welcoming.

GL: They have. Some say to me, and these are not usually the people who suffer from depression themselves, "Oh, you're so brave to take on the stigma of mental health." And I'm thinking, "I don't really feel a stigma! What stigma?" And "brave" means they don't quite think you're brave, more like "foolish." I tend not to pay much attention to that, because I think these are not people who've suffered from the illness. I had written in poetry in code up till then, and been very unprepared to spill my beans in public. I rather blew that with *Sunbathing in the Rain* by writing a very personal book, and also *Two In a Boat,* afterwards, which was about a sailing voyage with my husband and had a lot of very intimate material in it. But even though they are revealing books, they are still crafted narratives, and there's an enormous amount of crafted narrative; they're not splurges. With the depression book, I was very careful to use personal material only as it reflected on depression. I didn't want to write a book against all the people who'd hurt me ever: that wasn't the point. The point was my personal history was only of interest insofar as it helped illuminate the condition of depression. So I was very disciplined about that. Similarly with the second book as well. So I still have a fair amount of unexplored, unrevealed territory.

CM: And did you find it satisfying to write those stories in prose, to face that material in that way? Was it a different experience from writing in poetry?

GL: Yes, it is. I enjoy prose very much. It's like a holiday from poetry. And I do enjoy telling a story. I used to work in television in the BBC, and making documentaries was what I ended up doing, and it's very much the same skill, in a different medium. But if you're in a poem, writing overtly about your own personal history brings up difficult issues of what you have a right to say about other people. And you're in difficult terrain, where you've been arguing with other people who are still in your life. You have to remember I come from a small community, I have to live in that community; but on the other hand, part of defeating depression is saying what you have to say and saying what you feel. I had to balance the right to my own narrative with what I felt would have been wrong to reveal about other people without their permission. So that was awkward.

The situation with the boat book was different in that, without blowing the story, I had a very delicate negotiating job to do there with regards to my husband, who is portrayed in the book in one way. But then you find that there's a very good reason why he was behaving like that. So I had to think about how I was going to do justice to him, and justice to myself, and still stay married, which we are.

CM: Well, clearly! And so it worked. Did you find that having written the prose books affected your poems in any way? Did you find that they wanted to become less formal, or changed in any formal fashion?

GL: No. I think they have their own trajectory. In fact, for a period, after doing the prose, I went even more formal. I've just finished a long poem, an epic poem, that rhymes. I think it's in five-line stanzas, based on François Villon's measure. So I went even more formal, though I'm playing a bit more now with a slightly looser form. Prose and poetry are two rivers that run in different valleys.

CM: Nice image. I'm very struck by your technical skill and it's a joy to see someone who can handle a sestina, terza rima, villanelle, whatever, so well, and so lightly. There's no sense of, "Now I'm going to pull out the heavy weights. . . ." Your brain has long ago learned how to write in those forms.

GL: I've done a lot of sonnets. At one point I was doing a—this sounds bizarre, but I did—very long poem in Welsh, a sequence of sonnets about the history of the Philippine Islands, and my mother was saying, "Oh, you're turning out sonnets like sausages!" I've done a lot of sausage-making with sonnets. Yeah.

CM: How do your parents react to their daughter as the poet? Do they enjoy it? Do they find it strange?

GL: I think they find it strange. They don't really understand why I had to do it. By now they are used to the idea. But they were worried and mystified before. It's all very well to do it in an amateur way at school, but to then put yourself in danger, in poverty, and go abroad to study—that worried them, and I can see why. I don't know if they even read what I write, properly, anymore. My stepchildren are not in the least interested in poetry or in my books. So, family life carries on, no matter what. It's quite good in a way; it's not a big deal.

CM: You get a certain privacy. You can actually write what you want, because you can assume they won't necessarily read it.

GL: Yes. I recently wrote a poem about my stepgrandson, and I showed it to his parents, and they were thrilled. I didn't expect that. So they're going to frame it, and put it up in his bedroom. That pleases me enormously because it seems to me the use of poetry is to celebrate a child or . . . I like it that people take a joy in it personally, you know.

But I think the term "professional poet" is a contradiction in terms. I've heard Seamus Heaney say that. But there are ambitions that you get, as a poet. You think, "Artistically, I must try an epic." Or "I must try—" or "Now I must try a long line." I've tried it; I'm no good at it. You want to try everything out. It's an almost impersonal imperative. It's not really to do with "Oh, I must express my love for my dog." You see it more in technical terms, like "I would like to write something of this kind of length, with that kind of feel." And then the personal material goes into that. So, it's a wonderful way of getting away from the boredom of your own ego.

CM: So you're inspired as much by the joy of a new form as you are by, "I need to write about that tree outside my window."

GL: Oh, it's really all about the form, I'd say.

CM: I wanted to ask, listening to you read the poems about knitting and the one about St. Paul's, how it was to be given a poetry commission and being asked to "fill it." Was it a pleasure and a challenge, or is it a little uneasy sometimes?

GL: I love it! It doesn't bother me in the least—in the Welsh Eisteddfod competitions [an annual assembly of Welsh musicians and poets], what happens is they'll say, "Right, we want a two hundred word poem on the subject, say, of fire." Now this may seem draconian, but actually you learn very quickly if you say, "Now, OK, what can I make? How can I make that subject my own?" It leaves you fearless. So I'm not daunted by that. I welcome it as an occasion to write.

Some commissions are more worrying than others. I was commissioned once by a trade union to do a poem about the history of work from the earliest times to the present day, and that proved a bit challenging. But then I just thought, "Oh, I'll set it in an industrial museum, and I'll pretend to be a curator," so I looked from the earliest remnants of work to the digital revolution; that made sense of the whole thing. I have noticed that these public poems, these commissioned poems, don't always last very long. They're poems of the occasion. It's important to realize that they're not going to have a long shelf life.

CM: For you or for other people?

GL: For readers, I think. They tend to get clotted at the top, pretty quickly, even though they may serve the occasion very well.

CM: Which of your poems have readers returned to and praised to you over and over? Are there some that seem to be specially loved?

GL: The knitting poems. It can't just be the popularity of knitting. I think it must be people's memories of knitting when they were children. There are certain poems I get asked for. And there's no legislating for it. I'm having my poems translated into Dutch at the moment; I didn't know I had an opinion about this, but there were certain poems they had left out, and I thought, "No, this gets read a lot, that gets read a lot, they should be in." And very often they're the poems about language issues, a subject I tackled in order to get rid of it. But those are the ones that people want me to read all the time. That's interesting.

CM: You said earlier that you think of yourself as a religious poet. What religion were you raised with and where do you stand now with that?

GL: I was brought up Presbyterian, Methodist, and we went to church twice on a Sunday, a very Welsh type of upbringing. You know, white tights and velvet dresses—*waugh!* Then I went through the usual period of not being interested, in fact being hostile to it. And then I've come back over the years, have experimented with Zen meditation, which taught me a huge amount. I think it's an immensely useful tool to anybody who suffers from depression; it's a life skill. But I'm now in the Episcopalian church in Wales. I suppose I'm "high" rather than "low," which means I like bells and smells and kneeling and crossing myself, and I'm very happy there. I don't know if I'll stay. I guess I will. It partly depends on how politics in the church work out. But that suits me because I love the liturgy and the idea of not speaking words that are personal, but being part of a collective act of linguistic worship that is set down, and is poetic, appeals to me enormously. Much more so than personal witness in the more Presbyterian or fundamental or evangelical churches. That's not what I find helpful, partly, I think, because it goes with my own concept of poetry as impersonal. Even though you're using personal material, part of the transformation of poetry is to make that into something else, which is of interest to everybody, not just to yourself, one hopes.

CM: Yes. I was admiring that in your work yesterday. Your poetry is not confessional poetry in Robert Lowell terms. It is very deft, very formed, very delicately poised, and there's a certain distance from the writer. . . . .

GL: Well, I do worry a lot about it. Although, of course, Robert Lowell makes his experience universal in a different way. A confessional poet would be one about whom you'd think, "OK, take it to your therapist." That's the bad confessional side. But what can we use other than our own experiences?

CM: The other thing I loved that you said yesterday was that poetry isn't a pastel thing. It's red and black, and I was thinking of the Paleolithic caves and how they were always painted in red and black.

GL: Also, I was very aware that there was a resonance to saying it in Smith that isn't usually there. That it was perhaps an obvious thing to say in the shadow of Sylvia Plath attending here. I felt strange saying that. Here of course it's obvious. In other places, people, I think, are more sentimental about poetry.

CM: Yes. But there was a gratitude for your saying it. I don't think it was familiar enough to be boring. I think it was, "Yes! We agree with you, we're on the same page as you."

GL: Oh, poetry is not to be fooled with. It really isn't. I don't know if I read the part where it says, "unwritten poems are a force to be feared," but I have found it so in my own life. I'm more afraid of not having written a poem than of the reception of anything. The worst thing would be not to have written it.

CM: That gives you tremendous courage, in the sense of forever pushing forward to find it—

GL: Pushing. Yes, pushing. That's right. Because I'm so frightened of that knot in my stomach. I never want to go back. I may not have a choice, but, if it's down to any conscious act of mine, I would resist it. I was very grateful to Louise Glück; she came and taught a seminar at Columbia many years ago, and she was saying how she was tussling with despair, and that the difficulty was how to stay alive between poems. Nobody, at that time, ever spoke about that kind of issue. I was so glad that she did. I thought, "Oh, oh yes! I know that." And just the feeling that somebody else was going through it, somebody successful, gave me a lot of hope. In fact I saw her recently and was able to thank her for that. The tendency is to say, "Oh yes, it's easy." A more muscular way of saying, "Oh yes, it's easy." No, it's not like that. If you're doing it properly, you pay a price.

CM: It's been a price worth paying.

GL: Not too high, I hope.

CM: For you, I mean.

GL: Not at all.

W. S. MERWIN

Interviewed May 1, 2013

W. S. Merwin was born in New York City in 1927, the son of a Presbyterian minister. "He wasn't much good as a father," Merwin said, years later. "He wasn't much good as a minister." But there was a way he read the psalms or the Prophets or the Acts of the *New Testament* that made the child Merwin sit up straight. By the age of four, he already knew that he wanted to be a poet.

Merwin attended Princeton University on a scholarship, and later worked as a private tutor in Europe, becoming a prolific translator of Latin, French, Spanish, and Portuguese, as well as Russian, Japanese, and Sanskrit. He published more than fifty books over the course of a long career, and has twice won the Pulitzer Prize for poetry. Other awards include the Lannan Lifetime Achievement Award, the Bollingen Award, and the Ruth Lilly Prize, as well as the Golden Wreath of the Struga Poetry Evenings and fellowships from the Rockefeller and Guggenheim foundations. In 2010, he was appointed poet laureate of the United States.

As a small boy, Merwin had dreamed of living in the woods surrounded by tall trees. In 1976, he moved to Hawaii to study Zen. He and his wife Paula bought a piece of land on the northeast coast of Maui, surrounded by acres of tropical forest. "Now, in Hawaii, we live with trees all around us. We look out from every side of the house straight into trees. It's just wonderful to me," he says. "It's what I've always wanted."

Place

On the last day of the world
I would want to plant a tree

what for
not for the fruit

the tree that bears the fruit
is not the one that was planted

I want the tree that stands
in the earth for the first time

with the sun already
going down

and the water
touching its roots

in the earth full of the dead
and the clouds passing

one by one
over its leaves

Christian McEwen: Thanks so much for agreeing to this interview.

W. S. Merwin: I'm very happy to be here, and I think it's a good augury to have it on the first of May.

CM: Would you speak a little bit about your childhood? I read your book *Unframed Originals,* and that was of course published back in 1982, and

I read your poem "Testimony," which was published in 1999, and other more recent poems in *The Shadow of Sirius*. And I wondered what you know about your childhood now that you didn't know when you wrote those books.

WSM: "Know" in the sense of "have come to understand" or "have new information"?

CM: "Have come to understand."

WSM: "Have come to understand . . ." You know, I learned very early to simply write off my father. He was very harsh, very negative, very abusive. He never spoke to me except negatively, to tell me what I wasn't allowed to do. And to punish me if I did it. But I learned very early to pay very little attention. I mean, I tried not to do things that I would get whopped for. And otherwise, just bided my time. I didn't go into spasms of anger and hatred and all of that. I just wrote him off. And I don't think he was aware of that at all.

My mother came from a background which had great difficulty expressing the emotions directly. She was very attentive, very careful. She had lost absolutely everything in her life: her parents and her brother and her first-born child. She had come to believe that she couldn't keep anything she loved. And I was the first treasure of her life that she began to hope she could keep. And so she was attentive and loving in that sense. But she was extremely anxious that I might ever get hurt. Which again—was limiting. I wanted freedom. I realized that my childhood dreams were freedom from my father. The anger took the form of—"When the day comes, I just will vanish and I'll be gone." And that's what happened.

I mean, I don't wish my father ill. He was a sad, pathetic man who never quite made it. He always charmed his way into situations that he couldn't then handle. I think there are actually quite a lot of people who just—temperamentally—don't especially want a domestic life, and don't especially want children, and yet they're persuaded that's the natural thing to do. I think that's a very bad thing. But good parents are just wonderful to see. I have two stepsons who are absolutely wonderful fathers, in quite different ways. I don't feel jealous, I just feel admiration for it, and think that's the way it should be. I like children. I've never wanted any of my own, but I was delighted when Paula and I were together, to inherit two adolescent stepsons. I just love them. I couldn't have two better friends than the two of them. We aren't alike, and we don't have to be. But I love them and admire them, and their families, and everything to do with them. I feel very, very lucky. But I feel very, very lucky to have met Paula.

CM: I wondered if you'd say something about your early reading and what books were read to you as a child. You wrote about the children in books who had fishing poles and straw hats, and then you also wrote about reading Conrad, and how that awakened you.

WSM: It started when I was thirteen. He became one of my absolute favorites. He still is. He's one of my great joys. I love Conrad. And I love everything I know about him. He's a fascinating man.

But the early things . . .

My mother read poems to us. She read a poem of Tennyson's called "The Brook." I realize now that it's the only poem of Tennyson's I can stand. I don't really like Alfred, Lord Tennyson. I love Hardy, of the late Victorians. I have a passionate love of Hardy. Browning, I think, is the greatest of the great high Victorians. He's not easy, but I have great, great admiration for Browning. And some of Browning is very, very beautiful. Great character. I thought Tennyson was smug and closed off and self-righteous. You could just imagine him reading *In Memoriam* to the Queen. "You could rise on stepping stones / of your dead selves to higher things." I thought, "Oh God, please, take it away." And the *Idylls of the King,* no, not for me.

But that poem, over and over, "The Brook," that is so beautiful, and which is related to a poem of Stevenson's which he wrote at the same time, "Where Go the Boats?" Do you remember that lovely poem? "Dark brown is the river. / Golden is the sand. / It flows along for ever . . ." They're river poems, they're water poems. Water and boats. And that's a kind of freedom. It's a water freedom, you know. And those are actually poems I read over and over again.

Then, and the first book. . . . Well, there was a book about Indians. I taught myself to read out of the book about Indians. There were pictures of Indians living in winter camps, and I said to my mother, "Tell me about these people who live surrounded by trees." And she told me. She said, "This isn't really our land. We stole it from the Indians. And those are the people who really should be living here." I said, "Well, I would like to be living here with them. I like the idea of living with trees all around me."

Now of course in Hawaii, we live with trees all around us. And so they shall remain, as long as I'm alive. We look out from every side of the house straight into trees. It's just wonderful to me. It's what I've always wanted.

But the first book of fairytales that had real magic for me was *East of the Sun, West of the Moon*. A great Norwegian novelist was behind that. And Kay Nielsen—a very, very beautiful and unique Danish painter—did some of the great early illustrations to the book. Those are Norse fairytales, and in some of them you can recognize their sources, which are Mediterranean. But they've been changed so much by the time you get them up into Norway and Sweden that they're totally different. They're utterly magic. The title story, "East of the Sun, West of the Moon," is one of the great stories, one of the great, great stories.

And you know, just the titles! "The Princess on the Glass Mountain," and "Soria Moria Castle," and "The Giant Who Had No Heart in His Body." Ah, just extraordinary stories! I read them over and over again, and now I'm reading them over again, and they're just as good as they were then.

You know, I love myths. I think language is myth to begin with. The words are all myth. You look into a word and it's all there. And the myths of nonviolence. We were talking about these things earlier today. It's not necessary to be caught up in violence for its own sake. This was a thing that I came to in adolescence. Albert Camus, writing about the Algerian Revolution, said, "You must break the chain of violence, whenever and wherever you can. Don't wait for the right minute because the right minute never comes. Just break it."

I don't think we can get rid of violence. Anger is in all of us. And greed is in all of us. We can't get rid of it in ourselves. We can't get rid of it in the society. But we can oppose the organization of it. The use of it as a tool, and as a threat.

CM: It seemed to me, as I was reading your work, that there was an on-going tussle with what one might call metaphysics. What it meant to be alive on this planet. And I wondered if you'd talk about that, and about the kinds of consolations and philosophies that have worked for you.

WSM: The first philosopher that I read with understanding—well, understanding? with some kind of recognition, and recognition is always mysterious—was Spinoza. Spinoza helped me to deal with what happened between the age of seventeen and the age of eighteen, with organized violence and my objections to it. I'd started out by thinking I wanted to be a career naval officer. Because I wanted to wear summer whites and impress the doctor's daughter. And I began to think about it. "No, that won't do. That's not what you want to do with your life."

People had always asked, "What do you want to be when you grow up?" And I had always said, "I want to be a poet," from the time I could put words down on a page. I knew that. It had to do with the great moments of language that I'd heard. I wanted to find the way to them myself. And I always was going to do that, always, from four on. So that was there.

And then my mother, if she hadn't been a Presbyterian minister's wife, would certainly have been a Quaker. Because she had great, great sympathy with the Quaker philosophy—the whole mind approach of the Quakers. And there was a man named Paul Harris who came several times to give talks, when I was ten or twelve, and I guess he was very interested in me and I was very interested in him. We talked a lot about music. The only composer I'd ever heard—because of church music—was Handel. I loved Handel. Then a little bit later I discovered Beethoven. I love Schubert and Mozart and Bach and Monteverdi. But Beethoven is the one that I always come back to. The great incredible richness of Beethoven—everything from great gentleness and sweetness to great power. He was an amazing composer. I've always loved music. And I think of music and painting when I'm thinking about poetry, because sometimes those different arts, those different senses involved, are very revealing when you think about language.

And language of course is deeply mysterious. Nobody can ever know this, but the origin of language and origin of poetry I think must be the same. Because they come from the urge to say something that there is no way of saying. Of course there's never any way of saying it. There will never be a way. But there are things that approach the way of saying it.

I must say, if you love Shakespeare you'll love him all your life, and more as you get older, too. There's just nobody like Shakespeare—Shakespeare, and probably Homer. I don't read Greek, but I would suspect that those are probably the two great writers. I love Dante, obviously, and I've spent a lot of time with him over the years. But—I don't know of anything before Shakespeare that seems to me as great as the *Odyssey*. Because the *Odyssey* is about the truth. What is the truth? Odysseus is this great hero. He's very, very wily, Odysseus, very smart. And he can't tell the truth. Every time you ask for Odysseus, every time anybody tries to find Odysseus, he presents them with somebody else who isn't Odysseus. And finally he gets all the way back to Ithaca, to the homeland, whatever that metaphor means, in Homer. And he can't tell the truth because if he tells the truth, if he lets them know who he is, he'll be killed right there.

Then comes the great moment, when the beggar stands up in the doorway, throws back his rags, picks up the bow. That's the great turn, one of the great scenes in literature. That is poetry of an order with Shakespeare, and even in translation you can see that this is an amazingly powerful poem and a great revelation.

So when we talk about poetry, we're talking about that whole metaphorical side of language. Language is metaphor. Prose comes much, much later, and is simply the conveyance of information. There's nothing wrong with it. We use it, we need it. It's very useful for our ordinary lives. But it's very limited.

They look to many people as the same, because they use the same words. But there are different dimensions there, different views of the use of language. With poetry, every time you say it to yourself, or you read it over again, it's different. Every time you use a word in the way that it's used in the poem, it's different. And this is true through the whole history of the word, and the history of the word includes its etymology, its sources, its former uses. Nietzsche says something about how poetry is a mass of shared emotion. Language. It's all there in language. And if you listen in poetry, you can begin to make it out. I don't know that all poets would talk about it this way, but it seems to me we are dealing with something that is really magic, a very powerful substance. Really, straight out of the fairy tales.

CM: That's lovely. Thank you.

There are so many questions I want to ask you. I was very moved by what you have to say about listening and the power of listening. One of the things I find again and again in your poems is—a kind of listening to the non-human, a listening beyond human conversation.

WSM: Yes.

CM: To the conversation between the tree and the wave. To the conversation between the pieces of furniture in a room. And I wondered if you'd speak more about that.

WSM: When students ask, "What should I be guided by in reading?" I say, well, pleasure in the first place. You have to like it. Read the things you like. And then listen to them, and go on listening, listening to language, listening to poems. The only way you're ever going to get close to poems is by listening, not by getting very clever and reading a lot of criticism. That won't get you anywhere at all. It makes you sound very clever, and it maybe gets you good marks. But it's not getting close to poetry, it's not what it is about. I think that listening is where it all begins, where it all comes from. The origin of language and the origin of poetry comes from hearing something, not from understanding something.

When you see a picture of a woman with her mouth open whose husband has just been killed by a bomb in front of her, you know what the sound is coming out. It's just one long shriek. But you can hear it, you know what it means. It doesn't mean anything; it means pain. "I can't express this pain." That's what you hear.

And I think, if you say to students, "Listen," they automatically say, "Listen to what?' And I would say, "That's what you have to find out. Only you can tell you what to listen for. But listen. All you have to do is stop, and listen to what you hear." And if you hear the silence in the room, that's something. If you hear your own breath, that's something. If you hear the empty stream bed. If you hear the birds waking up in the morning. If you hear the car shrieking to a stop at the red light. Whatever it may be. You're listening to it. You belong. *Listening, listening, listening.* You realize that there's a whole fabric going on around you of silence and sound. There's a wonderful book by a man called Max Picard. It's called *The World of Silence*. You know that book?

CM: Yes. I adore that book.

WSM: Isn't it a wonderful book?

There's a little bit where he gets rather Christian, because he was a theologian to begin with. He starts talking about "language is a gift from heaven." And I think, "Well, I can't quite buy that." But most of it—I mean, "Silence and the animals. Silence and music. Silence and speech." It's an absolutely wonderful book. And you read it over and over again. I'm trying to get Shambhala to reprint it. And that book influenced Rainer Maria Rilke, the great Austrian poet. Rilke, I think, was one of the two supremely great poets of the twentieth century. Rilke and Yeats. They were so different from each other. But they had many things deeply in common.

This whole feeling about language, too. Yeats was thinking about language all the way through his life, including the lost languages, the old Celtic languages of Ireland. Rilke, of course, was not German, he was Austrian, and he saw German from a different point of view than the Germans.

That connection with language. . . . Shakespeare is right at the point when the English language is becoming aware of itself as a language. Chaucer was aware of it, but it was still Middle English in his day, it was still in formation. It became fully formed with Shakespeare. He's got the perfect form for it, which is the drama, and using poetry for that drama, which developed that breathtaking development of Elizabethan drama. There must be two great periods of drama. One of them, Greek, and the other one, Elizabethan, Shakespeare. There are wonderful periods elsewhere, but nothing comparable to those two—culminating with Ben Jonson and Webster and Tourneur. Absolutely wonderful! And their use of language. What they were doing with the language was marvelous.

By the time it gets to the seventeenth century, with the Puritans, it becomes a class system. The marvelous thing in Elizabethan English was it had nothing to do with class. The illiterate people recited poetry and listened to poetry, and had street ballads read to them, and listened to *Hamlet*, stood listening to *Hamlet* for five hours. And they couldn't read or write! Take the original audience of *Sir Gawain and the Green Knight*. Most of them couldn't read. This was read to them.

And I think this was true—I know this was true—of the whole Homeric tradition. Homer came at the end of this great tradition of bards who could recite this heroic material for hours on end. They grew up learning how to do it. That tradition still survives in the Balkans, and in the mountains of Pakistan. It won't survive more than another generation, because as people learn to read and write, as they become literate, they lose it, they can't do it any more. But there's a couple of books about that. There was Milman Parry, and two people at Harvard. There's someone who's been writing a book—parts of it have been in *The New Yorker*—about long oral recitation in Northern Pakistan. This ability to recite these long passages from Homeric material, heroic material. Heroic stories, and the things that Homer used.

People said that Homer didn't write those two poems, that they were all written before him like ballads. That's nonsense. All that material certainly existed, and it existed for a very long time. But it took a very great poet to write those two immense poems. The organization of them! It's breathtaking, the way they're put together. The eighth book of the *Iliad,* you know, having failed at the peace conference, and walking back, knowing that the war is going to start in the morning. As the day breaks, they're walking up along the beach, past all of the beached boats. And he's naming each of the boats, and where it came from, and how many men were on it. And they're talking about the names of the warriors. And it gets to the end, and they look up, and they said, at that moment, "The horses, the dogs rose up into their high place. It was the morning, the morning of the beginning of the war."

That didn't happen as a folk development. That's a great poet doing that. That's very deliberate.

CM: It's magnificent.

WSM: I find it very exciting, those things. There are peaks. I don't think it should cause anyone jealousy for their own tradition. We are lucky to have what we have. You know, there's a great history of poetry in China from the seventh century right through to about the tenth or eleventh century. It's absolutely wonderful. But it's different. It's lyric poetry. Very, very beautiful.

We're lucky, in our short-lived species, to be able to develop—think of the awful things we've done!—but we've developed these wonderful arts. They're there for us, they're there for everybody, if people could relate to them long enough. One of things about Smith, which is very reassuring and heartening to come to, is the level of poetry that's around this college. As long as I've known anything about Smith, it's been here, in the members of the faculty and the students, that enthusiasm about poetry. It's wonderful to see.

One of the marvelous things I've seen happen since the hippies and the Vietnam War, is that the audience for poetry has grown and grown. People come to hear it, instead of just reading it. It's not just the intellectuals who have it to themselves, it's all sorts of people who'd never been to a reading before. They hear poetry for the first time and they love it. That's marvelous.

We were talking earlier about activism. Actually, I abhor politics. I don't want anything to do with them. But I also abhorred the Vietnam War. And I thought, when you're given a chance, those of us who are free to speak have a duty to speak for those who can't. Peter Matthiessen and I used to talk about that together. He said, "I try to write something of that kind every year—speaking for the people who can't speak."

I'm not so good at that, but I've tried over the years to do it. I don't think one wants to get stuck in a rut, so that one becomes predictable and everybody says, "Oh, that's just you, you know." They recognize it, and they know just what to expect. It's much better to keep them guessing. I said this to [Robert] Bly years ago. I said, "When they knock on the door and ask you a question, you don't want to tell them straight out what the answer is. There ought to be a bit of a surprise in it for them too."

CM: Yes, absolutely.

One of the people we have in common, you and I, is the Scottish poet Alastair Reid. He's a dear friend of mine from childhood. One of your books is dedicated to him. And I wondered how your paths crossed.

WSM: We knew each other a long time ago, in Mallorca. He followed me tutoring Robert Graves's son William. Robert was a very difficult man, and he was very jealous of younger poets. And he found ways of arguing, or breaking with all of them. Mostly it had to do with Robert's flirtations with young women and his feeling that the young men were getting in the way, and sometimes that was perfectly true. In my case, it was too.

Graves was a very gifted and a very kind of twisted man, and *Goodbye to All That* is a remarkable autobiography. And *The White Goddess* with all of its nuttiness. . . . When *The White Goddess* came out, I remember talking with American poets at the time, and we were very excited by it. We thought it was fascinating, this take on that field of mythology, that early Welsh mythology, which is incredible.

When I was in Europe and had no money, I took a milk train across Spain to go and visit Robert. And while I was there, it was a piece of luck (I was tutoring in Portugal, I had a wonderful tutoring job there), William's tutor wrote and said he'd got another job and he wouldn't be coming. So Robert said, "Would you like to do that yourself?" And I thought about it, and I said, "Sure." I had to go back to Portugal and cancel my other job, and sort that out as diplomatically as I could, because I really loved the people there. But this was something I couldn't turn down.

As long as the friendship was a honeymoon, it was marvelous. And Robert certainly knew a lot about poetry. But I realized that the theories behind *The White Goddess* were not metaphors for him. Robert was a fundamentalist. He was taking the whole thing completely literally. And I was kind of shocked. I thought, *No!* In the first place, these were not meant to be taken literally. These are great metaphors. And you treat them as great metaphors. They're talking to you that way. But if you try to make them a kind of fundamental doctrine, I don't think this is what poetry is about.

Well, we had fundamental differences. And finally Robert, he broke with me, he would never speak to me. That was too bad. I went back and lived by myself in that village, in a little tiny valley, and had a wonderful winter or two up there. I translated the *Song of Roland, The Poem of the Cid,* and got started doing things for the BBC in London. And that was a great way of breaking in on translation. But I always had a great fondness for the place, and admiration, of a dwindling kind, for Robert.

Actually, my favorite poem of Robert's over the years turns out not to be one of his central poems at all. It's called "Cuirassier of the Frontier," about the mercenary soldiers of the Roman Army who stay away from the capital. The last line is, "A rotting tree lives only in its rotting." The poem is as good as that. But it's not one of his theoretical poems about the White Goddess. The late poems I don't like; I don't think they're terribly good. So it was a very dicey relation with Robert; it was for Alastair, too. But Alastair and I remain friends. I love Alastair's essays, I think they're wonderful. I've lost touch, and I don't want to. I'll write to him again and see what's happening. He always writes in longhand, you know. Beautiful longhand.

CM: Let's talk about translation, because you yourself have done enormous numbers of translations. I wondered what you thought you'd gained from all those other countries and other literatures.

WSM: I'll never know the full answer to that.

Copper Canyon's just brought out three volumes of selected translations, they go from 1948 to the present, so a long period: sixty, seventy years. When the third volume came out, I thought, it's time to make a real essay about what translation's become in our time.

One of the great pioneers and a great visionary, and a very difficult man, was Ezra Pound. He was a hero of mine, and I went to see him when I was eighteen. People find this hard to believe—but I did not know his politics. I learned them quite soon afterwards. If I'd known them when I went to see him, I probably wouldn't have gone to see him. He was following out a sort of perverted attachment to his own theories on usury, and so on and so forth. He was a very cranky and very opinionated man. He talked too much. But when I went to see him when I was eighteen, he took me seriously as a poet. And he taught me some wonderful things. One of the things he said was, "If you're going to be a poet, you have to take it and yourself seriously. You don't know if you have any talent at this point. But you have to work at it every day." And he said, "You have to write something every day. There's nothing you can write about every day. You don't have enough to write about every day. You think you do, but you don't, your life at eighteen is really not that interesting. It may become interesting as you go further away from it. But it isn't now." So he said, "Learn languages and translate. That's the best way of learning your own language there is." And that's absolutely true.

I'd already started translating for a young Spanish professor—a very homesick Spanish professor at Princeton. He wanted to translate Lorca's plays, and he got several of his students, including me, to help him with these translations. I wasn't very interested in Lorca's plays. I tried to be, for his sake. But I was interested in the poems, very much. And I tried to translate the poems on my own, with his help. So I'd already started when I saw Pound. And I went on and did try to learn old languages. And he said, "Go back to the source." And the source of all of our language, the source of all of our poetry, is the Troubadours.

This was a great beginning, some of the greatest poems. I mean, they were the great teachers and fathers of Dante. Dante revered that language of theirs so much that he could sing it, right in the *Comedia.*

And of course Arnault Daniel and the twenty-six cantos of the *Oratorio.* There's this wonderful passage with Arnault Daniel, who in Dante's view was the greatest of the Troubadours, and when Arnault answers Dante's question to him, Arnault answers in the whole rest of the canto, in the *Purgatorio;* it's not in Italian, it's in Occitan. I mean, that is the ultimate tribute, giving him his own language. It's a beautiful language.

I learned so much from translation. There is no such thing as real translation. Translation can't be done; it's the impossible art. But there are many forms of translation. How can you translate from a language you don't know? But Auden said, "This is the best way of doing it, because if you know the original, it just confuses you. It's much better to have it at several removes."

There are poems that have been translated over and over again. The one I tried to recite last night, that little poem at the beginning of the dedication of the marriage of Venus? That poem has existed since Egypt. And then been translated into Greek, and then probably into other languages, and then . . . "Drink to me only with thine eyes." That beautiful lyric, beautiful song. You forget that's it's a poem. It's a poem of Ben Jonson's, and it's not a poem, it's a translation of two little Latin poems. He's taken these two little poems, and made this exquisite lyric. "Drink to me only with thine eyes, / and I will pledge with mine; / Or leave a kiss but in the cup / and I'll not look for wine." You don't need music to go with that, that is so beautiful. It used to be that we all knew it by heart, and knew it was a song. That's wonderful.

Pound said at the beginning they didn't make a distinction between the words and the music. It's all teaching one—it's the most wonderful teaching. It's not theoretical at all. It's totally practical. "How do you say this in English?" And this is the best school, the best sort of test for poets. How good are you at this, at saying what can't be said? And that's what poetry's all about, you know.

CM: That's lovely. Thank you.

We are reaching the end, and I'm thinking of the students who will be reading this interview, and of Pound's advice to you to sit at the desk every day and do some work. And I'm wondering what you might say to the students about your own work habits and about what would serve them best as apprentice poets?

WSM: I think passion is terribly important. Something you really care about. This has to be something you really want to do. Poetry has been central to my life ever since I was four years old, so that I've been thinking about it all the time. So that yes, I do, I try to write every chance I have. I go back and make notes, and sometimes there'll be a phrase, and I know, the light came on and maybe if I keep it on long enough, I'll see what else is in the room that belongs with it, and maybe it'll be a poem. Those are the notes, and I look at them, and see, "Where does it lead to?" And sometimes, two years later, you see what it is, and that's—never letting go of it, never putting it down, hanging on to it, keeping it. It's you.

The only thing that changes is you. You change so much that you are no longer that person, and then you can let it go. But there's some of the language, and only you are the judge of what's still alive, what still is making that sound to you. I don't think anybody—any two people— evolve the same way of going about it. There is no "way of going about it."

But listening is essential. Going on listening to yourself, that's what you're finally listening to. Something that's happening in your own mind. And sometimes, a phrase of something that is leading toward something, will occur at the most inopportune moments: in the middle of an argument, or in the middle of some bad news or something ghastly that you heard on the radio or saw on television. All of a sudden in this other part of your mind, the light goes on, and there are these five words you know. You're off. You're somewhere else.

I don't know. This is true for me; I don't know whether it's true for other people. I think everybody has to work differently. But listening is terribly important. Stephen Kusisto, this wonderful blind poet who has just got a new book of poems, they're blind-man's poems, the imagery is not visual imagery, it's wonderful. His second memoir, which I haven't found yet, haven't read, is called *Eavesdropping*. It's about listening. Listening to the world. But I think poets do that anyway. I think the great Bardic tradition is doing that. You're hearing something that is coming from the deep past. And poems—I think this is the most important thing to recognize and accept—*poetry does not come from what you know*. All that you know is very important, and not to be put down or ignored or got rid of, but finally it is from the unknown that poetry comes to you.

Whenever I finished a poem, all my life, or have come to the end of it, and thought I had to let it go, I didn't know what else to do, I think, "Well, that's the best I can do. I may never write another poem." I don't know that I'll be able to write another poem. Poets that I know who say, "I'll finish my book of poems next year, about the middle of the year"—well, OK, good luck to you!

CM: [Laughs.] So the message would be to keep the door open to the unknown in whatever way you can.

WSM: Yes. Absolutely. Everything. Anything. You have no idea what is going to pop out of Pandora's box.

PATRICIA SMITH

Interviewed December 18, 2012

Patricia Smith was born in Chicago in 1955, the first in her family to be raised up North. Her father was a gifted storyteller, and Smith herself was very much a daddy's girl. "So I learned early on to look at the world in terms of the stories it could tell."

Smith's father was killed in a robbery when she was only twenty-one, leaving her tremendously bereft. In the years that followed, she made a name for herself as a performance artist, winning National Poetry Slam champion four times. She also worked as a writer-in-the-schools. The children would come in full of stories about the gunshots they had heard the night before, and she would tell them about her own complicated childhood. Her students were astonished and impressed. "Wow! You grew up like me, and look what you're doing!"

Smith has published six books of poetry. She was awarded the 2013 Lenore Marshall Poetry Prize for *Shoulda Been Jimi Savannah,* and has twice won the Pushcart Prize. She has also written and performed two one-woman plays. Her work has appeared in *Best American Poetry, Best American Essays,* and *Best American Mystery Stories.* She is a Cave Canem faculty member and currently teaches at Sierra Nevada College and at the City University of New York/College of Staten Island.

Ethel's Sestina

Ethel Freeman's body sat for days in her wheelchair outside the New Orleans Convention Center. Her son Herbert, who had assured his mother that help was on the way, was forced to leave her there once she died.

Gon' be obedient in this here chair,
gon' bide my time, fanning against this sun.
I ask my boy, and all he says is *Wait*.
He wipes my brow with steam, says I should sleep.
I trust his every word. Herbert my son.
I believe him when he says help gon' come.

Been so long since all these suffrin' folks come
to this place. Now on the ground 'round my chair,
they sweat in my shade, keep asking my son
could that be a bus they see. It's the sun
foolin' them, shining much too loud for sleep,
making us hear engines, wheels. Not yet. Wait.

Lawd, some folks prayin' for rain while they wait,
forgetting what rain can do. When it come,
it smashes living flat, wakes you from sleep,
eats streets, washes you clean out of the chair
you be sittin' in. Best to praise this sun,
shinin' its dry shine. *Lawd have mercy, son,*

is it coming? Such a strong man, my son.
Can't help but believe when he tells us, *Wait*.
Wait some more. Wish some trees would block this sun.
We wait. Ain't no white men or buses come,
but look—see that there? Get me out this chair,
help me stand up. No time for sleepin',

cause look what's rumbling this way. If you sleep
you gon' miss it. *Look there,* I tell my son.

He don't hear. I'm 'bout to get out this chair,
but the ghost in my legs tells me to wait,
wait for the salvation that's sho to come.
I see my savior's face 'longside that sun.

Nobody sees me running toward the sun.
Lawd, they think I'm done gone and fell asleep.
They don't hear *Come.*

Come.
Come.
Come.
Come.
Come.
Come.
Ain't but one power make me leave my son.
I can't wait, Herbert. Lawd knows I can't wait.
Don't cry, boy, I ain't in that chair no more.

Wish you coulda come on this journey, son,
seen that ol' sweet sun lift me out of sleep.
Didn't have to wait. And see my golden chair?

Christian McEwen: There's so much I admire about your work, but I'd like to start with your book *Blood Dazzler,* which came out in 2008, and which is about Hurricane Katrina. You describe Katrina from outside and also from within; you become her in some way. "I become a mouth, thrashing hair, an over-done eye." I was utterly blown away by the power of that book.

Patricia Smith: Thank you very much.

CM: How hard was it to write about Katrina? Did you have the sense you'd already come into your mastery as a poet, or was it the writing of the book that taught you how?

PS: Hmm. That's kind of a two-pronged question because as far as coming into my mastery, I was writing this book at the same time as I was getting my MFA. So I would write segments of the book, and I would automatically have another eye on them and it pushed me a little bit to keep going. But at the time I wasn't thinking, "Oh, I'm going to sit down and write a book about Katrina."

There was one situation that kept pushing me. It was the story of the thirty-four nursing home residents who were left behind. I had an aunt who died in a nursing home and my family was kind of charged with her care. I was only sixteen at the time, so I didn't really know what I was doing, and she was in the later stages of Alzheimer's. I would come into the room and my formerly God-fearing aunt would be throwing food at me and cursing like a sailor. But I remember she had a yellow button on the side of her bed, and no matter how rough things got, she could push that button and someone would come right away.

And when I read the story about the nursing home in St. Bernard's Parish, I just imagined: the lights are out, the water is rising, and the residents are pushing buttons—and nothing's happening. I could not get rid of that picture, so I decided that was the poem I wanted to write—not to make sense of it, but to process it in some way.

Because as witnesses, which writers are, these situations come to us and we need to write our way into and past them. So I decided I would work on that poem, and since I had worked in persona quite a bit—because I got introduced to poetry by getting up on stage, and persona is a very effective device—what I wanted to do was to wind the clock back a little bit and give each of those thirty-four people a little bit of their voice back, enough to say, "You don't know who I was, but I was . . ."

So I did that poem first of all, and—I had a lot of questions. I'm not from New Orleans. I don't have any connection to the Gulf. My only connection to Katrina was the same connection that you had, that anyone else you'd encounter on the street had who had processed it through the news and on television and on their computer, and whatever else they saw. The only difference was that as an artist I felt it wasn't just a witnessing, that I owed it to myself at least to say, "This is something else human beings are capable of, this is something else nature is capable of, and I need to be able to understand it with my own voice." That's how it starts to make sense to me.

I thought, someone's going to challenge me on this, and they're going to say, "You're exploiting this thing." I kept waiting for that and waiting for that, so I was a little tentative about writing it, but I'm very, very happy that I did.

In terms of mastery—OK, I was studying craft. I got involved in poetry by performing it, and I decided at one point that the entire canon belonged to me. At the time, I was plumping up my toolbox. If I picked up a poem I wanted to be able to read it, and not only to follow the narrative, but to find out what the author had done technically to help heighten my response to the poem. So in a lot of ways I was at the juncture of those two things. I had "How does the poem reach the open air?" in mind, but I also wanted to make sure it lasted on the page.

But once I got that poem done, I felt like it was the poem I set out to write.

CM: I was tremendously impressed by your mastery of form.

PS: Thank you, thank you. I was just beginning. It was me realizing that you can guide a reader though the reading of a poem. I always used to regret the fact that people could pick up my book, but they couldn't hear me do the poems. But then I found out that there were things you could do with the spacing on the page, there were things you could do with meter and rhyme that could slow a reader down, and that would set a tone beyond the actual words. The writing of *Blood Dazzler* was when those realizations were just popping for me.

Personifying Katrina, for instance, it was never a question for me. I felt there wasn't any other way to do it. But when I was doing the poem about Ethel Freeman, the woman who died in her wheelchair while she was waiting with her son for a bus to take them from the Convention Center, I thought about the way older people speak—they have comfort pockets in their speech and they return to familiar words and comfortable phrasing—and I go, "OK, what's a form that backs up onto itself and comes back to these phrases?" And it's a sestina.

CM: I love that poem. I have read so many sestinas and almost always they start to feel forced by the last third, or even half. And yours carried itself through right to the end.

PS: Thank you.

CM: It's magnificent. In fact, let's have you read that one.

PS: That's one of my favorite poems too.

[PS reads "Ethel's Sestina." See page 246.]

CM: It is superb. It's really a miracle, that poem.

PS: Thank you. I appreciate that.

CM: Were there forms you tried that somehow couldn't hold this very rich, very complicated, almost radioactive material?

PS: Were there forms? No, because I didn't start out saying, "Here's a form I want to use, let me squeeze the poem into it." I would wait to see what the poem was asking for. Some poems were meant to just sit on the page as they were. But once I had these skills in my toolbox, for instance if I was writing an elegy and knew there was a form that lent itself to that, then I would use it. So a lot of the poems that were just sitting there, and I wasn't sure why they weren't quite working, once I found out that they wanted to sound a different way, they wanted to reach the reader in a different way, if it wasn't a form that I already had knowledge of, then I would study it. So there weren't any forms I tried and couldn't find a poem for.

CM: And did you use persona as an entry-point to almost all of the poems?

PS: When I started out performing, with no idea of getting published, persona was very, very popular. I was in Chicago where the poetry slam began, and I got addicted to it. All of a sudden everything had to be in persona: anything I wanted to write about, I needed to find another voice. But you know, you have to temper it. You find out eventually where it's at its most effective. It can just sit on the page like anything else if it's not used correctly.

Once I had decided to personify Katrina—you can see how she's alternately remorseful and arrogant and giddy and doubtful—I didn't want to overdo it. I didn't want to personify everything. I wanted her to come in at different points in the book and say, "Here's what I'm feeling right now." In that sense it was a touchstone. For any other of the persona poems, I had to make sure that the persona was warranted. For instance, in the poem about Ethel. I wanted Ethel's story to be a triumphant story, not just an account of some poor woman who died in her wheelchair on the street corner. And I needed to inhabit her body to do that. I needed the reader to feel her body go to another place, and that wasn't something I could do as an outside witness.

When the other hurricane, Betsy, decided to chastise Katrina for overdoing it, it was clear that if Katrina was a woman, Betsy had to be a woman also. The few poems that came very close to being persona, and people talk to me as if they are persona poems but they're not, are the ones I did about the dog.

CM: I love those.

PS: About Luther B. I talk about them often and I say "persona," but they're not really from the dog's point of view. We sample the dog's thinking, but it's not a personal pronoun poem. It was really important for me to include those poems—I wasn't a dog person at the time. I didn't have a dog. I used to be the person who, if you'd come up to me and say, "My dog needs a hip replacement and it's going to cost $4,000," I'd go, "Are you crazy? It's a dog!"

But then during Katrina, I had to ask myself why there were people who wouldn't leave their homes unless they could take their animals. And I saw a picture of a dead dog draped over a power line, and I thought, "Someone somewhere is going to come back looking for that dog." So that's how Luther B. came about. And now I have two huge dogs, and of course I would step in front of an eighteen-wheeler for my dogs now. But I thought it was important that various perspectives made it into the book, that it wasn't just a one-note book, that the dog and the transvestite coming home from the club—that everybody had a moment. It was hard to realize when to stop because Katrina was an ongoing story; there wasn't a point where you said, "Oh, good, that's over." So I had to realize when the narrative arc had sort of played out and I could stop it.

CM: You mentioned the transvestite poem, which is also one of my favorites. Really brilliant. What strikes me over and over is the range of characters in the book, and the fullness with which you inhabit them. You have George Bush, you have Michael Brown, you have the old people, you have this transvestite, you have the hurricane itself.

PS: Well, it's like being behind the camera and scanning the entire story, and every once in a while you reach a moment and go *click!* and then you move on and then you click again. The frightening thing is that now I'm beginning to encounter students to whom I have to explain what Katrina is before I begin to talk about the poems. So I needed to have a book where you could turn and look at any side of it and get another aspect of a story. It wasn't just the storm and the damage, it was also the country's response to it, and the country's response to it was different depending on what part of the country you were in. There's the political response, and then you stop and go inside the storm, and then there's the dog, and then there's the person trying to identify the bodies that are coming into a certain building. You can only get the entire picture if the camera keeps moving.

If you keep the camera in one spot, you're just getting part of that picture—and I guess we can't teach everything in schools—but it's amazing to me that I am encountering people who go, "Oh, that was that storm, right?" *That was that storm.* Especially when Hurricane Sandy came, and the comparisons to Katrina started that forced people to go back and say, "Oh, what was Katrina?" I didn't expect it was ever going to be that kind of a story. I always thought that it was huge enough and it shook us enough that everyone who went through it should mention it to someone who didn't, whether it be a child or an adult. "This is something you really need to know about." So the one thing that makes me really happy about the book is, ten, twenty years from now maybe it will be in a remainder bin, and whoever picks it up might not buy it, but if they read the back at least they'll go, "Oh yeah, right, Katrina happened," and that might be all we can hope for.

CM: Yeah. American amnesia . . .

PS: America: the next big thing.

CM: The next big thing. You said that you were in New Jersey during Hurricane Sandy. What differences do you see between those two hurricanes and how they were treated by the media?

PS: There wasn't really a socioeconomic aspect to Sandy that was touted right away. It was more, "We are talking about the New Jersey coastline, we are talking about people losing their $500 million homes." It was very much an issue of property and land damage, and Katrina, at least as far as I was concerned—now someone else might look at it and see something else totally—had to do with human damage, and because the greater extent of that damage happened to be visited upon poor people and people of color, I looked at the story in an entirely different way.

I mean, I could have picked that up and moved it just about anywhere. I can remember when I was growing up, the area I was in was pretty much written off. Everyone was told to stay away from it. People looked at me as though I was some sort of freak because I used two-syllable words. They'd go, "You're not supposed to achieve, because you come from this neighborhood or from this school." So the sight of mothers being lifted in baskets with their children—that was part of it too. I think a lot of the country really didn't want to see that because it didn't just remind them of the storm, it reminded them of people they had never really needed to think about, and now didn't want to be forced to think about.

So as soon as the next big thing came along, it was like "Oh, oh, look this thing's happening over here and I think they had Mardi Gras, so New Orleans is OK now." It's so far off everyone's radar. No one's talking about it. But what happened with Hurricane Sandy—Lincoln and Cadillac car dealerships saying, "Was your car damaged? We'll give you a break and get you a new car"—there was none of that. A lot of residents during Katrina were told to get out fast, now, and had absolutely no way to get out. It was different, it was very different.

With Hurricane Sandy, you're still seeing stories about people who are wondering whether or not they can rebuild, but these are people who were firemen, policemen, bankers, and the help is there. So no one's really talked about the difference. The only time it was mentioned was, "We just want you to know that this was as serious, as forceful, as Katrina was." But then when it gets too close to who was involved in Katrina, who was involved in Sandy, we stop talking.

CM: Very interesting.

I wanted to go back to an earlier book of yours, *The Tea House of the Almighty,* which was published in 2006. And because of what happened in Connecticut this past Friday [the Sandy Hook Elementary School shooting in Newtown, Connecticut, on December 14, 2012], I wanted to ask you to read one of the poems you wrote for your sixth grade class.

PS: Oh sure.

CM: It's the one that includes the line, "I rejoice when they kiss my face."

PS: I just want to tell you a little bit about that. I was at a poetry conference in Ashville, North Carolina, and I read, and a woman came up to me and said, "I would love for my kids to hear you." And it wound up that she was a music teacher at a school in Miami, and she said, "But we don't have any money," and I said, "I'll come to you." I didn't have any place to stay, so I slept on a palette on her floor. And I went to see her kids, and they were amazing, although it was one of my first trips being a poet, you know, starting to travel, and so I go in with this great sparkly personality, "I'm here to teach you poetry!" and the area I was in had a very high incidence of drug use, so a lot of the kids had lost parents or sisters or brothers to AIDS and I come bounding in with an ear-to-ear grin, and they're looking at me like, "There's nothing you can say that's going to have anything to do with the way we live." And I had to work really hard, at least in the beginning, to convince them that their voices were legitimate.

I went back to that school probably every year for the next ten years, until that woman who initially had brought me lost her job and then they said, "Oh, we don't have to do poetry anymore." [Laughs.] Right, right. So that poem was written for the kids I met there, and in particular a little girl named Nicole who, during that first visit, was in school and her mother had died the week before. So that's the background.

[PS reads "I rejoice when they kiss my face."]

CM: A few years back, I had a gig as writer-in-the-schools in the South Bronx, and I asked the children to write poems about loss. But most of them were poems about death. "My older brother went down to the bodega to get a pack of cigarettes, and he got in a fight." You know, those stories. And when they read, the classroom became like a prayer meeting, with the children standing up one after another, "I have a dead one, I have a dead one too."

And what struck me was that most of the children didn't know each other's stories. They'd been carrying their own important dead person in their heart, but they didn't know the kid across the aisle had a similar story. It was tremendously powerful to help elicit that material. I had an enormous sense of gratitude that my role as a teacher allowed me to release those stories.

So, I know your father was killed in a robbery, and I was wondering whether that is something that you shared with the children.

PS: When you come into a classroom, especially if you're in a school where they don't bring in a lot of outside people, before you're anything else you're an authority figure. The students have been told to sit still, to be quiet; "Don't fidget and listen, fold your hands." So I see that as something I have to break through. I tell them about the type of neighborhood I grew up in, I sound the way I sounded then—I will sound the way I sound when I talk to my mom as opposed to the way I sound when I'm talking to you now, and they go *"What!* No one has ever stood up in front of us in a classroom and spoken that way." I have a poem about cooking with my father—the main movement of the poem is not the fact that he's dead, but it mentions it just enough, so kids are like *"What, what, what?"* So I let them get the news from me, and don't hesitate to tell them that story, and almost immediately it's *"Me too, me too."*

You really have to steel yourself against that in a way, when you see that level of trauma in one classroom. You see something happen in a place like Utah, and they fly psychologists in, and here the kids are kind of left to process on their own. For instance, the child Nicole in the poem, her grandmother all of a sudden had custody of her, had no idea what to do with a young child, and put her right back in school. There was no psychotherapy, there was no counseling. It was just, "You can't sit home all day, you know. I'm sorry your mom's gone, here."

If they could turn to the child next to them and be open enough and hear that they're not suffering [that would be great], but they don't communicate that way until someone they're supposed to be looking up to admits some kind of loss or vulnerability, or "I was once in your shoes." They come in buzzing about gunshots they heard the night before and I say, "Let me tell you about the west side of Chicago," and then it's like, "Wow, you know, you grew up like me and look what you're doing!" So it becomes more of a conversation.

[PS addresses the imagined children] "I'm not worried about you, right now, in this space, I'm not worried about you spelling your words right, I'm not worried about your double negatives. Nothing's going to be corrected, the only thing is that everyone's story is as important as everyone else's." And while you're drawing those stories out, "This is a problem I have, and some of the students have too." That breaks through this barrier so that I'm not interested in their stories as some kind of creative exercise, I really become *What am I going to do for this child? How am I going to pull this child forward a little bit?*

And then the kids want to go home with me, because I am the first person who has really shown interest in their story and not only that story, but the way they want to tell it. You ask questions because you're really curious about it, and they've never had that before, and so it's like, *"Can I come live with you?"* Especially young kids. You're in front of the class and all of the sudden they come up, and they start holding on to you and standing next to you while you're doing whatever you're doing. That's when I realized the power that language has to move you from one place in your head to a safer place, because not only are we doing it constantly, but we need to teach kids that, "Yeah, you might want to act out, or you might want to start skipping school, or you can pull out this notebook and you can write *exactly* what you feel, not writing for a teacher, and that is a story that belongs just to you; no one else can mess with that."

It takes a lot of time at the beginning to convince a group that everything that they say is OK. You can't go in with a form workshop—a workshop that you've thought of that's one size fits all—it doesn't work. You need to find out where you're going, what the neighborhood is like, what the teachers' attitudes are toward the kids, because I've been in places where they've ushered me into the room and left, with no introduction to the kids, no introduction to the student body, just plop me in front of the class.

So you have to be prepared for that, you have to do your own background work, and you just do it by going straight to the kids. "You know, tell me . . . " I know just how disconnected the people who teach every day can be, and believe me, I am in awe of teachers, but there are some that write off the community and write off the people in their classrooms.

I was at a high school, and there were all these couples just making out against the lockers, and I was like "What's going on here?" So I go and do this workshop and someone writes a poem that's not intensely sexual, just had sexual mentions, and there's this teacher sitting in the back of the room, saying, "We just can't have this kind of language." And I said, "Do you know what's going on in the back stairs of this school?" And he's like, "What do you mean, in this school?" And I said, "Oh, it's like that, huh?" I guess part of it is that you come in with another eye, and if you're in the trenches every day, you can steel yourself against things and not see them after a while.

But these are kids we're talking about, they're individual kids, and you can't clamp on the "oh poor disadvantaged" story and assume that's going to do. You have to pull each one of them out in a different way, and the good thing about being in a school two or three days is that you can at least begin that process. The problem is, then I go, "Here's my email address, here's my mailing address, send me this poem," so you can keep some sort of contact going, because as soon as you leave that hole's gonna snap shut and the kids are gonna wonder if you were ever really there. So you give a little bit of yourself.

CM: So you always go in from the point of view of the story, you don't try and teach particular forms?

PS: No, no. Now we might want to play for a while. I go, "How old are you?" "Eight." And I go, "OK, so I want you to write a poem, eight lines, eight syllables each line." Everybody has a great time, and everybody is counting on their fingers and all that, but there's got to be an open space in the time we're together to say, "OK, here's your story, here's what a poem is. There is a way for you to move this into this space."

It's often something you can't do in one day, but once I've been able to do that, I then take the children's poems into other classrooms, and say, "You know this was written by an eight-year-old," and then the poem reflects something they're all talking about or thinking about. And they all say, *"How old?"* "He's your age." You know, not "Here's Langston Hughes." They're so used to that: you opening up a big thick book and reading them something and they go, "Oh, OK." But to have a folder and to show them the actual written poem on the lined paper that some child did, and to have one of them read it and say, "Oh. I've felt this way. This means I can do this too."

We just have to stay aware there are these different entry points, and they are not the same for every kid. There's always kids in the back of the room that are kind of glaring at you and doing things, and I used to get discouraged when I would see that, but then those are the kids that when you're on your way out, or you're in the parking lot and by your car, will run up to you and give you a little sweaty poem that they've been carrying around, which they couldn't do in front of their peers. So leaving that space open and not saying, "Well, you in the back of the room, I need you to behave. . . . " If that's where they need to be to maintain, let them be there. If you're not finding an opening, they're looking for one.

CM: I love using children's poems to elicit other children's poems. That's so powerful.

PS: It took me a while to learn that, but as I got a body of work—I wasn't going to throw them away, so I would just keep copies, and I realized that's what they need to see. *Somebody just like you wrote this.*

CM: One of the things that came up with Sandy Hook—I think I heard this on the radio—was, "Of course, these children have never heard gunfire before," and I thought *"Ah-ha!* That's very interesting." When I was teaching in the South Bronx, the teachers were always saying, "Children to the center of the school, children to the staircase, children away from the windows," because there was a gunfight going on outside.

PS: I know the area. I've done a reading and a workshop in Newtown High School before, and it is kind of rarified air, it is very classically New England. It can look very much like a haven, and I understand that, I understand the people who said, "I moved from wherever I moved from because of the area's reputation."

But at some point, I had the news on as backdrop, and it was another one of those "Into a pristine morning . . . " reports, you know, and, "This isn't supposed to happen here."

And I understand why people say that, but I'm from Chicago and there's so much violence there right now, and kids in the crossfire, and no one ever says, "Well, yeah, of course it happened here." I mean it doesn't work both ways, and I'm sure if those parents could remove their children that they would. But they can't, so it is rapidly getting to a point where that's not something we're going to be able to say anymore: "It can't happen here." It can happen and it has happened everywhere. It's time for us to let that go.

I haven't faced it yet as a poet, as an artist, as a writer. When something like this happens, there's a huge story and I start to look at little aspects of it: *How small can I make this story?* You can make it one family, you can make it one child, you can make it one moment—and I'm not even saying I'm going to write something, but I kind of have to go through this process in my head to feel safe enough to write something. After I wrote *Blood Dazzler,* every time some big event would happen someone would say, "Oh, are you going to write about that? Are you going to write about Haiti?" It's like, I'm not the disaster writer. If there's something within that story that you can connect to as a person and then pushes you as a writer then that's fine, but sometimes—often—that doesn't happen.

You know, I'm still a little numb, I'm still a little numb, I can't. And then I found something about ten Iraqi children—girls—were killed. . . .

CM: Gathering firewood.

PS: Right, gathering firewood. And I wanted to go, "When you say 'protect the children,' you have to mean that." Our scope needs to be a lot larger.

Let's stop the regional bias and the socioeconomic bias, and realize saving children means saving children.

CM: Thank you. Yes.

We've been focusing on your books, and I wanted to spend at least a little time on your own story, your own immediate family. I wondered if you'd speak about your son, your writer son.

PS: My son, yeah, he's writing. He gets these notebooks and he fills them up with, I won't say science fiction, but these otherworldly stories. What he tends to write, it's kind of escapist, you know. He doesn't write rooted in the real world, and I think there's probably a reason for that. He's a kid, he was a kid for a long time, and he was kind of enamored of street life because I represented something else. I put him in what he calls "a house behind a white picket fence," which I've never had by the way, and sent him to these private schools, and that was my way of assuring a success. But it didn't take into consideration who he actually was. I think I was trying to pound that peg into the wrong-shaped hole, and so he just rebelled against it, and he was in jail for a while. Someone will say, "Where's your son?" and I'll say, "Oh, he's in Boston, or he's in . . . " while my friends' sons are traveling Europe with their jazz bands and stuff.

What happened with him went a long way toward pushing me forward as a poet, once I realized that there were a lot of things behind me, as there are a lot of things behind all of us that we kind of pave over and go, "Oh God, thank God I don't have to look at that anymore." But they don't go away, they kind of rumble beneath the surface and they beg to be confronted. So my experience with him went a long way toward giving me the courage to look at not only my relationship with him and how it evolved, but also my relationship with the family, and within myself. It gave me the courage to look at those things, andat least begin to write about and address them in my own work.

CM: Thank you.

There are a couple of people who show up in your more personal poems. I'm thinking of figures like Mamie Tuttle, holding court on her lopsided wooden porch, or Sergei, waving his gun, and I wondered how it was to use real life stories, as opposed to public information, in the poems, whether it felt different or difficult.

PS: Oh, it didn't feel difficult; as a matter of fact, it feels like that's the way I should do it. I never thought about doing it any other way. I mean I didn't sit in a classroom and have someone tell me, "These are the choices you have to choose from," instead of me going and trying to find my own way. So before I'll call myself a poet, I'll call myself a storyteller.

My father, when he came up from Arkansas during the great migration and got his job working at the candy factory in Chicago, he brought with him what I call "the tradition of the back porch." At the end of the day he'd sit and he'd go over his entire day, and all of the people at work would become characters, and the next night I'd be like, "Well what happened with so-and-so?" and we'd talk about somebody else. So I learned early on to look at the world in terms of the stories it could tell, and to look at someone that I knew and see not only how they fit in as part of my story, but to be intensely curious about theirs.

So I know that I could write something about a woman who used to do hair—open her kitchen door and just have a chair sitting there, an old Sears dinette set chair and do hair, and there would be a little line of people walking around. A lot of people who grew up the way I did would recognize that. But I really need to see Mamie, I need to see her, and I think using her and using her name and picturing her while I'm writing is a form of tribute. It kind of sets them in place, and somebody who grew up my way could still look at it and say, "Oh! The woman who did that in my neighborhood was . . . "

Part of it, too, is that after my father died, my mother and I kind of looked at each other like, *"And you would be who?"* Because when she left the South, she really wanted to leave the South, she didn't want to talk about it anymore, she didn't want to admit being from there, so it shut off a lot of my history, and I don't want to do that anymore. So if putting those situations in place and putting those names in place helps somebody after me say, "Oh! well this is how she lived," then that's what I want to do.

CM: There's a lot of very brave storytelling in your work: the poem in the voice of the abused child, the poem about music and sex, terrific stuff, but stuff that one imagines the Mama might not . . .

PS: My new book is called *Shoulda Been Jimi Savannah,* which is the title poem. My mother told me later in life that my father wanted to name me Jimi Savannah when I was a baby, and I said, "You talked him out of it, didn't you?" It would've been a great poetry name.

But that is the book. I think I've come a long way in that it started out being a book about Motown, because I love Motown; then I realized it was a book about being first-generation up North, and there are poems in there about my mother, who was never really satisfied with my color or anything else about me. In her favor, what she wanted—she's up North and she's got this child to raise and she's kind of confounded, so in her head it's "Be as much like the mainstream as you can, speak the way white people speak, look the way white people look, 'Oh my God you're too dark, oh we've got to press all—everything—out of your hair.'"

And one of the poems is about my mother in the summer. When I'd get darker she would put Lysol on a washcloth and scrub the back of my neck because it was too black. Now, I put that poem in the book and I can see the horrified recognition by a lot of people. My mom used to put Tide detergent in my bathwater because she thought that would make me lighter. So my vow to myself, now that I'm about halfway through my poetic career, *is that what I'm waiting for?* If indeed I'm telling my own story so people can see the parallels to their stories and go tell theirs, then there's no reason for me to hold back on any of it, because while I'm telling it, I'm trying to make sense of it myself.

I've been holding on to that information for a long time. There are things in there about my father, about the hardships they had finding themselves in Chicago with this child. They would instinctively know how to raise a child in the South, but all of a sudden there were all these rules: how do you tell her where to go, what time to be home when the streetlights come on, how do you send her to school halfway across—you bus her to school halfway across the city because it's a white school and a white school is better, well, no, you bused me across the city to a really bad white school.

So my mother will not read these poems. If you went to my mother's apartment you would see my books on a doily on the corner of her dresser, spine ucracked because she knew from way back when she saw me read once, that I do—I mention my family. It doesn't matter if it's good or bad, just the very secretive culture, where everybody had the crazy cousin locked in the basement, and you would see signs of women being abused and your parents would shush you away and nobody would talk about it. There's a lot of whispering and that's how I came up. So for me to stand on a stage in front of strangers, or to put out a book that just anybody could pick up and talk about my mother coming from the South and sitting on barstools and trying to look like a Christian woman who was just leaving, that horrifies her so she can say, "She writes," but she won't [read my work]. So we're not very close because she cannot recognize my passion.

Imagine having something you've decided to do with your life and then what's supposed to be your closest and most supportive relative says, "I won't have anything to do with it." My mother could call right now, pick up the phone, and say, "You know, the post office is hiring." This whole idea of writing creatively for a living has never made sense to her. She used to call me and say, "Have you gotten paid yet?" And I'd go, "Well, I don't get paid like that." None of it means anything to her. I can come to a reading in Chicago and say, "Hi, I'm in town," and she goes, "What are you here for? Why aren't you at home taking care of your husband?" I love that part.

I don't have any brothers or sisters, so my writing is doubly important to me because I'm kind of chronicling my own life—what I can piece together of its past, which includes trying to piece together my parents' past. So that's what I've been trying to do in this book [*Shoulda Been Jimi Savannah*].

CM: I look forward to reading it.

PS: Thank you.

CM: Just two more questions. One is, given that you got really so little encouragement from your mother, and that your father had died—

PS: My father was killed when I was twenty-one.

CM: I misunderstood, I beg your pardon.

PS: I had gotten my first writing job, I was writing for a newspaper—no, it wasn't even writing. I was like an editorial assistant.

I was at work, my mother came. They called me outside, and they said that my mother said my dad hadn't come to work that day, and someone had—had broken into his place and shot him. And I said, "No, they didn't break in," because he shared an apartment—he lived there and there was another guy who lived there, so it was like an apartment with two doors, and the other guy had brought a relative up from the South, a nephew or something that had just gotten out of jail, and told him he could stay.

And my father loved big cars, and this guy saw my father driving this big car and thought he had money, so all I know is—my father—his back was turned like he was going back into his part of the apartment and he had gotten shot in the back of the head. And the guy had taken his car keys, gone out to the street, dropped my dad's car keys by the car, got on a bus, and then was bragging to people on the bus that he had just killed someone, and the police were waiting for him when he got off.

It was probably the hardest thing ever because I was—I was the dictionary definition of a daddy's girl. I didn't even know my mother; she was not very emotionally affectionate. My dad listened to all my stories. So—I pretty much decided at that point that I wanted to be a storyteller, like he was a storyteller. But yeah—he worms his way in and out of a lot of pieces.

CM: And in the years since, where have you found the support that he gave you?

PS: I'd like to personally thank my fifth grade teacher, Carol Bernawski. She honestly went to my parents, told my parents that I should try not to get into the school I was supposed to go to, but somewhere else. She told me I was good enough to do it, she was great. She had red hair and little crinkly—I never saw anybody's eyes really sparkle, her eyes really sparkled, little blue eyes. You know how you can get to a point and look back on it and realize how pivotal one year was in terms of how you thought of yourself? I was in a school where everybody was supposed to fail. She said, "Guess what? You didn't fail, you know you didn't fail, and there are other things you can do." She suggested I go to this big private school, which just kind of intimidated my parents, so I wound up not going, but I love that she existed.

And then I got things from the poetry community, the performance poetry community. There was kind of a chasm, the academics and the performance people looking at each other, glaring at each other like they didn't all use language, so we very much just turned into ourselves and said, "Don't worry, we're doing the right thing, we're doing the right thing." We got up on stage and read things that were sometimes intensely personal because that was how we were processing, so for that reason I'm closer to some poets than I am to my mom.

CM: Thank you.

The first group of people who will be reading this interview will be the Smith poetry students.

PS: Hi, Smith poetry students! What's up? *Woo woo!*

CM: So I wondered if there was anything you'd like to say to that particular age group—eighteen, nineteen, twenty, twenty-one—by way of encouragement or advice.

PS: OK, yeah, I'm going to be revolutionary. All right, Smith poetry interns, you are at a *really, really, really* good school. However, I should warn you that the school is not all that there is, that sometimes in a quest to legitimize your own voice you will let someone else shape it, you will let someone else tell you where it should go, how loud it should be, how soft it should be, and your voice is the only thing that you truly own. So you can learn things while you're in school to do with that voice, you can learn devices that can make that voice stronger, but in the end, you're the only one who can tell the story and the story has to sound the way you want it to sound.

Go out and live, get your heart broken a lot, you know, just go out and do stuff, so that there's texture to the life that you are talking about.

CHASE TWICHELL

Interviewed March 4, 2010

Chase Twichell was born in New Haven, Connecticut, in 1950, the eldest of three sisters. The family spent almost every vacation in the Adirondacks, just south of Montreal, and Twichell grew up with a passionate love of nature. As a child, she identified more strongly with animals than with human beings. She saw herself as a tomboy, too, "a tree-climber, and a fisher, and a camper," like the son her father had always wanted.

At fourteen, Twichell was sent away to boarding school in Maryland. She began to keep a notebook (for her eyes only) and read poetry constantly, "everything from Yeats to Ferlinghetti to Milton to Allen Ginsberg." In the years that followed, she attended a number of different colleges, graduating with an MFA from the University of Iowa. She also studied graphic designing and letterpress printing, and in 1999 founded the Ausable Press, which was acquired by Copper Canyon in 2009.

A long time Buddhist practitioner, Twichell has published seven books of poetry, winning the Claremont Graduate University's Kingsley Tufts Poetry Award for *Horses Where the Answers Should Have Been*. She has received numerous other honors and awards, including fellowships from the Guggenheim Foundation and the National Endowment for the Arts. Her poems have appeared in *The New Yorker, The Paris Review, Poetry,* and *The Nation*. She and her husband, the novelist Russell Banks, live in Keene, New York, deep in the Adirondack wilderness.

Horse

I've never seen a soul detached from its gender,
but I'd like to. I'd like to see my own that way,
free of its female tethers. Maybe it would be like
riding a horse. The rider's the human one,
but everyone looks at the horse.

Christian McEwen: I wondered if you'd talk a little bit about your growing up. I'm thinking of a few lines in *Perdido*, "I had as a child a mind / already rife with sacred greens / I could neither harvest nor ignore." And I wondered if you'd comment on the power of place and landscape in your life.

Chase Twichell: I had the great good fortune to grow up in the Adirondack wilderness, which is the largest significant wilderness east of the Rockies. And I grew up in the middle of it, at least in the summers. We lived in Connecticut, and my father was a schoolteacher, but we spent all summers there and many weekends, and always spring vacations and Christmas vacations, so it was really the holy locus of my childhood. I was a very lonely child. I was the oldest of three daughters. My parents had a rocky marriage. And I think that most of my childhood—and I could probably say the same of myself today—I identified more strongly with animals than with human beings. Both painting and poetry were early avenues for me into kinds of consciousness that let me take a vacation from, or escape from, the normal human consciousness of the household.

And so those lines, "I had a mind / already rife with sacred greens"—I read Keats early on as a kid, I came across him in a children's book, and I think my encounter with him was significant because it gave me a piece of information that was very important to me, which was, "There are other people out there in the world who speak a language different than the one that most people speak," and which I on some childish, inarticulate, gut level, identified with. And so the phrasing of things, words, came to me when I was a child, and I would write them in a notebook, and even though I didn't know what they meant or what I was going to use them for, they were like secret treasures that were possible doors into another kind of consciousness. I was aware from earliest memories that language had that possibility. That there were ways that you could use language as a door to go somewhere else.

CM: Thank you, that's a beautiful, lucid answer.

You spoke about your love of animals and the early love of language, and I was struck in some of your poems by a kind of cross-species communication. Conversation with animals, conversation with place. I wondered if you'd comment on that.

CT: Well, I used to believe when I was a child that I was actually half dog. I mean that quite literally. [Laughs.] I felt more comfortable with the family dogs than I did with the family. I used to announce that I really didn't speak human languages, I only spoke dog, horse, *et cetera,* and I would go to great lengths to assert—until I was maybe eleven, when my credibility began to suffer for it—that I really was able to communicate with dogs. I was also around a lot of wild animals when I was a kid, and they became emblematic, also, of a life that was wordless in the usual human sense, and that relied upon other ways of communicating. And so to me, even though I was joking about learning to speak animal languages, animals did seem to me to have a language, and the world itself, the natural world, had a language, or many languages between them, to which I think I became sensitized very early, partly because I was in the wilderness, partly because I was a kind of dissociated, lonely little kid and I spent a great deal of time in nature, in the woods. And so I think that my identification with animals and with the natural world was really a bedrock part of my identity from a very early age.

CM: Thank you.

Connected to this is the theme of the tomboy, whom I love and identify with myself. I adored that poem, "Girl Riding Bareback," and I'm thinking of the lines, "Arrows of sun falling harmless on a girl / and the big imaginary animal of herself." And I wondered if you'd talk about that tomboy girl and the ways in which she's still present in your poems.

CT: That's a really huge question.

I'll start off answering it small, and stop me if I start expanding beyond the pale. I was a tomboy. I think that my father wished I were a boy. I grew up with pitching practice and abhorred dolls, wouldn't be caught dead in a dress, wore high-top black Keds until I was about fifteen. And I simply did not identify with little girls. Most of my cousins were boys; my crowd was boys; I was a tree-climber, and a fisher, and a camper, and—not a fighter.
. . .

And there's another element in there, aside from wanting to be the creature that my father wanted me to be. I . . . I had some bad experiences when I was a child, as a girl child. I was never physically injured, but I was, um, put in some compromising situations. I realize I'm dancing around the subject here a little bit, and it's quite overt in the poems, so I don't know why I'm being coy about it. But I did suffer some sexual abuse when I was a child. It was, um, mostly being photographed. There was a person in my life who was an amateur photographer, an older man, who as far as I can remember—and I was pretty young, and so—any of this stuff, I hesitate to call it facts, because some of it's facts and some of it is speculation and so forth—but I think he basically made kiddy porn in his basement . . . and that I was, well, I know that I was part of that.

And so the tomboy becomes, in the poems, a defended creature, a creature that insists it's not a girl, that these things do not happen to boys. And it was a way of creating a kind of armor or shell around myself, an alter-identity, alternative identity, so that I could still be a child, but not be the child to whom these things had happened. Because I certainly wasn't an adult yet. I'm talking about age four, five, six, seven, somewhere in there. And then perhaps a little older. So the tomboy becomes a stand-in for the wounded child; the tomboy can fight; the tomboy can be someone who did not live through what I lived through but is still me. And is also part dog. [Laughs.]

CM: There's a lot of layers to this.

CT: Yeah. That's why I said it was a really big question. And in fact it was interesting. I didn't realize how many times I used the word "tomboy" in the new poems. In all my books I've crept around the edges of this. I had an interesting experience putting this book together [*Horses Where the Answers Should Have Been*] because it's a *New and Selected,* and so I had to go back through all the early books and figure out what should live and what should die, which was not easy. And what I realized was although I thought that I had avoided writing about this—and I made a conscious decision; I didn't feel ready to write about it, it seemed prurient, sensationalistic, and I just didn't know how to handle it—but I realized in going back through all the books that in fact I managed to get it in there anyway, and there are poems that allude to it, or that hint at it, without really coming right out about it. So one of the decisions that I had to make in writing the new part of the *New and Selected,* and also in the last book, *Dog Language,* was that I had to quit pussy-footing around and deal with it. If I was going to mention it at all then it was time to deal with it. And after all I'm almost sixty years old, I turn sixty in a couple of months, and if I haven't dealt with it by now, when am I ever going to do it? So I decided to come out of the closet about it.

CM: Thank you.

You spoke about Keats and the lusciousness of finding the right language, or people who spoke a language other than the home language. Could you say more about the ways in which poetry entered your life as a young person, and what encouragement you had, if any?

CT: That's a complicated answer also, but an interesting one. My father was a classicist; he taught Latin. And so I grew up on the classic tales and had the *Odyssey* read to me as a bedtime story, slightly synopsized by my father, cutting out all the boring parts and concentrating on things like the Cyclops, and Scylla, and Charybdis. I think he added a great deal of his own personal detail. But I was captivated by the language and the song of it, the ongoing human song. So that was one element. My parents were both literate, well educated, and poetry, although it was not a regular part of my life, was certainly not something that was foreign to me.

I went to a grammar school in New Haven, Connecticut, and when I was in fifth or sixth grade, our art teacher became ill, and at the last minute the school hired a graduate student from Yale, a guy named George Chaplin, who was in the painting program there. And this guy was a genius. He'd never taught before, but he ended up being my art teacher through eighth grade. The first thing he did was change all the furniture in the art room so that all the chairs faced the wall, and no one could see what anyone else was doing. And then he put a bathtub, a claw-footed bathtub, in the middle of the room, and he used to scrounge through the dumpsters at Yale at the end of every semester and collect all the old canvases that they'd thrown away, and all the oil paint, and we had an entire bathtub full of half squeezed tubes of really good oil paint to paint with, and we only painted on canvases that had already been screwed up by somebody else, so there was never any possibility of fearing the blank page. And since he didn't know how to teach fifth graders—I think I was ten—we did Josef Albers color studies and did some pretty sophisticated stuff, but for us it was just fun, it was just games.

By the time I left that school in eighth grade, I was pretty seriously obsessed with painting. I would go home after school every day and paint. And I can bring my mother to tears by reminding her of this because she feels so guilty, but my parents decided that it would be bad for me to continue studying art because it might socially isolate me and I was getting a little weird. So I was forbidden to take art classes when I was sent off to school. I got my revenge by starting to write poems. And that was when I really did begin to write my first poems as a sort of "screw you" gesture to the world. If I couldn't get there through paint I was going to get there some other way.

For years I had the feeling that I'd given up my true calling, but eventually poetry supplanted painting, and it became my secret life in high school. I had a notebook that was for my eyes only. I read poetry constantly, to the great detriment of my other schoolwork. And by the time I got out of high school I really was as obsessed with poetry as I had been with painting. So that was the early avenue in. And I read everything. I read everything from Yeats to Ferlinghetti to Milton to Allen Ginsberg. Everything. And at that time I probably didn't have much sense of what the differences were. All I knew was that there was this big, wild circus of a world out there and I wanted to be part of it.

CM: Were you alone in that great world circus, or did you have other friends who were also passionate readers and apprentice poets?

CT: No. Creative writing was not taught at my high school, which was a very repressive, small boarding school in Maryland called St. Timothy's. We had one creative writing class the entire time I was there, and it was taught by a teacher who didn't have any particular connection to creative writing, but was just teaching it because somebody should teach it. I always felt completely misunderstood by him. I felt that I knew far more about poetry, and did know far more about poetry, than he did. It wasn't until I went to college that I really was able to take creative writing classes and have real teachers. And that's when someone began to encourage me for the first time.

CM: I wanted to ask you a little bit more about your childhood. I'm thinking of the "cherries in the chilled silver bowl." That side of life: the finger bowls, the linen tablecloths. Both what was hard about that world and what was gracious and delicious.

CT: Well, I did grow up with a privileged background. My grandparents on one side were an old New York State, New Haven, Long Island WASP-y family. And the other side were from California, from northern California; my grandmother was born in San Rafael and came east when she married. And I did grow up in two grandparental houses that had finger bowls and chimes that rang here and there, and little bells for the next course, and people waiting on table, and so forth. So I came from that kind of WASP background. In a way it was of course an advantage: I got to go to great schools, and so forth, and I never had to worry about having enough to eat, or a roof over my head, or tuition, or any of that stuff.

But on the other hand, it was a very isolating kind of background. It made it hard to just fall in with the crowd. And of course I got teased about it a lot as a kid. Kids can be pretty brutal. But I never felt it was really a handicap. For one thing it gave me social confidence, because the training in households like that starts very early. I will always be grateful for that. I really feel comfortable in pretty much any social situation, whether it's a black tie, fancy-dancy affair where I have to talk to socialite types and whatever, or whether it's just the roadhouse down the block. I really do feel pretty comfortable in any social milieu. I'm married to someone who grew up in a house without plumbing or heat, and who was a wrong-side-of-the-tracks kinda guy. And we've managed to find middle ground that's very comfortable for both of us. But I did grow up with, I think, real exposure to art, to really good paintings and good books and good music, all of which I'm very grateful for.

CM: Since you mentioned your husband, who is the novelist Russell Banks, how is it to be married to another writer?

CT: Divine. [Laughs.] It's great. He's ten years older than I am, and of course works in a different genre, so we've had to fight none of the battles that are so famous between two poets, two fiction writers, whatever, especially if they're of the same generation, duking it out over careers. Also, he is way, way, way ahead of me in his career, and would be even if he were ten years younger. [Laughs.] He's at a completely different stage of career life than I am. So that's always been very easy for us. We've never been competitive, never jealous. Which is really lovely. Also, we didn't get married till late, so we didn't have to go through any of those adolescent, life-changing marital wranglings that a lot of people have to go through when both parties are writers.

CM: I was very moved by your poems about childlessness, unborn children, poems like "Nostalgia for the Future" and "The Shades of Grand Central." I wondered whether you'd comment on those.

CT: You know, I was always ambivalent about having children. I was never one of those young women who fantasized about the children that I would have and how many I would have, *et cetera*. It always remained a kind of anxiety-provoking, mysterious area of my life. I pretty much decided fairly early on that I would not have children, because I was hyper-aware of the over-population in the world, and I was not convinced that I would be a good parent. I was working through a lot of things. And I never met, during those years, a man with whom I wanted to have children. So it was not something that I grieved over.

And then when I met Russell, he had four grown-up daughters and a vasectomy, so that settled that. I inherited four daughters and a stepgranddaughter, which has more than fulfilled my maternal instincts, and being a grandma is the best part ever. You get to skip all the hard part, like twenty years of hard part, and go right to the fun part. But it was never a big sacrifice for me. There was a time in my life where I tried on the idea of it having been a big sacrifice, and it just slipped right off my shoulders. So I honestly can say I never suffered over it. In fact, I felt relieved. I simply cannot imagine how I would have been able to write my books and have children at the same time. And yes, there are times when I think, "Oh no! I'm getting old. When I'm in a nursing home, who will come and visit me? Who will balance my checkbook for me?" But maybe I'll just hire someone when the time comes. [Laughs.] Or draft one of my fabulous stepdaughters.

CM: [Laughs.] There you go.

I was so relieved to read your poems like "City Animals" and "Shades of Grand Central," because I felt such admiration for the way in which you face the anguish of every day and combine personal pain with the larger pain of the world. I feel like I don't often see that done with such skill and such integrity.

CT: Well, thank you.

Those poems came out of a book called *The Ghost of Eden,* which took me a long time to work up to, partly because ecology was a trendy subject to write about, so I wanted to avoid that at all costs of course. And also it was a subject that was extremely painful to me, because I did grow up in a pristine wilderness, and have personal, long experience with the world as it once was, and have had, during the course of my life, to say goodbye to it. It simply doesn't exist anymore. Anywhere. Every single inch of the earth is polluted. I was just listening to something on PBS the other day about what's in mother's milk. . . . I mean, all these evil chemicals start at conception practically. It's just a fact of our lives.

And it's something that enrages me so profoundly that I found myself speechless about it for a long time, and in a state of real grief. When I finally worked up the courage to begin the poems in *The Ghost of Eden* I realized that not only did I have to write them, but that—a volcano was about to erupt. And I tried to curtail it. I said, "All right, I'm going to write ten or twelve of these, and that's it, that's my contribution to the poetry of ecology and then I'm going to move on." And every single poem in that book said, "Sorry, pal, you're not done yet," and did a U-turn, and I ended up writing an entire book. Which amounts to a kind of ecological diatribe.

It was really interesting because after I finished the book I felt myself to be numb in a way that I'd never felt before. I thought of it as numbness at the time, and I really worried about it. I thought, "Well, I'm exhausted from writing this. Maybe I'll wake up in a little while." And it went on and on for more than a year, and I really wondered if I had done something to myself by writing the book, if I had accumulated a kind of armor that was preventing me from feeling what I felt I should be feeling. I was asking myself, "Where did this righteous rage go? Surely you're not going to let go of it, turn into an ecological wimp at this point?"

And then I began to realize very slowly that the work that I did in writing that book was the work of grieving. I had gone through the grief and come out in another place.

It was as if the person for whom I grieved, which in this case was the earth, had died and I had survived its death, and was continuing to live on. And it reminded me of something Keats wrote in a letter, and I used that quote as an epigraph in *The Ghost of Eden.* "I have an habitual feeling of my real life having past, and that I am leading a posthumous existence." That was what it felt like, and it was a great relief to me to be done with it, because it used to take so much out of me. Though even now I sputter with rage when I watch the news, and I think what a very dim-witted species we are in terms of our home, our only home, this planet.

CM: Perhaps you could read just one of those poems. I particularly love "Touch-Me-Not" and "The Rule of the North Star," but choose whichever suits you.

CT: "Touch-Me-Not" is long, but I'm happy to read it.

CM: Let's go for long this time.

CT: OK. For those who don't know, touch-me-nots are a form of wild, shrubby plant, and the flowers are like little orchids, and when they go into the seed stage they make fat little pods, and the way they propagate is, if an animal brushes up against them, or you touch one, it kind of explodes, and that's the basic metaphor.

[CT reads "Touch-Me-Not."]

CM: Is there anyone who's tackling subjects of that scope among your contemporaries, or whose work you especially admire?

CT: Hm,m . . . I always go brain-dead when someone asks me a question like that, and I think of ten thousand people and none at the same time. The greatest twentieth-century poet of ecology was Robinson Jeffers. I go back to him all the time. I think Gary Snyder has always been a kind of covert crusader without ever preaching about it, on matters of ecology. And then there are poets like William Heyen, who's written about it quite powerfully. And of course poets like Wendell Berry who's made it his subject. Among younger poets (I mean my age!) I think Tony Hoagland has been brilliant in his handling of it inside out—the view from the mall. Most poets that I think of, though, have touched on it and left it, touched on it and left it, rather than really immersing themselves in it. And for me the difficulty has been to avoid any kind of preaching about it, because politics don't seem to work. It has to be a much more intimate contact with the earth, a real intimate knowledge. And a lot of people simply didn't grow up around nature, and can't see as clearly what's happened.

When I stand on our front porch—we live still, in the Adirondacks, in a very remote area—and visitors will come and say, "Oh, look at that. Those trees are so beautiful. I love the reddish ones." And I think, "Yeah, the reddish ones, those are the beeches with blight, those are the red spruces dying from acid rain, that pretty color that you like so much is the maple thrip that's moving in." When I look at it, I see the diseased world. I can no longer simply see it as beautiful. I remember having an argument with my father while he was still living, and he grew up here, but he absolutely could not accommodate the notion that anything about it was spoiled.

I remember one day we were at someone's house and looking out, and there had been a forest fire really far away, I think in Canada, and there was a kind of haze, and there was a purple quality to the sunset that was very abnormal, and I was saying to Dad, "Wow. Look at that, it's amazing that this pollution could travel this far." And he looked at me and he said, "That's not pollution. Those are"—I remember his exact phrase, he said, "That's not pollution: those are wisps of mist." And I just looked at him.

And I said, "Well, maybe you're right." It was not wisps of mist. It was decimation. Well, of course now I'm getting a little carried away.

So . . . circling back around to your question, there are individual poems I can think of that are moving to me in that way. But maybe the poets were just smarter than I and didn't let themselves get saddled with the subject for a whole book.

CM: So you've done that subject, in a sense. You don't feel pressured to write more poems of that kind?

CT: Actually, it creeps back in all the time. But I feel that I got it out of my system. I don't think that I could say it better now. But the spoilage of the world is now simply part of the landscape, in my life and in my work. I look back at some of the early poems, in which nature was still a pure god, and nature was my god when I was a kid; it was the thing through which I was able to be in touch with the numinous. It was the higher power. Pure and simple. And I still, I see it still as a holy thing, but as a thing that's damaged, surely beyond repair. I'm sure that the human race will survive; I'm sure that our planet will survive. But it's never going to survive the way it was made; it's never going to survive in its healthy form. It's compromised forever, I believe. And I'm glad I lived this span of years, that I was born when there still literally were places untouched on the planet. Untouched. Virgin. And now there are none. And that happened in sixty years.

CM: I wanted to ask you when the Zen practice entered your life. Because it did seem to me that from really early on you had what one might call the gift of seeing, and that probably goes back to the love of nature and the love of painting. This eye, this enormous, encompassing eye. The honoring of the natural world, the naming, the knowing of the names, which many children now simply don't have.

CT: You know, with hindsight I can say, "Yes, it's true, it goes way back." But at the time I wouldn't have been able to articulate it in that way. As for Zen, I had a flirtation with it when I was in college. I was very interested in it, and I took courses in comparative religion and in Chinese and Japanese religion and so forth, and I began to sit zazen by myself, without a teacher. I was quite fervent about it but ignorant, and I had a couple of really scary experiences in which I had small hallucinations. In fact, they are extremely common. They're called *makyo,* and they're simply a sort of side effect of sitting zazen. The corner of the rug will seem to curl up, or you'll imagine that someone is standing just outside of your peripheral vision, but no one is there. Little things like that. But at the time they were quite scary to me, and I thought, "Oh, I'm going nuts. I better stop doing this."

It wasn't until after I finished writing *The Ghost of Eden,* the ecological tirade, and found myself in that state of unanticipated, um . . . what word shall I use? There was a kind of equanimity that I was not used to at all, and it felt very alien to me, and what it reminded me of more than anything was what I had read about, about Buddhism in particular, and about Zen in ultra-particular, and the way that meditation had once made me feel a little bit. So I got really curious about it. This would have been in the early '80s. So I went and found all my old Buddha books down in the basement and started reading them, and it was truly amazing: lights went on, one after another. I began to gobble up books because here was proof that all along I wasn't alone, that there were lots of people in the world going back centuries and centuries who had intuited the same relation between human and world that I had in my own childish, inarticulate sort of way.

I guess every religion defends its truth, but I can say that when I started to read about Zen I recognized in it what I had already instinctually come to believe was the truth. So for a couple of years I read and sat by myself, and then I realized that I needed to find a teacher. The notion of having a teacher is very important in Zen. It's considered mind-to-mind teaching. You learn from someone else. There have been plenty of cases historically of people, Buddha himself, figuring it out alone, but most people benefit greatly from the guidance of a teacher, and from a sangha, a group of fellow Buddha-heads.

So I decided to go online and do research, and my plan was to locate maybe ten or a dozen Zen centers in the Northeast and visit all of them, and then make a decision about what was right for me. The very first place I went to was Zen Mountain Monastery, which is just southwest of Albany. I opened the door, walked in, and I recognized that it was my home. And it was a very odd sensation. And I thought, "Oh, this is so New Age, I can't stand it. I walk in the door and I'm home. I can feel my eyes glazing over." So I was very suspicious of that reaction in me and I thought, "Oh, now you're suddenly going to become a joiner? You're going to become a religious person? *Ha ha ha!*" But I was completely captivated by the place. I was amazed by the monastics, amazed by my fellow practitioners, by the practice itself, and by the time I left—I went for an introductory weekend, in which they just kind of plunk you into the system and you learn a little about this, a little about that, and just kind of get a taste of what the whole thing is about—I was signed up. I suppose it was like a seventeen-year-old boy wanting to get into the army and faking his age. I just knew that it was for me. And I never did ever go to any of the other centers to check them out.

It's been fifteen years since I became a formal student. I was there for about eight years, and then I dropped out for a while for various complicated reasons, and I just reentered as a formal student last year. But that is my home away from home.

CM: Can you say something about how Zen practice has shaped or transformed your poems?

CT: I'll try to give you the bouillon cube version. [Laughs.] Zen has called into question the whole role of language in human consciousness. That's a rather large statement to make, I realize. But I used to believe that language was itself the tool by which one came to consciousness about things. And that it was through language that it was possible to articulate what was previously unknown to oneself. And I still believe that language plays that role: that by writing the poem you figure out what the poem is about. You can't know in advance.

I think that's one of the most common misconceptions that people have about poetry—that you get an idea for a poem and then you sit down and write it. Whereas poets know, in fact, *if only that were true!*

But I have come to see language almost as an obstacle in the writing of a poem. Because the thing that I'm trying to express, which is unknown to me before and during the writing of the poem, is something that language corrals or closes down, and I've never found a way to make an exact translation or paraphrase into words.

My husband, Russell, and I argue about this ad infinitum; in fact we refer to it as Argument Number One. Once we get into it we'll just say, "Oh, it's Argument Number One. We know where this is going." Because he still believes that language is the tool that takes you all the way to the articulation. Whereas I think language is a tool, one of many, that takes you to that place. And so the problem, and the fascination, that comes up is, "How do you use language to say what cannot be said in words?" I think Russell believes that anything can be said in words if you can get it right. But it has been my experience that there are states of mind and kinds of human perception and consciousness that are simply not translatable into language. But language can point at them. Language can turn your head so that your eyes are looking in the right direction. There's that old Zen maxim, you know, of the finger pointing at the moon. I think a poem can be the finger pointing at the moon, but it can't be the moon.

So that's kind of the quandary that I'm working with.

As a result my poems have gotten skinnier; they're almost anorexic now, and I'm much more interested in the holes in them and the spaces between them, the slats in them through which one can look, and less interested in their surfaces, so that I'm almost completely intolerant of decoration now. For instance I used to love those winding, mossy ways of Keats, and just the lushness of physical description. Much of what I loved when I was younger is something that I would not be particularly enamored of now. I'm really interested in poems that somehow manage to become transparent so that you see through them to something else. And I've been reading, as a result, mostly anonymous ancient Asian stuff in translation, and so my head is full of that now.

When I was the editor of Ausable Press, which I was from 1999 to 2009, I read probably eight hundred unpublished manuscripts a year, so my head was full of unpublished contemporary American poetry. And in the time since I stopped doing that, I find that my mind is in a completely different place; when I let it float it goes somewhere else entirely. It's exciting to me, but I also feel kind of out of it as far as what's going on in the contemporary world.

CM: It's so interesting the way you describe it. I have to say, I have an enormous fondness for your ornament and your clear, exact seeing. But there's room for both.

CT: Yeah, and who knows? I mean when one moves through life as a poet, things that I discarded years ago are now the newest thing I'm just discovering. [Laughs.]Things reassert themselves, and so who knows what'll happen? That's what makes it interesting about going back and looking at old work. Of course there are the poems where I think, "Oh, I was so vain to publish that. I only published it because of that cool bird image," or whatever, and I realize that the poem doesn't go nearly as deep as I wish it had gone in retrospect. But then there are the ones where I think, "How the hell did I write that? I couldn't write that now. I wish I could write that poem now but I can't; I don't know how." And it's kind of wonderful when that happens.

CM: It's terrific.

This is doubling back into personal history, but I wondered how it was for you to come out as someone who suffers from depression in poems like "Neurotransmission" and "The Fifth Precept."

CT: Mm-hmm. It was . . . it was actually a kind of a relief to me. There are three subjects that I try to bring out of the closet on a regular basis. One is that I'm a cancer survivor. One is that I'm a depressive, bipolar II. And the other one is the childhood sexual abuse stuff. And, what I have found is that people are very wary about talking about any of those things, but if someone starts the conversation, it is extraordinary how responsive people are. I once gave a reading in Texas, at a little conference called Round Top. There were maybe fifty people in the audience, and I would say it was roughly half men and half women, maybe a few more men. And that was one of the first readings I did in which I just sort of took a deep breath and said, "I'm coming out with this stuff." And I stated that I had had this experience as a child and so forth, and then I read some of the poems, which were new at the time, and which were pretty rough.

And after the reading, out of an audience of fifty, eleven women and one man came up to me privately and said, "It happened to me too. It happened to my daughter. It happened to my sister. It happened to my mother when she was young." I mean, that's close to a quarter of the audience. And statistics do say that one out of four women is sexually abused in some way or another as a child. Look around a room of twenty people; that means you've got company. But it's not something that's common knowledge, and it's certainly not something that people feel comfortable talking about.

And depression too, because I've been depressed since I was a child, and I've been taking psychoactive drugs for twenty-five years—thank you, pharmaceutical industry—I just feel it's really important to make it part of the common discussion and consciousness. Because it's something that people feel guilty about, they're embarrassed by it, and they suffer so unnecessarily because they're afraid to get help. And I know from having been there that it's life-threatening. It's a life-threatening illness. If you are severely depressed and you don't get help, a high proportion, a scarily high proportion, of people commit suicide. It is that painful; it's that dangerous. A lot of people think, "Buck up. You know, think happy thoughts." They don't understand that it's a biochemical malfunction of the first order.

And so for me, it's actually been kind of exciting and a relief to be a crusader for it. Because I'm not embarrassed. I mean, there are times when the word "bipolar" scares people. I'm not a manic-depressive. I'm bipolar II, which is a completely different diagnosis. So I don't walk around saying, "Hi, I'm bipolar II." Whereas I am likely to say, "Oh yeah, I'm a depressive; I have to take my pill now." That doesn't bother me at all. But I do realize that there's a kind of alarm that goes up in people when they hear the word "bipolar," so I do have a little spiel about what the difference between bipolar II and bipolar is. But it's just part of coming out in the world and being who you are—or being who I am, I should say—without apology. And it's a great relief not to have to keep secrets.

CM: Yeah. Thank you.

I wanted to ask you what you read that had nothing at all to do with poetry. I'm imagining from the accuracy of your natural history that you read books about landscape and so forth.

CT: I actually don't. I actually don't. My husband says I behave like a graduate student, which I do—I read a ton of books about Zen. I read anything I can get my hands on about Zen, and I like to read big, juicy novels. I read a lot of poetry too. But I really like to get in bed at night with a novel and just disappear into another world.

CM: There's a line in one of your poems where you said that your ambition was once to "write the star-lit poems of our age." And I wondered what your ambition was now, particularly as it's been inflected by the Zen practice.

CT: Well, it's funny because that is a line that actually got changed fairly late in the revising of the poem. In the original version I said my ambition was *not* to write the star-lit poems of our age, and then as I was working on it—I'd been working on it for a few months—I thought, "Who are you kidding? Who is this liar, liar?" Of course I wanted to write the star-lit poems of our age. Who doesn't? What young poet doesn't want to be the Emily Dickinson of the twenty-first century, or whatever? When I was younger there was always the possibility that maybe I could write the great poems of our century. And then as you get older you realize that the poems that you're writing are just your poems, and no one in this century is going to make any decisions about what the great ones were—we'll have to wait a couple hundred years to figure that out—and that it was really kind of a silly ambition, even though I was being sort of tongue-in-cheek admitting that I'd once had it.

But what I'm more interested in now is writing poems that simply express what it means to have human consciousness. I would like them to be little arrows of insight—and "arrow" is the wrong word even. There's no equivalent in words. I would like them to be little windows, or holes, through which one can glimpse what's really true. The way things really are. What Shunryu Suzuki, the Zen master, described as "things-as-it-is." [Laughs.] I always loved the way he used to twist the language to keep you from just hearing it in a simple form and make you hear it some other way, and he said, "Just look at things as it is." [Laughs.] I would like to write poems about things as it is. In fact, that's going to be the title of my next book, *Things as It Is.*

CM: I wondered if there's any advice you have for poets who are just starting out, and perhaps also for those who are older and may be a little discouraged?

CT: What always comes to mind when I'm asked a question like that is the advice that I give myself more often than any other advice, and the advice that I constantly find myself giving to students when I look at their poems. When one is in school, and putting poems in front of workshops, the assumption is that the thing on the paper is a poem—an unfinished poem, but a poem—and that the group is there to advise the poet on what ought to be done to it to make it more successful. What that does not take into account is the fact that what is on the page at that time is almost entirely arbitrary. Had the poem been written on Wednesday morning after a sleepless night instead of Tuesday night after two beers, it would be a completely different poem. And to allow a poem to close down prematurely is one of the greatest mistakes that a poet can make.

So one piece of advice I give is, "Don't let go of the roughness of the draft until you really know what's going on or what the poem wants to do or what your basic question is." Because a poem can't just express what you already know. It can't just be an opinion about something or a description of a feeling. It has to go somewhere. It should take the reader somewhere, but in order for it to do that it has to take *the writer* somewhere. In order to trick yourself into going somewhere you haven't been before, you have to be really patient, and you also have to be really open to being stupid, being inarticulate, getting it wrong, getting it backwards, going off on long sidetracks, being inaccurate, all those things. You have to be willing to just put it out there and give yourself enough room for it, the thing, whatever it is, the poem's real subject, to reveal itself. So Piece of Advice Number One is: "Don't start polishing the poem and shaping it up until you know what animal you've got." I see so many poems on worksheets and from student poets that are starting to be closed in and closed down and finalized when they don't have any idea what the poem is about. Or it may not even be about anything yet. And so that's part one.

And there's an adjunct to that, the "Don't start polishing" part. Because if you start to polish a poem before you know that information, you are basically building a house you'll have to tear down. And so resist the impulse to do that as long as you can. Because that's the fun part. Once you know what the poem is supposed to do, then you know how to write it. But until you know that, you don't know how to write it. Which is why so many poets say, "I know there's something happening here, but I don't know what to do to it next. Should I cut it? Should I expand it?" And that's because they haven't gathered enough raw stuff for that thing to become clear. And so I'm always saying to myself, "Don't stop yet. Maybe there's more."

CM: So allow the chaos at much greater length—

CT: Learn to tolerate chaos. Learn to generate and tolerate your own chaos.

JEAN VALENTINE

Interviewed February 25, 2013

Jean Valentine was born in Chicago in 1934, the middle child in a family of three. Her mother read nursery rhymes aloud to her when she was small. "I think that's when I first loved poetry," says Valentine. "Those nursery rhymes. And I had an older sister who loved books; that was a great gift too."

Valentine began to write in third or fourth grade. At eighteen, she was a student at Radcliffe with "a bookbag full of poems." When one of her professors suggested she write from her dreams, it "was like a huge door opening, which has never closed." To this day, she keeps a notebook next to her bed and writes down bits and pieces as they come to her. "It could be just a scrap of conversation. But oftentimes, it'll get me into a poem."

Valentine won the Yale Younger Poets Award in 1965 for her first book, *Dream Barker,* and has since published more than a dozen books of poetry. *Door in the Mountain: New and Collected Poems* won the National Book Award for Poetry in 2004. *Break the Glass* was a finalist for the 2011 Pulitzer Prize for poetry. Now in her eighties, Valentine looks back with some astonishment at all she has accomplished. For five years she wasn't able to write, and that was hard. "Since then," she says, "I have found things more joyful. I would never say it's easy. . . . But it's more—more of a pleasure. There's some light coming to it. I can't be too articulate, but yes . . . I feel that that has happened. Yes."

Listening

for Fanny Howe

My whole life I was swimming listening
Beside the daylight world like a dolphin beside a boat

—no, swallowed up, young, like Jonah,
sitting like Jonah in the red room
behind that curving smile from the other side

but kept, not spat out,
kept, for love,

not for anything I did, or had,
I had nothing but our inside-
Outside smile-skin . . .
My paper and pen . . .

But I was made for this: listening:
"Lightness wouldn't last if it wasn't used up on the lyre."

Christian McEwen: I wondered if you'd speak a little bit about your childhood. I remember, in *Door into the Mountain,* a father who "raged like Achilles" and a mother who—was not uncomplicated.

Jean Valentine: That's true. My father was in World War II, and he saw action in the Pacific, and he came home with what they now call PTSD. My mother was not uncomplicated, but she was in a hard situation as well. She had to do everything herself, and there was rationing and so forth. So she was working hard during the war too. And then she had this husband who went away for a year and came back pretty wrecked.

It's not much when you think of the war. But it's what our story was.

CM: How many children were you?

JV: Three. An older sister and a younger brother.

CM: When you were small, your mother used to read aloud to you.

JV: Oh, that meant so much to me, to all of us, I think. She read us nursery rhymes. That's what I remember. I think that's when I first loved poetry—hearing our mother read to us. Those nursery rhymes. And I had an older sister who loved books, and that was a great gift too. She'd give me a book by Yeats or something. You know, not as a young child, but as an older teenager. She'd tell me good poets to read. She loved poetry as well.

CM: How wonderful to have that companionship.

JV: It was wonderful.

CM: There's a poem of yours—I think it's called "Eighteen"—where you say you had "a green bookbag full of poems." And I wondered if those poems were by, as it were, Yeats, or whether by then they were your own poems.

JV: Probably my own, although I don't remember that poem. But when I was eighteen, I was in my first year of college. And I had a bookbag. Probably if I said, "full of poems," it meant my own, 'cause I was very—I was very mad about poetry.

CM: When did you actually begin to write?

JV: I guess around eight or nine. We were given quite a peaceful childhood, in spite of everything I told you before. We went to public school in California. There was no homework. And so we could just read at night, and I used to say that I was writing poems.

CM: Were you sharing them with other people then?

JV: Probably with my sister. And then when we went back to the East Coast, I'd show teachers what I was doing. I got a tremendous amount of encouragement from teachers. God bless the teachers! Right along, from probably sixth grade onward.

It meant the world, 'cause, you know, it gave you a feeling maybe you could do something.

CM: Were there any other children who were writing poems?

JV: No, I was the only one. Until I got to college. Well, maybe I should say I was the only one I knew of. Because people could be quite quiet about what they were doing if they were writing poetry.

CM: And who were you reading in those days, apart from Yeats?

JV: Well, I found great delight in e. e. cummings. I think it was because we were being taught everything that was correct in school of course, and he was doing everything incorrectly! I was rebellious too, and I liked that. He was very charming, and he was different from anybody else I'd read. Yeah, I loved him for a while. That would be in high school.

CM: And then you went to college. And then suddenly you're in London. You ended up in London in 1956. In a big green bedsit. I wondered what you were doing there.

JV: Oh, God knows! I graduated from college and I had some friends who were going to Europe, and I was given a gift by my father of going along with them, so we went to Italy and had a wonderful time. I didn't know what I was doing in life at all, but I had a couple of friends who were in London. And so I stopped there on my way back. I thought, "Well, maybe I'll stay here." I got a job working for the U.S. Navy in Grosvenor Square. So I did that for a while, and had a love affair that didn't turn out, and went on home again. But I did live there for about six months. And I really did love it. It was an adventure. 'Cause I was on my own for the first time.

CM: It must have been quite strange. 1956 was the year I was born, and there was still rationing, I think. And there was a lot of debris still around, from the war.

JV: Yes, there was, there was. You could still see those buildings, bombed-out buildings where the stairs had been, and just great pits. Yeah, it was very strange. And I had come from peaceful Cambridge or Boston. Also, I had a job, as I said, with the U.S. Navy. I could go to the PX and I could get American gin and I forget what other alcohol, and I could get cartons of cigarettes. They were very expensive to the British, and very cheap if you went to the PX. So I was very beloved by my friends, 'cause I could turn up with whatever they liked to drink or smoke. And that was an education for me, because I saw people who would ordinarily be doing much better than I was, grown-up people, and it was hard for them still.

And just walking around London, and seeing all that. They still had the fog, I remember! I experienced the London fog, which now, people don't. I'd read about it in Dickens. It's quite something. I loved being on my own for the first time. I was also lonely. But I had some friends, and I loved it. It was quite a wonderful few months for me.

CM: Were you reading any British writers in those days?

JM: Yes. I was. I actually got the chance to meet Louis MacNeice—I don't know if you'd consider him a British writer. But he was living in London. He had one of those townhouses. And a teacher of mine from Harvard had been given a floor in the townhouse to live in, so I went over to see him, and he introduced me to Louis MacNeice. Reading Louis MacNeice was wonderful. I just can't remember who else I was reading then. I was writing.

CM: Borges says somewhere, "Writing is nothing more than a guided dream." And I remember your lines in *Little Boat,* "My dream life is more vivid than my waking life." So many of those poems read as if they'd been taken directly from dreams. All that beauty and elusiveness and strange authority. I wondered if you'd talk about that.

JV: Thank you.
You know, I was taking a course at college with a poet named Edwin Honig, and he said a couple of things that I never forgot. One was, he said to me, "Are you conscious of how much you write about money?" [Laughs.] And I said, "No, do I?" So he pointed that out to me, and that was interesting.

He also said you could write from your dreams. And at that, I really sat up. So I must have already been really loving my dreams. Or at least been affected by them. Because that was like a huge door opening to me, which has never closed. And who knows if I would have done it otherwise, you know? Somebody is just there at the right moment. Someone says the right thing. But anyway, I love dreams, and I love their power. I still to this day keep a notebook right by my bed and write down anything. It could be just a scrap of conversation. But oftentimes it'll get me into a poem.

CM: And how has it been to mine your dreams in that way? Do the dreams welcome being written about? Or are they so private that it's odd to have the reader's eyes on them?

JV: Well, if I did feel that, I would not publish them. I would not try to print them.

When I was young, I didn't know if anyone would understand anything I wrote. Then I got encouragement from my teachers as I say; I remember Honig encouraged me, and another teacher that I had in college encouraged me very much. It's getting better now in my late seventies. But I've pretty much all my life thought, *"Is this too weird for a poem? Is this something that makes sense to you?"* and I've shown my work to friends who are poets. Almost all my life I've been lucky enough to have poets to show the work to.

Not in my first book; I didn't know a single poet. Then I got the editor of the Yale book, and he was just incredibly generous and went over every poem in the book that I had questions about. He was a real teacher to me. So I guess I always have to check with somebody. *"Is it too weird, is it too unknowable?"* Occasionally, some things don't seem so bad to me, or so odd. But some things do. And so I check them over with friends.

CM: It sounds as if the dreams have continued to be a tremendous resource and a great joy.

JV: A joy and a half. Yeah. I can't imagine not having them. Although you have periods when you don't wake up with wonderful dreams. But usually they've come along.

CM: I read in one of your interviews—and this is a direct quote—that you "always tried to hear the sound of the words, and to take out everything that didn't feel alive."

JV: Hmm.

CM: And I wondered if you'd talk about sound and syntax in your poems, because they are splintered—they're very fragmented—and yet, they work beautifully. So, what is your aim?

JV: Well, thank you.

I just—I get bored with ordinary language when I'm trying to write poems. Not in ordinary speech. But when I'm trying to write a poem, I want it, as the quote says, "just to be as alive at it can be." So what can I add to that? Again, if it makes sense to me, then I'll try it on other people. If it's really odd, or what I think might be too fragmentary, too splintered, I've been blessed with friends who'll look at it and tell me what they think. And sometimes they say, "Yeah, I don't know what you're talking about."

So then I'll have to make it better.

But I do find ordinary speech is pretty splintered, pretty fragmentary. Even ordinary speech, you know. So it's usually pretty alive, or can be made so. I'm not sure I have anything interesting to say about it, except it's just what I like to do. I think it's a matter of pace. I like a lot of poetry that's perfectly slow, especially older poetry. But it doesn't interest me to write. I like to read it. God knows, there are wonderful poets. But, for some reason, I get bored with writing work that's just in a very expected, slow pace. I don't think it's how people speak or how they think, actually. So that's what I'm after.

CM: I did find a few traditional forms in your poems. I found a villanelle, among the older poems, and now and again you rhyme. There's a poem called "Advent Calendar" and another one called "To My Soul." And then the "Free Abandonment Blues." But mostly, as you say, you seem to resist those usual forms.

JV: Well, I love to be soaked in them. I was lucky to have the education to be soaked in those forms. When I was in college, the teachers said, "Write sonnets." That's just what they said. And that's good advice, I think. I'd still give it to students if they would do it. Because a sonnet is not a hard form. It's not as flexible as it was for the Italians—or is for the Italians—but it's pretty flexible. And you know, it's sort of comforting. It's been expected in our ears for centuries, so that must make it sort of comforting. I like it.

Just now, I've got a sequence of poems, and I looked, and I saw, "Gee, there are fourteen poems." So I thought, "That's wonderful. Fourteen poems! Fourteen, that's such a good old number!" I mean it is, and it isn't. It's really in my head. But it was comforting to me that something came out in that way by itself.

I don't think it has to do with reality, really. But there's something about being raised trying to write those things. Or for three or four years anyway. Probably more years than that. It gives you a sense of stability, I think, where the rest of the thing is not stability. It's looking for things in the sky, and under the earth, and in your dreams, and wherever you can. And often, you know, in unsettling emotions. And you want those. You want to try and get them into the air. So, I think if you go for a settled form, it can be grounding for you. I don't do it that often. But I'm all for it. It has been grounding for me. Sometimes.

CM: I just read fifty sonnets by a young poet called Jill McDonough, all about executions. I don't know if you've seen her book. It's quite challenging in some ways. But devastatingly well made. And it does exactly what you say: it grounds material that would otherwise be perhaps unbearable.

JV: Good for her. I haven't read that. I want to. Yes. Form can contain things a little bit. That are just unbearable.

And we had Elizabeth Bishop going ahead of us, who writes in a lot of forms. She's a good teacher for that, because she's not writing the expected thing, usually. But she has a lot of form to hold on to. I have another poet friend, Joan Larkin, and she has said that the sonnet form can be like a banister, or a handrail, to walk her through painful material. She's done crowns of sonnets and all kinds of very difficult formal things.

CM: I wanted to ask what religion you had as a child. Because there's a presence of the spirit through your poems. And I wondered where you began, and where you are with that now.

JV: For some reason I don't remember or understand, it's been important to me my whole life. There's a new book out: poets talking about God. It's called *The God in the House*. And Ilya Kaminsky, whom I worked with on the Tsvetaeva translations, was one of the editors. So I had a go at talking about that. About matters of the spirit.

It had to do with looking for something outside of the house, or outside of the run of things, when I was a child. And then with the war, I think. I went to the neighborhood church because they were nice. Some kind of Protestant church at the end of the street. I don't remember which. I just went by myself. They were nice. And that was very important.

That wasn't grown-up experience at all. But I was always very much looking for something more than was apparent, and I think had been since I was quite small. It didn't come from my family, although it might have come from the family of my babysitter. They were at the heart of my life when I was young, because there was a stable next door and I loved horses. And my babysitter was the daughter of the family, and the family welcomed me in. They may have been ardent Catholics for all I know, or at least practicing Catholics.

My own family didn't really practice a religion. It was a comfort to them; maybe not a comfort but important. Sort of like lightning. It was exciting, and also from someplace else. I can't articulate this very well. But it stayed with me, more or less in that form. I don't think I've become more mature about it. But if my life didn't hold that other part, I'm not sure if I'd be half as happy as I am. You know what I mean? It's very hard to describe. I don't know what my beliefs are exactly.

A poet asked me recently—we were sitting around having tea, and he asked, "Do you believe in the afterlife?" and I thought later, *"Did he actually ask me that?"* You know, it was so unusual. I don't know if I do or not. But I believe in something, and whatever it is, it feels interesting to me.

Another person who was there said, "Well, we mustn't ever make the mistake of feeling safe. All evidence to the contrary." And I said to myself, "OK, but why not?" I think it's a Buddhist thing; she's someone who'd done a lot of Buddhist study. I think it's about going toward the danger rather than running away from it. And then the sword turns into a flower.

You know, that teaching. So I think that's what she was saying, and I think that's in me by now, 'cause I've studied with a lot of Buddhist teachers and I love them. I think they're wonderful. The teachers I've sat with have been just amazingly sane and—life forces! I do feel very alive about that. About the spirit. Yeah.

CM: Do you meditate regularly? Has that become your form?

JV: I was a Catholic convert for a while. And I've met many wonderful people in different faiths. But I think the most clear to me now, if it could be said to be clear, would be the Buddhist. I think the sitting is very good, for me. New York, of course, is paradise if you're looking for a Buddhist teacher—they're on every block. And there are some wonderful ones.

CM: Absolutely. It's my tradition also. . . .

JV: Oh, so you know what I'm talking about.

CM: It's very rich.
   And then too, sitting in meditation and being open to the changing mind is not so different from opening oneself to dreams. In either case, it gets you out of the rational.

JV: Exactly.

CM: Out of the practical mind.

JV: That's right. That's very articulate. Thank you. You've articulated something for me. It is. Because you are going under the surface of the water, I guess. You are allowing something to come in that's probably always there.

CM: Right.

JV: In both cases.

CM: And yet, one of the names you mention in your poems—someone who was a dear teacher of mine, and whom I loved very much—was Grace. Grace Paley.

JV: Ah.

CM: I remember Grace saying long ago that she wasn't interested in traditional religion. But, she said, "That doesn't mean I don't believe in mystery."

JV: Yeah. Oh yes, she did!

CM: And I loved that. Speak a little about Grace and your friendship with her, because she's a dear person.

JV: That's right. She certainly did believe in mystery.

She was teaching in Sarah Lawrence when I got my job there. And we taught in offices next to each other. *How lucky was I!* Our offices were right next to each other for probably fifteen years. It was just wonderful. Also I got to ride in with her. Not out to school, but home in the afternoon or evening. So we became good friends. And then I stayed in touch when she moved to Vermont. When she retired. Although not as close touch, of course. Oh, she was so important to me! You know, I'd have these ideas, and she'd just laugh at me some of the time. [JV imitates Grace Paley's voice:] *"You know, Jeannie . . ."*

But she was also very generous. I don't know if you experienced this. I was completely out of it politically. And there I was working at Sarah Lawrence College, which was very, very political at that time, especially the corner where I had my office, which was right next to Grace. She had on the back—on the bumper—of her car, "No More Nukes!" And this is how out of it I was. I said, "Grace, what are nukes?" I did. And she didn't make fun of me at all. She said, "Oh, Jeannie, those are the nuclear bombs." And in that car, driving home, I got my education. There were some very smart people in the car, of whom I'd never have asked a question. But since she was there, I would say, "Grace, what is this thing about the personal and the political?" That was a riddle to me. I didn't mind saying so to Grace, because she was so kindly. And she would say, "Well Jeannie, think about money. . . ." I said, "Oh, OK." It was a teaching. It got me so that I understood what it was about. She was a wonderful teacher in that way. In the way of being a friend, so you could ask dumb questions and she wasn't going to laugh at you. She really would teach you what was going on.

CM: I worked at the Teachers & Writers Collaborative when I lived in New York. And Grace was one of the people who helped get that institution off the ground. So I wrote a piece about the Collaborative, and I interviewed Herb Kohl about Grace. And he said, "She always had a story." He'd call her up, and she would have a story that would be the answer to whatever your current conundrum was.

JV: Oh, how wonderful. That's right. I bet that's right.

CM: She was very generous to me. She showed up in London when I was living there, and then in Vermont. Our paths kept crossing.

JV: Oh, I'm so glad. For both of you.

CM: And she was just so generous. There was no, what in Britain I suppose you would call, "side."

JV: Exactly, no side to her. Absolutely none. One time she said to me, "Does my slip show?" She was about to go and do a reading at the college. This was when I first met her, and I was very timid—I said, "No." With a laugh. She said, "You wouldn't tell me if it was. You wouldn't tell me if it was showing!" I said, "I guess I wouldn't. But it isn't!"

She was so funny reading people, in a dear loving way. Always wonderful. The last time I saw her was at her home in Vermont. One of her former students and I were both teaching at Vermont College, and we drove over, and we had supper with them. And Bob [Paley's husband] cooked supper. She wasn't well at all, and Bob was pretty old. And they said—Didn't you often feel like you were in a Russian story with her?

CM: Yes.

JV: And they looked at each other, and they just beamed, and there was a candor, and one of the kids was there, Nora or Danny. I don't remember. And Grace and Bob looked at each other, and he put this beautiful supper on the table, and they said, "This is our *lucky* day." It was just so beautiful. Wonderful. I'll never forget her.

CM: Oh, blessings!

JV: Well, I'm glad we have memories of Grace in common. She's funny because she's one of the people I never think is not still here.

CM: There's a poem of hers where her shadow is stretching out over the water at the far tip of Manhattan. She writes that she wants it to be impressed forever on the map of the city. And I feel as if—it is.

JV: It is. Yeah.

CM: I did feel, reading your poems, that you had a tremendous network of friends and mentors and students and allies, and how important they all were. I don't even know how to ask this question. But who else is large in that world? Obviously Grace is a major player. But who else has been a solid friend?

JV: Gosh! I've had many solid friends through teaching, both students and faculty people. Jane Cooper was one. The first two poets I met were Jane Cooper and Adrienne Rich. I didn't know a poet in the world. And my first book came out. It was so much quieter in those days. And they both got in touch with me. So those were both very solid friendships, and very important ones as you can imagine. That was like my friendship with Grace, because they were good readers. They were tuned in, they were generous, they were helpful, and they were in places that I wasn't, and it was very helpful to go to the places that they were studying and reading about and excited about. I got enormous help in teaching, from Jane Cooper and Grace, especially.

I think some of the poets that I haven't known as friends have been friends, in the sense of their work, even if I met them only slightly. You know, I met Bishop a couple of times, and I met Lowell a couple of times. Well, I met Berryman, but . . . he was too ill to be a friend. But it wasn't important to *meet* somebody like that so much as to keep reading them. Well, that's friends in work, really, where you really just love their work so much, and you follow it, and follow it, and see what's happening there.

I loved the way that Bishop's work got more and more open the further along she went. It became emotionally more open. I said that once to Larry Levis, I said, "I wish she hadn't died. I wish she had just continued, and kept on writing more and more open poetry." And he said, "No, she was perfect." [Laughs.] He just loved her so much. He wouldn't hear a word that could be different. And that was dear too.

Solid friends. I've certainly had them. Very few of them have been poets. Often they've been writers. And students. Going into teaching changed my life. I just was so lucky, I think, to get that work. 'Cause I didn't know what I wanted to do, or what I could do. All I knew was that I wanted to write poetry. But what a gift to be born in a time and a place where you could go teach poetry and be paid for it, and pay the rent, and keep on writing. That's wonderful. Yeah, that's wonderful!

CM: What did teaching give you that you didn't have beforehand?

JV: Well, it actually gave me friends. I had these conversations like we're having now. I had wonderful conversations about poetry with people. I never had those before. Nobody really was interested. Or if they were, I was too shy to approach them. But I could talk about poetry three days a week if I wanted to. In fact I did. That was my job! So that made it much less lonesome, you know. And oftentimes, when those students would grow up, they'd come back with some work and we might become friends. When I say "grown up," they were in college. But they'd go on, and go on writing oftentimes, you know.

And then, the faculty sometimes become friends. Like Jane, like Grace. And so my life became much less lonely. I had lived with a man who was a fiction writer, but he didn't read poetry. And then I had children. I was doing office work where I could find it. And all of that was good, but it wasn't so good. It was bringing in a bit of money but it wasn't giving me company. Having students is wonderful, I think. It has been for me, anyway.

CM: I wondered, reading between the lines, or sometimes along the lines, whether depression was something you'd had to deal with in your life. I wondered—whether it was just the sorrow of being a human being on the planet, or whether there was something more serious.

JV: Yeah, I think depression. I'm not sure I want to talk about it in an interview. I certainly have [been depressed] yeah. But I'm not depressed now.

CM: Well, blessings on that. I guess I wondered if poetry had been—a way of finding a form for it, maybe. Using it as a lens, rather than just a grief.

JV: I was just thinking about that, actually. This might be a way of tackling that subject. I was having dinner with some friends just before I came up, and they were talking about this *Silver Linings Playbook* movie, which I haven't seen. It's about manic depression, which I didn't have, thank God, and how that could be made better, or healed, even, by an artistic discipline. The fellow I was talking to was a psychiatrist, and he had a student who had embraced one of the arts; I forget which one. But using that as a discipline had enabled him to live with whatever form of depression or manic depression he had.

And I went home that night—it was just a couple of nights ago—and I haven't seen the movie, or read the book, but I thought, "Well, maybe poetry did that for me." Because I did have depression, but I was so in love with poetry. For a period of five years, I wasn't writing, and that was hard. But I got through it. So, maybe poetry has been that for me, you know. And if so, it's another reason to love it.

CM: Ah . . .

There are some lines in *Little Boat* where you say, "The door is fallen down / to the house / I used to try & pry open, / in and out, / painfully, / stiff tears." And I wondered whether poetry has in some ways grown easier as you've grown older. More fluent? Or maybe just more mysterious?

JV: Hmm. I think both. I wouldn't say easy. But I think more joyful. More fluid, is that what you said?

CM: Yes.

JV: Yeah. Definitely. I had that five years when I had a lot of change and grief in my life, and I wasn't writing. That was like a turning point, and since then, I have found things more joyful. I would never say it's easy. You just have to go a long way to get anything you like. But it's more—more of a pleasure. There's some light coming to it. I can't be too articulate, but yes, I think that's a good question, and I feel that has happened. Yes.

CM: I'm so glad.

This is backtracking a little, but I wondered what it was like for you in those early child-rearing years, before you began to work at Sarah

Lawrence and found those other teacher-poets, other allies. I remember an essay Eavan Boland wrote about Sylvia Plath, where she asks, "What is it that changes when a woman poet becomes a mother?" I wondered if you'd speak to that.

JV: Well, it's a good question. I think for me—I think I was made more human by being in a marriage and by having children. The marriage didn't last. I had troubles along the way. But I think it made me much more human. Much more open to others. It was a matter of getting up early in the morning to have a couple hours in the day. But I did have a couple of hours in the day, you know. I didn't have the kind of desperate time that Plath had, with cold and isolation. I didn't have that, thank God. But I think it's made me feel much more in the human race, to have married and had children. Even though my marriages haven't lasted, the children have, and they have children. One of them has children. I think it put me in the human family a little more, which I'm very grateful for.

It didn't give me as much time. But I don't think I ever really lacked for time. Because poetry isn't like writing a novel. I can't imagine what it's like to write a novel! So gaps were OK. I think it was another opening to love.

CM: Thank you. Thank you.

In some of your more recent poems, you've been talking, as it were, on the cusp of your own mortality, knowing you're not going to be here forever, as of course none of us will be. I love those poems: the poems about the soul, the poems about your own material existence. "My shining, your shining life draws close, draws closer." And I wondered where you are with that subject, that knowledge that all of us have, that we have less and less time, and that we don't know when that time will end.

JV: I had two friends who died in March [2013]—Adrienne was one, Adrienne Rich, a lifelong friend, and then another friend whom I knew was ill. It's not quite the same as someone dying young. There comes a time when you're more or less expecting it, they're more or less expecting it. But I think I've been writing more elegies. That's probably natural if you get to be the age I am. I don't think they're elegies for myself. Maybe you just become more elegiac because you see things going by. Your own life, but also other people's lives. You know more and more people who have died, or are dying.

Also, I wonder, when that happens to a person, if they begin to see that their own death will be coming along. If they become more conscious of the other deaths around them, like the death of the earth if that's what's going to happen. I feel much more moved by that. So when I write an elegy, I don't feel as if it's an elegy only for that person. I feel like there's a lot of change going on.

There are a lot of things that are going away. Old churches, certain ways of governing, things like that. Some of it might be the weather, and some of it might be the polar ice caps. So I feel that if I write an elegy, it's not just for this friend, or just for my own age. Maybe people tune into that more when they get to be a certain age. Or is it the time we're in? I was just having lunch with a great-niece of mine, and she was saying, "We've had extinction five times on this earth already." And I said, "Have we?"

I wonder what they were writing about in those days, you know. Or drawing pictures about. If they had time.

CM: I'd like to ask you one last question. And I'm thinking of your great-niece, and of other apprentice writers, too. If you were to talk to a young woman trying to be a poet now, in her own muddle and privacy, what would you advise her, what would you like her to know?

JV: Oh, I'd like her to know she can! And she must never lose heart. [Laughs.] Never lose heart. And find someone who understands her. Find another poet, maybe who's older. Somebody who knows what she's doing. That's been so important for me. To be understood, you know. By somebody. If even one person understands you, you can grow, you know.

CM: Grace said once, "You can get by on a very little rice."

JV: Oh, it's true! You can get by on a very little rice. That's perfect. Exactly. But just find a couple of grains.

ACKNOWLEDGMENTS

This book could never have come into existence without the steady kindness and encouragement of Annie Boutelle, founder of the Poetry Center at Smith College, and of the current director, Ellen Doré Watson. Thank you both, so much, for trusting that *Sparks* could indeed catch fire.

Thanks to Francesca Rheannon for editing several of the early interviews, and to Daisy Mathias, who sat patiently through every one of the interviews that followed (listening intently, "minding the levels"), and who later edited at least a dozen, and played them on her weekly radio show, "Poetry à la Carte."

Thanks to Jeff Heath, who welcomed Daisy and me to the Smith College Center for Media Production and made it possible for us to record the interviews; and to Jennifer Blackburn at the Poetry Center for her calm and efficiency in all things anxious and administrative.

Thanks to Smith College students Hannah Shadrick, Yumna Ghandour, and Sophia Deady for their help with the transcriptions, and to the Gladys Justin Carr Poetry Internship, established to preserve the Poetry Center's legacy, which in turn allowed those students to be paid.

Thanks so much to Susan Karwoska, David Stoler, and Amy Swauger at Teachers & Writers magazine; to Gerry Cambridge at the *Dark Horse*; Supriya Bhatnagar at *The Writer's Chronicle*, and Ted Delaney at *Mount Hope* magazine for publishing examples of the *Sparks* interviews.

A number of the interviews included here have already been published, occasionally in a slightly different form. An edited version of the interview with Rita Dove appeared in *Teachers & Writers* magazine (Volume 43, Number 3, Spring 2012). The interviews with Yusef Komunyakaa, Aracelis Girmay, and Jean Valentine appeared in 2015 in the online version of the same magazine. The interview with Gwyneth Lewis appeared in *The Dark Horse* (Number 30, Spring/Summer 2013), as did the interviews with Matthew Dickman (Number 31, Autumn/Winter 2013) and Edward Hirsch (Number 32, Spring/Summer 2014). A portion of the interview with Maxine Kumin appeared in the *Advocate* (March 13, 2014). The full interview with Maxine Kumin was published by *The Writer's Chronicle* (Number 47, December 2014), as was the interview with W. S. Merwin (Number 4, February 2015). The Chase Twichell interview will appear in *Mount Hope* magazine (Number 8, Fall 2015).

Heartfelt thanks to the Eva Eastman Foundation for its initial support of *Sparks from the Anvil,* and to the great generosity of Will Hurd, who sustained the project for the next four years as grants dwindled under the onslaught of the recession. Thanks also to the Marsha Day Memorial Fund of the Astraea Foundation, to Susan Davis, Clauda Slacik, Susie Bourque, and Velma Garcia, and to the Poetry Center at Smith College for their crucial support in the publication of this book.

Thanks too to everyone at Bauhan Publishing for their hard work and constancy, in particular, to Sarah Bauhan, Mary Ann Faughnan, Henry James, and Nerissa Osborne.

Thanks to Sarah Rabkin, whose work at the Regional History Project at the University of Santa Cruz was the original inspiration for *Sparks,* and to its director, Irene Reti. Thanks too to Esther Ehrlich, for her early encouragement, and to numerous other friends and fellow writers, especially Barbara Bash, Penny Gill, Parker Huber, Mariel Kinsey, Simon Korner, Henry Lyman, Maia, Maria Margaronis, Pat Musick, Susie Patlove, Verandah Porche, Amy Pulley, and Jennifer Taub.

My apologies to those poets whom I could not include for lack of space, in particular the Iraqi poet Amal Al-Jubouri, the marvelously wise and antic Ko Un, and Annie Boutelle's special favorite, the Irish poet Eavan Boland.

Finally, many thanks to those whose words you have just read, especially the elders among them: Maxine Kumin, W. S. Merwin, and Jean Valentine. I did love talking to you.

Poem Permissions

"Ethel's Sestina" by Patricia Smith from *Blood Dazzler,* Coffee House Press; used by permission of the author.

"Horse" by Chase Twichell from *Horses Where the Answers Should Have Been: New and Selected Poems,* Copper Canyon Press, 2010; used by permission of the author.

"Listening" by Jean Valentine from *Door in the Mountain: New and Collected Poems,* 1965–2003, Wesleyan University Press, 2004; used by permission of the author.

Photo Permissions

Photo of Annie Boutelle by Ellen Augarten.
Photo of Michael Dickman used by permission of the poet.
Photo of Matthew Dickman by Laura Murphy.
Photo of Patrick Donnelly by Carl Nardiello.
Photo of Rita Dove ©2014 by Fred Viebahn.
Photos of Nikky Finney by Rachel Eliza Griffiths.
Photo of Aracelis Girmay used by permission of the poet.
Photo of Edward Hirsch by Michael Lionstar.
Photo of Jane Hirshfield by Nick Rozsa.
Photo of Maxine Kumin by Susannah Colt.
Photo of Gwynneth Lewis by Keith Morris.
Cover photo of W. S. Merwin by Matt Valentine, courtesy of Copper Canyon Press.
Interior photo of W. S. Merwin by Sarah Cavanaugh, courtesy of The Merwin Conservancy.
Cover photo of Yusef Komunyakaa by Tom Wallace.
Interior photo of Yusef Komunyakaa by Rachel Eliza Griffiths.
Photo of Chase Twichell by Emma Dodge Hanson.
Photo of Patricia Smith by Beowulf Sheehan.
Photo of Jean Valentine by Max Greenstreet.

Bibliography

Annie Boutelle
Poetry
Becoming Bone. Fayetteville, AR: University of Arkansas Press, 2005.
Nest of Thistles. Lebanon, NH: University Press of New England, 2005.
This Caravaggio. Amherst, MA: Hedgerow Books/Levellers Press, 2012.
How They Fell. Fort Lee, NJ: Cavankerry Press, 2014.

Other
Thistle and Rose: A Study of Hugh MacDiarmid's Poetry. Scotland: Macdonald Publishers, 1980.

Matthew Dickman
Poetry
All-American Poem. Port Townsend, WA: Copper Canyon Press, 2008.
50 American Plays, with Michael Dickman. Port Townsend, WA: Copper Canyon Press, 2012.
Mayakovsky's Revolver. New York: W. W. Norton & Company, 2012.
Wish You Were Here. Tucson, AZ: Spork Press, 2014.
24 Hours. Paris: Onestar Press, 2014.

Michael Dickman
Poetry
The End of the West. Port Townsend, WA: Copper Canyon Press, 2009.
Flies. Port Townsend, WA: Copper Canyon Press, 2011.
50 American Plays, with Matthew Dickman. Port Townsend, WA: Copper Canyon Press, 2012.

Patrick Donnelly
Poetry
The Charge. Keene, NH: Ausable Press, 2003.
Nocturnes of the Brothel of Ruin. New York: Four Way Books, 2012.

Other
The Wind from Vulture Peak: the Buddhification of Japanese Waka *in the Heian Period,* with Stephen D. Miller, Ithaca, NY: Cornell East Asia Series, 2013.

Rita Dove
Poetry
The Yellow House on the Corner. Pittsburgh, PA: Carnegie-Mellon University Press, 1980.

Museum. Pittsburgh, PA: Carnegie-Mellon University Press, 1983.
Thomas and Beulah. Pittsburgh, PA: Carnegie-Mellon University Press, 1986.
Grace Notes. New York: W. W. Norton & Company, 1989.
Selected Poems. New York: Pantheon, 1993.
Mother Love. New York: W. W. Norton & Company, 1995.
On the Bus with Rosa Parks: Poems. New York: W. W. Norton & Company, 1999.
American Smooth. New York: W. W. Norton & Company, 2004.
Sonata Mulattica: A Life in Five Movements and a Short Play. New York: W. W. Norton & Company, 2009.

Other

Fifth Sunday. Lexington, KY: University of Kentucky Press, 1985.
Through the Ivory Gate. New York: Pantheon, 1992.
The Darker Face of the Earth: a Play. Ashland, OR: Story Line Press, 1996.
The Poet's World. Washington, DC: Library of Congress, 1995.
The Penguin Anthology of 20th Century American Poetry (sole editor). New York: Penguin Books, 2011.

Nikky Finney
Poetry
On Wings Made of Gauze. New York: William Morrow & Company, Inc., 1985.
Rice. Toronto: Sister Vision Press, 1995.
The World Is Round. Atlanta: InnerLight Publishing, 2003.
Head Off & Split. Evanston, IL: Tri-Quarterly Books/Northwestern University Press, 2011.

Other

Heartwood. Lexington, KY: University Press of Kentucky, 1998.
The Ringing Ear: Black Poets Lean South (anthology). Athens, GA: University of Georgia Press, 2007.

Aracelis Girmay
Poetry
Teeth. Willimantic, CT: Curbstone Press, 2007.
Kingdom Animalia. Rochester, NY: BOA Editions, 2011.

Other

changing, changing. New York: George Braziller, Inc., 2005.

Edward Hirsch
Poetry
For the Sleepwalkers. New York: Knopf, 1981.

Wild Gratitude. New York: Knopf, 1986.
The Night Parade. New York: Knopf, 1989.
Earthly Measures. New York: Knopf, 1994.
On Love. New York: Knopf, 1998.
Lay Back the Darkness. New York: Knopf, 2003.
Special Orders. New York: Knopf, 2008.
The Living Fire: New & Selected Poems, 1975–2010. New York: Knopf, 2011.
Gabriel: A Poem. New York: Knopf, 2014.

Other
Transforming Vision: Writers on Art, author of introduction, and selector. Boston: Little, Brown and Company, 1994.
How to Read a Poem and Fall in Love with Poetry. Boston: Houghton Mifflin Harcourt, 1999.
Responsive Reading. Ann Arbor, MI: University of Michigan Press, 1999.
The Demon and the Angel: Searching for the Source of Artistic Inspiration. New York: Mariner Books, 2003.
Poet's Choice. Boston: Houghton Mifflin Harcourt, 2006.
A Poet's Glossary. Boston: Houghton Mifflin Harcourt, 2014.

Jane Hirshfield
Poetry
Alaya. New York: Quarterly Review of Literature/Quarterly Review of Literature Poetry Series, 1982.
Of Gravity & Angels. Middletown, CT: Wesleyan University Press, 1988.
The October Palace. New York: HarperCollins, 1994.
The Lives of the Heart. New York: HarperCollins, 1997.
Given Sugar, Given Salt. New York: HarperCollins, 2001.
After. New York: HarperCollins, 2006.
Come, Thief. New York: Knopf, 2011.

Other
The Ink Dark Moon: Poems by Ono no Komachi and Izumi Shikibu, Women of the Ancient Court of Japan, editor and translator, with Mariko Aratani. New York: Scribner, 1988.
Women in Praise of the Sacred: Forty-Three Centuries of Spiritual Poetry by Women, editor and translator. New York: HarperCollins, 1994.
Nine Gates: Entering the Mind of Poetry. New York: HarperCollins, 1997.
Mirabai: Ecstatic Poems, editor and translator, with Robert Bly. Boston: Beacon Press, 2004.
Hiddenness, Uncertainty, Surprise: Three Generative Energies of Poetry. Northumberland, UK: Bloodaxe Books, 2008.
The Heart of Haiku. Amazon Kindle Single, 2011.

Yusef Komunyakaa
Poems
Dedications & Other Darkhorses. Laramie, WY: R.M.C.A.J. Books, 1977.
Lost in the Bonewheel Factory. Spokane, WA: Lynx House, 1979.
Copacetic. Middletown, CT: Wesleyan University Press, 1984.
I Apologize for the Eyes in My Head. Middletown, CT: Wesleyan University Press, 1986.
Toys in a Field. New Orleans: Black River Press, 1986.
Dien Cai Dau. Middletown, CT: Wesleyan University Press, 1988.
February in Sydney (chapbook). Matchbooks, 1989.
Magic City. Middletown, CT: Wesleyan University Press, 1992.
Neon Vernacular: New and Selected Poems. Middletown, CT: Wesleyan University Press, 1993.
Thieves of Paradise. Middletown, CT: Wesleyan University Press, 1999.
Talking Dirty to the Gods. New York: Farrar, Straus and Giroux, 2000.
Pleasure Dome: New and Collected Poems. Middletown, CT: Wesleyan University Press, 2001.
Taboo. New York: Farrar, Straus and Giroux, 2004.
Warhorse. New York: Farrar, Straus and Giroux, 2008.
The Chameleon Couch. New York: Farrar, Straus and Giroux, 2011.
Testimony: A Tribute to Charlie Parker With New and Selected Jazz Poems. Middletown, CT: Wesleyan University Press, 2013.

Other
The Jazz Poetry Anthology, editor with Sascha Feinstein. Bloomington, IN: Indiana University Press, 1991.
The Insomnia of Fire by Nguyen Quang Thieu, translator, with Martha Collins. Bloomington, IN: Indiana University Press, 1996.
Blue Notes: Essays, Interviews, and Commentaries, edited by Radiclani Clytus. Ann Arbor, MI: University of Michigan Press, 2000.

Maxine Kumin
Poetry
Halfway. New York: Holt, Rinehart and Winston, 1961.
The Privilege. New York: Harper, 1965.
The Nightmare Factory. New York: Harper, 1970.
Up Country: Poems of New England, New and Selected, illustrated by Barbara Swan. New York: Harper, 1972.
House, Bridge, Fountain, Gate. New York: Viking Press, 1975.
Progress Report (sound recording). Watershed, 1976.
The Retrieval System. New York: Viking Press, 1978.
Our Ground Time Here Will Be Brief: New and Selected Poems. New York: Viking Press, 1982.

Closing the Ring: Selected Poems. Lewisburg, PA: Bucknell University/Press of Appletree Alley, 1984.

The Long Approach. New York: Viking Press, 1985.

Nurture. New York: Viking Penguin, Inc., 1989.

Looking for Luck. New York: W. W. Norton & Company, 1992.

Connecting the Dots: Poems. New York: W. W. Norton & Company, 1996.

New and Selected Poems, 1960–1990. New York: W. W. Norton & Company, 1997.

The Long Marriage. New York: W. W. Norton & Company, 2001.

Bringing Together: Uncollected Early Poems, 1958–1988. New York: W. W. Norton & Company, 2003.

Jack and Other New Poems. New York: W. W. Norton & Company, 2005.

Still to Mow. New York: W. W. Norton & Company, 2007.

Where I Live: New and Selected Poems. New York: W. W. Norton & Company, 2010.

Other

To Make a Prairie: Essays on Poets, Poetry, and Country Living. Ann Arbor, MI: University of Michigan Press, 1980.

In Deep: Country Essays. New York: Viking Press, 1987.

Women, Animals and Vegetables: Essays & Stories. New York: W. W. Norton & Company, 1994.

Always Beginning: Essays on a Life in Poetry. Port Townsend, WA: Copper Canyon, 2000.

Into the Halo and Beyond: The Anatomy of a Recovery. New York: W. W. Norton & Company, 2000.

Lofty Dogmas: Poets on Poetics, editor, with Deborah Brown and Annie Finch. Fayetteville, AR: University of Arkansas Press, 2005.

Gwyneth Lewis
Poetry

Parables and Faxes. Northumberland, UK: Bloodaxe Books, 1995.

Zero Gravity. Northumberland, UK: Bloodaxe Books, 1998.

Keeping Mum. Northumberland, UK: Bloodaxe Books, 2003.

Chaotic Angels. Northumberland, UK: Bloodaxe Books, 2005.

A Hospital Odyssey. Northumberland, UK: Bloodaxe Books, 2010.

Sparrow Tree. Northumberland, UK: Bloodaxe Books, 2011.

Other

Sunbathing in the Rain: A Cheerful Book on Depression. New York: Flamingo, 2002.

Two in a Boat: A Marital Voyage. London: Fourth Estate, 2005.

The Meat Tree. Brigend, Wales, UK: Seren Books, 2010.

W. S. Merwin

Poetry

A Mask for Janus. New Haven, CT: Yale University Press, 1952.
The Dancing Bears. New Haven, CT: Yale University Press, 1954.
Green with Beasts. New York: Knopf, 1956.
The Drunk in the Furnace. London: Macmillan, 1960.
The Moving Target. New York: Atheneum, 1963.
Collected Poems. New York: Atheneum, 1966.
The Lice. New York: Atheneum, 1967.
Animae. San Francisco: *Kayak,* 1969.
The Carrier of Ladders. New York: Atheneum, 1970.
Signs, with A.D. Moore. Iowa City, IA: Stone Wall Press, 1970.
Asian Figures. New York: Atheneum, 1973.
Writings to an Unfinished Accompaniment. New York: Atheneum, 1973.
The First Four Books of Poems. New York: Atheneum, 1975.
The Compass Flower. New York: Atheneum, 1977.
Feathers from the Hill. Iowa City, IA: Windhover, 1978.
Finding the Islands. San Francisco: North Point Press, 1982.
Opening the Hand. New York: Atheneum, 1983.
Selected Poems. New York: Atheneum, 1983.
The Rain in the Trees: Poems. New York: Knopf, 1988.
Travels: Poems. New York: Knopf, 1993.
The Vixen: Poems. New York: Knopf, 1996.
Lament for the Makers: A Memorial Anthology, compiler. Berkeley, CA: Counterpoint Press, 1996.
Flower and Hand Poems 1977–1983. Port Townsend, WA: Copper Canyon Press, 1996.
East Window: The Asian Poems. Port Townsend, WA: Copper Canyon Press, 1998.
The River Sound: Poems. New York: Knopf, 1999.
The Pupil. New York: Knopf, 2000.
Migration: New and Selected Poems. Port Townsend, WA: Copper Canyon Press, 2005.
Present Company. Port Townsend, WA: Copper Canyon Press, 2005.
The Shadow of Sirius. Port Townsend, WA: Copper Canyon Press, 2007.
The Collected Poems of W. S. Merwin. New York: Library of America, 2013.
The Moon Before Morning. Port Townsend, WA: Copper Canyon Press, 2014.

Other

West Wind: Supplement of American Poetry, editor. London: Poetry Book Society, 1961.
The Miner's Pale Children. New York: Atheneum, 1970.
Houses and Travelers. New York: Atheneum, 1977.
Unframed Originals: Recollections. New York: Atheneum, 1982.
The Lost Uplands: Stories of Southwest France. New York: Knopf, 1992.
The Folding Cliffs: A Narrative. New York: Knopf, 1998.

The Mays of Ventadorn. Washington, DC: National Geographic, 2002.
The Ends of the Earth. San Francisco: Shoemaker & Hoard. 2004.
Summer Doorways: A Memoir. Berkeley, CA: Counterpoint, 2006.
The Book of Fables. Port Townsend, WA: Copper Canyon, 2007.
Unchopping a Tree, drawings by Elizabeth Ward. San Antonio, TX: Trinity University Press, 2014.

Translations
"Eufemia" by Lope de Rueda, in *Tulane Drama Review*, December, 1958;
"Crispin" by Lesage, in *Tulane Drama Review,* 1958.
Punishment without Vengeance by Lope Felix de Vega Carpio, 1958.
The Classic Theatre, contributor, Eric Bentley, editor. New York: Doubleday, 1961.
The Satires of Persius. Bloomington, IN: Indiana University Press, 1961.
Some Spanish Ballads. London: Abelard, 1961, (published as *Spanish Ballads*, New York: Doubleday Anchor, 1961).
The Poem of the Cid. London: Dent, 1959 / New York: New American Library, 1962.
The Life of Lazarillo de Tormes: His Fortunes and Adversities. New York: Doubleday Anchor, 1962.
Medieval Epics, contributor. New York: Modern Library, 1963.
Poems and Antipoems by Nicanor Parra. With Denise Levertov, William Carlos Williams, and others. New York: New Directions, 1968.
"Yerma" and "Blood" by Federico García Lorca, 1969.
W.S. Merwin: Selected Translations, 1948–1968. New York: Atheneum, 1969.
Products of the Perfected Civilization: Selected Writings of Chamfort (and author of introduction). New York: Macmillan, 1969.
Transparence of the World by Jean Follain. New York: Atheneum, 1969, reprinted by Copper Canyon Press (Port Townsend, WA), 2003.
Voices: Selected Writings of Antonio Porchia. Chicago: Follett, 1969, reprinted by Copper Canyon Press (Port Townsend, WA), 2003.
Twenty Poems and a Song of Despair by Pablo Neruda. London: Cape, 1969, (reprinted, with introduction by Christina García, illustrations by Pablo Picasso, by Penguin Books, New York, NY, 2004).
Selected Poems by Pablo Neruda, (with others). New York: Dell, 1970.
Selected Poems by Osip Mandelstam, (with Clarence Brown). New York: Oxford University Press, 1973, (reprinted as *The Selected Poems of Osip Mandelstam*, New York Review of Books, New York, NY, 2004).
Sanskrit Love Poetry, (with J. Moussaieff Mason). New York: Columbia University Press, 1977, (published as *Peacock's Egg: Love Poems from Ancient India*, by North Point Press San Francisco, CA, 1981).
Vertical Poems by Roberto Juarroz. San Francisco: Kayak, 1977.
Iphigenia at Aulius by Euripides, (with George E. Dimock, Jr.). New York: Oxford University Press, 1978.

Selected Translations, 1968–78. New York: Atheneum, 1979.
Robert the Devil. Iowa City, IA: Windhover, 1981.
Four French Plays. New York: Atheneum, 1984.
From the Spanish Morning. New York: Atheneum, 1984.
Purgatorio by Dante Alighieri. New York: Knopf, 2000.
Gawain and the Green Knight: A New Verse Translation, New York: Knopf, 2004.
Collected Haiku of Yosa Buson. Port Townsend, WA: Copper Canyon Press, 2013.
Selected Translations: Translations from 1948–2010. Port Townsend, WA: Copper Canyon Press, 2013.

Plays
Darkling Child, (with Dido Milroy), produced 1956.
Favor Island, produced at Poets' Theatre, Cambridge, MA, 1957, and on British Broadcasting Corporation *Third Programme,* 1958.
The Gilded West, produced at Belgrade Theatre, Coventry, England, 1961.

Patricia Smith
Poetry
Life According to Motown. Sylmar, CA: Tia Chucha Press, 1991.
Big Towns, Big Talk. Cambridge, MA: Zoland Books, 1992.
Close to Death. Cambridge, MA: Zoland Books, 1993.
Teahouse of the Almighty. Minneapolis, MN: Coffee House Press, 2006.
Blood Dazzler. Minneapolis, MN: Coffee House Press, 2008.
Shoulda Been Jimi Savannah. Minneapolis, MN: Coffee House Press, 2012.

Other
Africans in America: America's Journey through Slavery, co-authored with Charles Johnson. Boston: Houghton Mifflin Harcourt, 1998.
Janna and the Kings (children's book). New York: Lee & Low Books, 2003.

Chase Twichell
Poetry
Northern Spy: Poems. Pittsburgh, PA: University of Pittsburgh Press, 1981.
The Odds. Pittsburgh, PA: University of Pittsburgh Press, 1986.
Perdido. New York: Farrar, Straus and Giroux, 1991.
The Ghost of Eden. Princeton, NJ: Ontario Review Press, 1995.
The Snow Watcher. Princeton, NJ: Ontario Review Press, 1998.
Dog Language. Port Townsend, WA: Copper Canyon Press, 2005.
Horses Where the Answers Should Have Been: New and Selected Poems. Port Townsend, WA: Copper Canyon Press, 2010.

Other

The Practice of Poetry: Writing Exercises From Poets Who Teach, edited with Robin Behn. New York: HarperPerennial, 1992.
The Lover of God: Poems by Rabindranath Tagore, translated with Tony K. Stewart. Port Townsend, WA: Copper Canyon Press, 2003.

Jean Valentine

Poetry

Dream Barker and Other Poems. New Haven: Yale University Press, 1965.
Pilgrims. New York: Farrar, Straus and Giroux, 1969.
Ordinary Things. New York: Farrar, Straus and Giroux, 1974.
The Messenger. New York: Farrar, Straus and Giroux, 1979.
Home. Deep. Blue: New and Selected Poems. Farmington, ME: Alice James Books, 1989.
The River at Wolf. Farmington, ME: Alice James Books, 1992.
The Under Voice: Selected Poems. Ireland: Salmon Publishing, 1995.
Growing Darkness, Growing Light. Pittsburgh, PA: Carnegie-Mellon University Press, 1997.
The Cradle of the Real Life. Middletown, CT: Wesleyan University Press, 2000.
Door in the Mountain: New and Collected Poems 1965–2003. Middletown, CT: Wesleyan University Press, 2004.
Little Boat. Middletown, CT: Wesleyan University Press, 2007.
Break the Glass. Port Townsend, WA: Copper Canyon Press, 2010.
Shirt in Heaven. Port Townsend, WA: Copper Canyon Press, 2015.

Prose

The Lighthouse Keeper: Essays on the Poetry of Eleanor Ross Taylor, editor. Geneva, NY: Hobart & William Smith, 2001.
Dark Elderberry Branch: Poems of Marina Tsvetaeva. A Reading by Ilya Kaminsky and Jean Valentine. Farmington, ME: Alice James Books, 2012.